# THE NEW CLARENDON BIBLE

OLD TESTAMENT

VOLUME V

———

# THE JEWS
# FROM ALEXANDER
# TO HEROD

# THE JEWS
# FROM ALEXANDER
# TO HEROD

BY

D. S. RUSSELL

OXFORD UNIVERSITY PRESS

*Oxford University Press, Ely House, London W. 1*

GLASGOW   NEW YORK   TORONTO   MELBOURNE   WELLINGTON
CAPE TOWN   SALISBURY   IBADAN   NAIROBI   DAR ES SALAAM   LUSAKA   ADDIS ABABA
BOMBAY   CALCUTTA   MADRAS   KARACHI   LAHORE   DACCA
KUALA LUMPUR   SINGAPORE   HONG KONG   TOKYO

FIRST PUBLISHED 1967
REPRINTED LITHOGRAPHICALLY IN GREAT BRITAIN
AT THE UNIVERSITY PRESS, OXFORD
BY VIVIAN RIDLER
PRINTER TO THE UNIVERSITY
1970

# PUBLISHER'S PREFACE

WHEN it became necessary, a year or two ago, to contemplate revision of the Old Testament volumes of the Clarendon Bible series, the publishers were faced with two important decisions: first, on what text the revision should be based, and second, whether any significant change should be made in the form and plan of the series.

It seemed to them, after taking the best available advice, that the Revised Version could not expect to hold the field for much longer in face of the developments in scholarship which have taken place since its publication in the eighteen eighties, and which have been reflected in more recently published versions. On the other hand, the New English Bible Old Testament is not yet published, and even after its publication it will be some little time before its usefulness for schools and universities can be evaluated. In these circumstances, the Revised Standard Version has seemed the obvious choice, the more particularly because of the recent decision by the Roman Catholic hierarchy to authorize the use of their own slightly modified version in British schools. The publishers would like to express their gratitude to the National Council of Churches of Christ in the United States of America for the permission, so readily given, to make use of the RSV in this way.

With regard to the form of the series, the success of the old Clarendon Bible over the years has encouraged them to think that no radical change is necessary. As before, therefore, subjects requiring comprehensive treatment are dealt with in essays, whether forming part of the introduction or interspersed among the notes. The notes themselves are mainly concerned with the subject-matter of the books and the points of interest (historical, doctrinal, etc.) therein presented; they deal with the elucidation of words, allusions, and the like only so far as seems necessary to a proper comprehension of the author's meaning. There will, however, be some variations in the content and limits of each individual volume, and in particular it is intended that a fuller treatment should be given to Genesis, and to the Psalms.

The plan is to replace the volumes of the old series gradually over the next few years, as stocks become exhausted.

# PREFACE

F o r over thirty years G. H. Box's *Judaism in the Greek Period* has held an honoured place as Vol. V in the Clarendon Bible (Old Testament) series; throughout that time many readers have found it of great value as a concise introduction to an exciting, if difficult, era. It is accordingly with due deference that the present writer has accepted the invitation of the Clarendon Press to produce a volume which will cover the same ground but will take into account the many developments and discoveries of the past generation. During that time many things have happened to make necessary a reassessment of the material available, the most spectacular being the discovery of the priceless Scrolls at Qumran on the west coast of the Dead Sea. Such discoveries have brought a new understanding to the history and religion of the intertestamental period as a whole, and have cast fresh light both on the development of Judaism and on the origins of the Christian Church.

Much of the story covered by this book is illustrated only by a series of 'still' pictures which the historian has to try to interpret as well as he can. Many obscurities and uncertainties remain, but, thanks to new scholarly insights over the past thirty years or so, much that was once 'frozen' has suddenly come to life, presenting to the reader a fast-moving and often dramatic story.

In this book the scope of Dr. Box's volume has been enlarged to include the years between Pompey's capture of Jerusalem in 63 b.c. and the death of Herod the Great in 4 b.c. Greater space has been given to the development of religious ideas and religious parties within Judaism, whilst a somewhat different selection of writings has been made to illustrate the literary activity of the times.

The period covered in these pages, from Alexander to Herod, may not represent the high-water mark of biblical thought and endeavour; nevertheless it is of supreme importance, for the

account it gives is in many ways a continuation of the Old
Testament record and an anticipation of the New. Of special
significance is the development of that Hellenistic culture
which, for good and ill, had a deep influence on the life and
faith of the Jews. Sometimes Hellenism and Judaism clashed
head-on; at other times they compromised. In either case the
results were momentous both for Judaism itself and for the
Christian Church. This intertestamental period deserves and
demands much closer scrutiny than in the past; it is hoped that
this small book will do something at least to assist the process of
investigation, and that the reader will be encouraged to pursue
his interests further by reference to other works noted in the
bibliography.

The author is greatly indebted to many scholars, as is evident
throughout this book, and in particular to Professor P. R.
Ackroyd, who read through a draft copy and made a number
of most valuable suggestions. He is grateful also to Mrs. J.
Davies, Mrs. W. J. Graham, and Miss M. Wass for their expert
help in preparing the manuscript, and to his colleague, the
Revd. George Farr, for kindly checking the final copy.

D. S. RUSSELL

*Northern Baptist College*
*Manchester*
*July 1966*

# CONTENTS

## PART ONE
## THE HISTORY

PART TWO

THE RELIGION

PART THREE

# THE LITERATURE

# LIST OF ILLUSTRATIONS

# LIST OF SELECTED PASSAGES

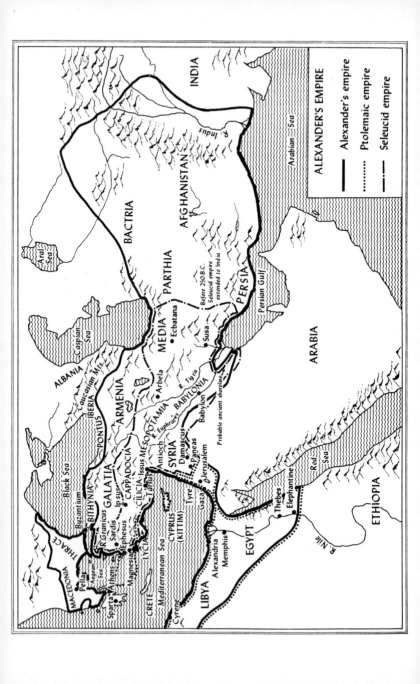

ALEXANDER'S EMPIRE

———— Alexander's empire
·········· Ptolemaic empire
— · — Seleucid empire

INDIA

R. Indus

Arabian Sea

BACTRIA

AFGHANISTAN

Aral
Sea

PARTHIA

PERSIA

Before 250 B.C.
Seleucid empire
extended to India

Caspian
Sea

MEDIA

Persian Gulf

Ecbatana

Susa

ALBANIA

Caucasus Mts.

ARMENIA

Arbela

R. Tigris

ARABIA

IBERIA

PONTUS

MESOPOTAMIA

BABYLONIA

R. Euphrates

Babylon

Black Sea

BITHYNIA

GALATIA

CAPPADOCIA

Ip sus

Sardis

Probable ancient shoreline

Byzantium

R. Granicus

Ephesus

CILICIA

Issus

Antioch

Tarsus

SYRIA

Damascus

Paneas

THRACE

LYCIA

Jerusalem

Red
Sea

MACEDONIA

Magnesia

CYPRUS
(KITTIM)

Tyre

Pella

Aegean
Sea

Gaza

Athens

Mediterranean Sea

Thebes

Elephantine

Sparta

CRETE

Alexandria

EGYPT

ETHIOPIA

Cyrene

Memphis

LIBYA

R. Nile

## PART ONE

# THE HISTORY

## I

## ALEXANDER THE GREAT

### 1. *His career*

'SOME men are born great, some achieve greatness, and some have greatness thrust upon them.' Alexander of Macedon qualified on all three counts. Born into a noble family in 356 B.C. he inherited, twenty years later, the throne of his father Philip II, having already given clear evidence of his skill in government and his prowess in battle. But the greatness he achieved was infinitely more than the greatness he inherited, for within the short space of thirteen years he made himself master of an enormous empire, stretching from Macedonia in the west to India in the east, from Armenia and Bactria in the north to Egypt and Arabia in the south. It is not surprising that his greatness was even further enhanced by legends of every kind, conferring upon him fame and honour surpassing those that history ascribed to his name.

Although a Macedonian in origin, Alexander was culturally a Greek. For two generations or so before his time the Macedonian court had been deeply influenced by Greek ideas and had entertained Greek scholars, artists, and men of letters of many kinds. At the age of 13 he became a pupil of the famous philosopher Aristotle, from whom he acquired an insatiable thirst for knowledge. Aristotle taught him not only the art of ruling, but also the whole range of the 'liberal arts', including philosophy and metaphysics, ethics and politics, science and medicine. These interests remained with him throughout his life, as is evident not only by the philosophers who accompanied his armies into Asia, but also by his zest for the 'natural sciences' and his concern for the physical health and well-being of his fighting men. He was convinced of the complete superiority of the Greek way of life, and carried with him on his campaigns copies of Homer's *Iliad* and *Odyssey*. He claimed descent from old Greek heroes on both sides of his family. Hercules was the renowned ancestor on his father's side, and Achilles on his mother's side. This heroic ancestry casts light on certain events of later years in which Alexander claimed for himself divine descent.

In his own character he combined the practical sagacity of his father Philip and the passionate nature of his mother Olympias. He was a man of boundless energy, at times merciless and cruel and without a trace of conscience. Though a careful schemer and a skilled general, he sometimes acted on impulse, following resolutely the decision of the moment, prepared to slaughter without pity or remorse all who stood in his path or who in any way roused his suspicion. He was a military genius who inspired his troops with his own irrepressible enthusiasm and supreme confidence. His military tactics, in which the striking power of the cavalry was a prominent factor, made for easy and rapid movement, and help to explain the remarkable progress of his campaigns.

Having established himself in Macedonia, following the death of his father Philip in 336 B.C., Alexander took steps to consolidate his position in the Greek states to the south. That same year he asserted his authority over the members of the Hellenic League who were made to acknowledge his leadership in succession to that of his father. The following year he strengthened his position in the north, where his authority was being seriously threatened. Meanwhile more trouble was brewing in the south, in the city of Thebes, following a false rumour of Alexander's death. With great haste he sped to the trouble spot and, failing to gain a peaceful settlement, razed the city to the ground and sold many of its inhabitants as slaves.

Having thus secured his position on his own borders Alexander then set his face to the invasion of Persia. In 334 B.C., with a force of 35,000 men, he crossed the Hellespont and entered Asia Minor. There, on the banks of the River Granicus, near the ancient city of Troy, he defeated a Persian army sent against him by Darius III. This success opened the way to the conquest of the whole of Asia Minor, for the defeated army was the only sizeable Persian force in that whole area. Alexander had little difficulty in overrunning and 'liberating' one city after another. Occasionally he met with opposition, as at Halicarnassus, which he burned to the ground; but for the most part his march southwards and eastwards was unimpeded until he came to the borders of Syria. There at the 'Cilician Gate' (a narrow mountain path leading from Cilicia into Syria) near Issus he met Darius, who had mustered his armies to halt Alexander's perilous advance (333 B.C.). Darius was routed and fled for his life, leaving behind members of his own family and certain prominent Greek emissaries who were taken captive, together with much booty.

The way was now open for Alexander to continue his triumphant march southwards through Phoenicia in the direction of Egypt. The seaports of Arvad, Byblos, Berytus, and Sidon handed over their fleets to him, but at Tyre he met with stiff opposition. Only after a seven months' siege was this island fortress taken (332 B.C.). The capture of Tyre and the capitulation of the other Phoenician seaports meant that the Persian fleet had now no harbours from which to operate. Alexander continued his march southwards into Palestine,[1] meeting no serious opposition until he reached Gaza, which he captured after a two months' siege (332 B.C.).

The same year he entered Egypt, where the people welcomed him as a liberator. The satrap of Memphis readily opened the gates of that city to him; Alexander thereupon sacrificed to

[1] For evidence concerning Alexander's campaign in Palestine see pp. 12 ff.

One of the 'Cilician Gates' or Passes in the Taurus mountains near Issus where Alexander routed Darius in 333 B.C. This victory opened the way for Alexander to advance southwards through Syria and Palestine into Egypt.

Apis, the sacred bull, and was acclaimed as the successor of the Pharaohs. Continuing his progress to the coast he planned out a great new city at the mouth of the Nile to be called by his name. Alexandria was soon to replace Tyre as the great trading port of the Mediterranean and was to become the cultural centre of the ancient world. At this point Alexander, together with a number of his followers, made a hazardous journey to the oasis of Amon, where he consulted the famous oracle, just as he had consulted the equally famous oracle of Apollo at Delphi on a previous occasion. The priest of Amon greeted him as 'son of Amon', an official designation of every Pharaoh, and (so the story goes) declared that he would have dominion over the whole world. The government of Egypt was then reorganized and the administration of land and taxes put on a more secure footing. Leaving the control of the country in the hands of a small army of occupation he retraced his steps northwards to Syria (331 B.C.), which he now placed in the charge of a Macedonian governor.

Asia Minor, Syria, and Egypt now lay at his feet. But the Persian army still remained intact. Striking eastwards he crossed the Euphrates and the Tigris and advanced to meet Darius near the village of Gaugamela. Darius' army, whose infantry and cavalry were reinforced by fifteen elephants and many chariots fitted with scythes, was utterly routed, and the Persian king fled eastwards to Ecbatana (331 B.C.). Alexander did not pursue him, but instead turned his attention to a number of wealthy cities whose capture would give him complete control of the once great Persian empire. First he received the capitulation of Babylon, whose rulers and priests and people greeted him as a great deliverer, showering on him garlands and gifts from the city's treasuries; Alexander in turn set about rebuilding the ruined temples of the god Marduk. Within a month the Persian capital, Susa, was in his hands, with its legendary riches. From there he advanced to Persepolis, where he set fire to Xerxes' palace, thus avenging the burning of Athens by Xerxes many years before. After wintering in Persepolis he advanced northwards to Ecbatana, which he

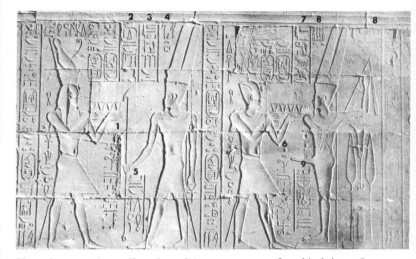

Alexander presenting a gift to the god Amon: two scenes from his shrine at Luxor.

In the left-hand scene the figure of Amon-Re is the normal one: in the right-hand scene the figure is that of an ithyphallic god, Amon-Re Ka-mutef, identified with Amon. Each scene is a separate entity divided by columns of hieroglyphs giving the royal titles, the name of Alexander, and the statement that he is 'beloved of Amon-Re'.

In each scene the god has a crown with two small plumes, originally feathers, but in historic times solid and, in the small statues known to us, gilded or of gold. The King, Alexander, in the left scene is wearing the crown of Upper and Lower Egypt, the white (mitre-shaped) crown within the red crown; in the right scene the King wears a blue crown. The bird above him here is the protective god Horus, who holds in his talons the symbols of life and dominion. The protective formula, which starts behind the King's head, and reads down vertically, says 'All protection and life surrounds him, like (that of) Re'. The god Amon-Re Ka-mutef has a flail over his upraised hand. Behind him is a shrine on top of which are, at each side, a stalk of romaine lettuce (thought to be an aphrodisiac) with a flower, or perhaps a fan, between them.

The details numbered in the picture are as follows:

1 and 6. Offering pellets of natron or incense as part of a purification ceremony. The pellets are shown on top of four jars which the King is holding on a tray; presumably the jars contain burning charcoal.

2. Words spoken by Amon: 'I have given to you all health which issues from me'.

3 and 4. Amon-Re, King of the gods, Lord of Heaven, Ruler of Thebes.

5. Words spoken by Amon: 'I have given to you the crook and the flail (emblems of kingship) like (those of) Re'.

7. Amon-Re Ka-mutef (meaning 'Bull of his mother', i.e. self-begotten).

8. Who is before his sanctuary.

9. Words spoken by Amon: 'I have given to you the lifetime of Re in heaven'.

captured with all its treasures. The conquest of Persia was now complete. Alexander, having achieved his aim and having amassed enormous wealth, was at last acknowledged as the 'Great King' and successor to the Persian royal house. Within a few months Darius was killed by one of his own princes, and Alexander remained in a position of undisputed authority.

His ambitions, however, were not yet fulfilled. With visions of a world empire before him he advanced through Parthia to Arachosia (Afghanistan), Bactria, and Sogdiana (Turkestan), and on to India itself, where he occupied the Indus valley (the Punjab). There his army refused to accompany him any farther, and Alexander was forced to retrace his steps. Half his soldiers set sail from the Indus to the Persian Gulf in a fleet of new ships (325 B.C.); the others returned by land. Alexander thereafter made Babylon his centre of operations and there ruled over his subjects after the style of the Persian kings whose place he had taken.

His end came swiftly and unexpectedly. In 323 B.C. he planned a naval expedition round Arabia with a view to conquering the countries of the west. Before his ships could sail, however, he was taken with a fever in Babylon and died ten days later. In less than thirteen years, and at the age of 33, he had changed the course of world history, and prepared the way for a new era in the life of mankind—and not least in the life of the Jewish nation.

### 2. *His policy*

Alexander set himself the task of bringing together into one the civilizations of east and west, on the basis of that Greek culture which he himself had inherited and of which he was an avowed champion. National, political, and cultural barriers were thrown down in his triumphant march eastwards, and men of diverse customs and traditions were made to feel that they belonged together within 'the inhabited world'. Such Greek culture had, of course, been widely known in western Asia at any rate before the time of Alexander, as archaeological discoveries have made plain: as early as the seventh century B.C. Greek mercenaries and traders had found their way into Egypt, Syria, and Palestine, and in the succeeding centuries this influence spread further east. But Alexander, with full intent, accelerated this process and set himself to teach Greeks and Asiatics to accept each other as partners in a common culture. He did this in the main by two methods.

First, he established Macedonian colonies and new Greek cities all over his great empire, a policy which, as we shall see,[1] was continued by his successors. Many emigrated from the overcrowded Greek peninsula, whilst disbanded Greek soldiers and adventurous Greek merchants were sent far afield to become natural carriers of Greek civilization. The rapid spread of *koiné* or 'common' Greek greatly facilitated the process of Hellenization and within a relatively short time it became the lingua franca of Alexander's empire. Second, he used the practical means of mixed marriages between Greeks and Asiatics to bind these diverse cultures into one. Persian princesses with considerable dowries were offered in marriage to his own chief officers, whilst a handsome gift awaited every soldier who married an Asiatic woman. Alexander himself married Roxane, the daughter of Oxyartes, whom he had taken captive in Sogdiana. Such measures caused no small resentment among his people, and this was accentuated when he placed Persian satraps and other officers of state in important posts in preference to his own Greeks and Macedonians. It is clear that the ways of the Orient had a strange fascination for Alexander and that, from a fairly early stage in his conquests, he had fallen under its spell. On ceremonial occasions he put

[1] pp. 23 ff.

*Caption to map opposite*

Alexandria, founded by Alexander the Great in 331 B.C. The port and harbour, overlooked on the east by the towering Pharos lighthouse, were of great commercial importance in the ancient world. But the city was even more famous as a centre of learning and literature, attracting scholars and writers from many lands. The site of the celebrated Museum and Library is uncertain. The Greek translation of the Old Testament, called the Septuagint, is said to have been prepared here on the island of Pharos.

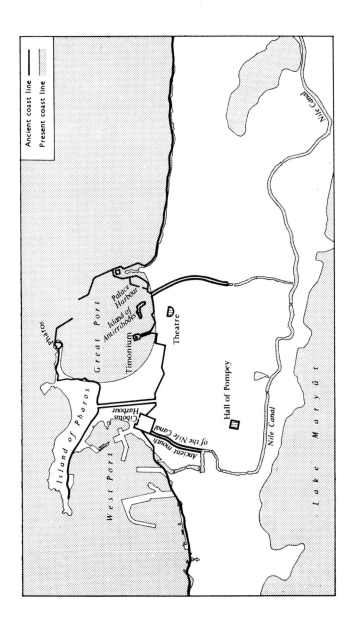

Ancient coast line
Present coast line

Island of Pharos

Pharos

Great Port

West Port

Cibous Harbour

Ancient mouth of the Nile Canal

Palace Harbour

Island of Antirrhodes

Timonium

Theatre

Hall of Pompey

Nile Canal

Lake Maryût

Nile Canal

on Persian dress and introduced Persian customs into his court, in particular encouraging the habit of prostration. In Persian eyes this was no more than a mark of supreme respect; but in Greek and Macedonian eyes it was no less than a sign of worship and implied that Alexander was allowing himself to be treated as a god. This impression had been strengthened by his nephew, Callisthenes the historian, who claimed that the oracle at Amon had announced that Alexander was not Philip's son at all, but the son of the god Zeus-Amon himself. It must have appeared to many of his followers that their leader, in his desire to win the sympathy of his oriental subjects and to be regarded by them as their protector and friend, was himself more Persian than Macedonian, not only in his habits but also in his convictions. Unrest developed in the Macedonian ranks, which Alexander had to quell with strong measures.

His dream of a single world-wide empire based on a unity of language, custom, and culture began to be realized even in his own lifetime. But the measure of his success can be gauged only by the extent to which this dream was achieved during the reigns of his successors.

### 3. *His relations with Palestine*

Very little is known about the history of the Jews during the period between Nehemiah and Ezra and the conquests of Alexander the Great. They were to be found in two main centres—in Babylonia, where they had been taken into exile many years before, and in Judaea, which at this time was very restricted in size, consisting of Jerusalem and the open country with its villages immediately surrounding the mother city. There were Jews also in Egypt, but prior to the Hellenistic period these were of little cultural or religious significance. As the Hellenistic age advanced, however, the Jewish Dispersion in Egypt, as we shall see, became of ever-increasing importance, whilst that in Babylonia receded into the background.

At this time Judaea was a small indigenous state hemmed in on every side by other small nations whose territory was regarded as part of Coele (Hollow)-Syria, the name given to the depression between the Lebanon and Mount Hermon which continues along the Jordan valley to the Dead Sea. Subject to their Persian overlords and harassed by their neighbours, the Jews found economic progress and political aspiration well-nigh impossible. Information concerning their method of government during this period is scanty, but it seems likely that they enjoyed a certain measure of independence and that the High Priest, together with the heads of ancient priestly families who had amassed for themselves considerable wealth, were in control of administrative affairs, and were permitted a fair measure of jurisdiction over the people. The political autonomy of Judaea would be strictly limited, however, by the presence among them of the Persian satrap, who alone would have the right, for example, to mint coins[1] or to muster troops, and who was answerable for civil and military discipline to his Persian overlord. Although the satrap was appointed by the Persian king there is no reason to believe that at this early period, or indeed for some considerable time afterwards, the High Priest was also a Persian nominee. Appointment to this office would require the royal approval, but there seems little reason to doubt that the Jews were given the right to elect their own High Priest, who, according to a deep-rooted tradition, should be of the house of Zadok, i.e. the office was a hereditary one, the eldest son succeeding his father. Recognition would be given to the High Priest as civic and religious leader not only by the Jews in Judaea but also by those in Babylonia. Another factor uniting these two communities was their common language, Aramaic; the fact that the Palestinian Aramaic represented a different dialect from that spoken in Babylonia was no great barrier between them. In spite of the widespread use of Greek it remained the commonly spoken language of Palestinian Jews till long after New Testament times.

[1] A few such coins have been found, dating from the fourth century B.C., bearing the name of the Persian province of *Yehud*, i.e. Judah, where they were minted. They are made of silver and are in the Greek style.

Concerning Alexander's conquest of Palestine very little is known. The biblical evidence, for example, gives only the barest references to him, The claim made by some older scholars that the Book of Habakkuk is to be read against the background of Alexander's Palestinian campaign is now generally discredited, but a number of others see reference to it in Zech. 9–14 and especially in 9[1–8].[1] A clearer allusion, even beneath its symbolic disguise, is to be found in Dan. 8, where Alexander's Greek empire is likened to a he-goat that 'came from the west across the face of the whole earth, without touching the ground' (8[5]).[2]

Somewhat more detail is given by the Greek and Roman writers who record Alexander's life and exploits, but their information too is scanty and obscure. Little is said beyond the fact that, after his two months' siege of Gaza, he destroyed the city, then subsequently restored and repopulated it, stationing there a Macedonian garrison. Thus Gaza became the first Greek city on Palestinian soil. There are indications that several other Greek cities were also founded about this time by Alexander or by one or other of his generals, a policy which was to be pursued with vigour in the following generations. Such absence of information no doubt indicates that there was in fact little or nothing to report. It is clear that he did not waste any time in Palestine, nor did he meet with any serious opposition there apart from that at Gaza. The capitulation and control of Palestine he left in the hands of his generals and his strategically placed Macedonian garrisons, one of which was stationed in Samaria, now established as a Greek city. This step was taken as a result of an outbreak of violence there that had resulted in the murder of his lieutenant Andromachus.

The Jewish historian Josephus[3] supplements these accounts

[1] See commentary, pp. 202 f.          [2] See commentary, pp. 236 ff.

[3] Josephus was born in A.D. 37 and died some time after A.D. 100. His earliest work, *The War*, was written shortly after the Fall of Jerusalem in A.D. 70, first in Aramaic and then, with the help of collaborators, in Greek. It is divided into seven books and uses, together with other sources, a life of Herod by Nicolas of Damascus. The first of these books gives a survey of Jewish history in Hellenistic times; the others tell the story of the Jewish

with certain information found in various (often legendary) forms in Hellenistic Jewish writings and in rabbinic sources. The fullest account is in *Antiquities* XI. viii. 1–6, which tells how the Jews in Jerusalem were angry with Manasseh, brother of the High Priest Jaddua, for having married the daughter of Sanballat, governor of Samaria. They urged him to divorce her or else cease to officiate at the altar. Sanballat thereupon promised to use his influence with Darius to make him High Priest and to appoint him as governor of Samaria in succession to himself; furthermore, he would seek permission from Darius to build on Mount Gerizim a Temple similar to the one in Jerusalem. Unfortunately for him Darius was defeated at Issus by Alexander, who marched south and besieged Tyre. Sanballat thereupon acted prudently and promptly. He came to Tyre with 8,000 soldiers, offering to transfer his allegiance from Darius to his victor. Alexander was greatly pleased and, on hearing Sanballat's request, gave him permission to build the Temple on Mount Gerizim. Sanballat then returned home, built the Temple, and appointed Manasseh High Priest. Shortly afterwards he died.

Meanwhile, during the siege of Tyre, Alexander had sent a letter to the Jews in Jerusalem requiring them to give him men and the supplies which had formerly been paid as tribute to Darius. The High Priest Jaddua refused to comply, affirming that he could not break his oath to Darius not to take up arms against him. Alexander was greatly incensed and, after capturing Tyre and Gaza, advanced against Jerusalem. The Jews were in a panic, but God showed Jaddua in a dream what he should do. The city gates were opened and

Revolt against Rome in the war of A.D. 66–70. About twenty years later he produced his *Jewish Antiquities*, a monumental work in twenty books, the latter ten of which deal with the period from the Exile onwards. A smaller work, *The Life*, was added to this at a later date as an appendix. Later still he wrote a powerful apologia in defence of Judaism called *Against Apion*, which is in part a reply to the slanders of a heathen critic of that name. These writings, though biased by reason of his desire to please his Roman and Hellenistic readers, and also inaccurate in places, provide one of the chief sources of Jewish history in the post-exilic and intertestamental periods.

Alexander III of Macedon, known as Alexander the Great, 356–323 B.C., by the Greek sculptor Lysippus (325–300 B.C.). Probably modelled on a contemporary likeness.

the populace went out to meet Alexander, the people clad in white festal garments and the priests, with Jaddua at their head, in their priestly robes. When Alexander saw them he fell down before the High Priest on whose golden-plated mitre there was inscribed the divine Name. Alexander then entered

Jerusalem and offered sacrifices to God in the Temple under the direction of the High Priest. Permission was given both to them and to their fellow Jews in Babylonia and Media to live according to their ancestral laws, and exemption from taxation in every sabbatical year was granted to them.

On leaving Jerusalem Alexander was met by the Samaritans, who asked him to visit their Temple also and to give them similar exemption from taxation. Alexander, however, refused to commit himself. He sent the Samaritans away but retained Sanballat's soldiers, so that they might accompany him to Egypt.

There are many discrepancies in this story which suggest that it is chiefly legendary in character. The references to San-ballat, Manasseh, and the Temple on Mount Gerizim have their roots in history, but the fact that Sanballat was a contemporary of Nehemiah in the second half of the fifth century shows that Josephus' chronology here cannot be trusted.[1] It is most unlikely, moreover, that Alexander would have had the time to visit Jerusalem following his capture of Gaza and before going to Egypt, for reliable sources indicate that, on leaving Gaza, he arrived in Egypt within seven days. No march at this time is mentioned by any writer other than Josephus. It has been suggested that Alexander may have come into contact with the Jews when he (or his general Perdiccas) set out from Egypt to quell the rising in Samaria, and that Alexander may then have transferred to the Jews stretches of Samaritan territory, as recorded elsewhere by Josephus (cf. *Against Apion* II. 4). The kernel of truth contained in the story is that in Judaea the Jews in all probability were allowed to continue with their accustomed freedom in religious affairs, and that in Samaria there may have been a certain readjustment of territory following the unrest of the people there.

---

[1] It should be noted, however, that papyri from Samaria show that the name 'Sanballat' was borne by later governors also. It is just possible that Josephus may be referring here to one such from the time of Alexander; but this is improbable, as it assumes a repetition not only of the name but also of identical historical events.

# II

## PTOLEMIES AND SELEUCIDS

### 1. *The political scene*

FOLLOWING Alexander's death his empire became the spoil of his generals, four of whom staked their claims and assumed the title of king. These were Cassander, ruler of Macedonia; Lysimachus, in control of Thrace since the partition; Antigonus, who held the whole of Asia Minor and northern Syria; and Ptolemy Lagi, who ruled Egypt and southern Syria. Within a short space of time these were joined by Seleucus, one of Alexander's successful generals, who had subsequently served with Perdiccas and with Ptolemy. By 311 B.C. he had so asserted his authority that he became the acknowledged master of Babylonia, this year marking the beginning of the Seleucid dynasty.

During this time and for many years to come the land of Palestine was to remain a bone of contention. First Ptolemy took possession of it and annexed it to his satrapy in Egypt, only to have it wrested from his grasp by Antigonus (315 B.C.); winning it back at the battle of Gaza (312 B.C.), he had again to withdraw, leaving Antigonus in control. In 301 B.C., however, a decisive battle was fought at Ipsus in Phrygia in which Antigonus was defeated and killed. An agreement had already been reached that, on the defeat of Antigonus, Coele-Syria should be given to Ptolemy; but since he had not taken part in this battle it was now decided to annex it to Seleucus. Ptolemy, however, forestalled him and took immediate possession of the land, an action Seleucus and his successors were never to forget. Seleucus gained much from the victory at Ipsus, however, despite his loss of Palestine, and over the next twenty years he laid claim to a substantial part of Alexander's great empire. But the issue was by no means settled and the

Ptolemy I Lagi, surnamed Soter (Saviour), 376–283 B.C.

Seleucus I, surnamed Nicator (Conqueror), 350–281 B.C.

Bronze busts from Herculaneum, now in the National Museum, Naples. One cannot be certain that these busts are contemporary; they are probably based on earlier portraits and certainly date from the first century A.D.

great powers continued in intermittent warfare for many years. Palestine remained in the control of the Ptolemies throughout most of the third century B.C.; but in the end they had to relinquish it to the Seleucids in the person of Antiochus III (the Great) (223–187 B.C.). After several unsuccessful attempts Antiochus at last captured all its fortified cities in 199/198 B.C., and at the Battle of Panion, near the source of the Jordan, finally won control of the whole land. The Seleucids had now gained possession of what, from the beginning, they had considered theirs by right. The bewildered inhabitants of Palestine, the Jews among them, awaited the outcome of these changes with no little apprehension. The years to come would fully justify their fears.

Meanwhile Antiochus, though victorious over the Ptolemies, had trouble in another quarter. In 192 B.C. he found himself at war with Rome, and at the Battle of Magnesia (190 B.C.) suffered a crippling defeat. He was forced to pay an enormous indemnity and to hand over twenty hostages, among them his own son, who was later to become king as Antiochus IV (Epiphanes). Three years later he died a broken man, and was succeeded by his son Seleucus IV (187–175 B.C.), who, after an uneventful reign, was murdered by his chief minister, Heliodorus, who declared Seleucus' son king. The news of Seleucus' death, however, had reached the ears of his brother Antiochus on his way home from Rome. He immediately arranged for the disposal of his young nephew and proclaimed himself king (175 B.C.). A reign had begun which was to have dire results for the entire Jewish nation.

## 2. *Relations with the Jews*

The political events outlined above, from Alexander to Antiochus IV, are described all too briefly and in tantalizingly cryptic form in Dan. 11.[1] Other historical records fill in details, but the information is very limited indeed. The Greek writer Hecataeus, for example, reports that many Jews, including the High Priest Hezekiah, followed Ptolemy I into Egypt after the Battle of Gaza; the historian Agatharchides states that the same king captured Jerusalem by guile and carried off many as slaves to Egypt; the Letter of Aristeas claims that he transported 100,000 in this way, 30,000 of whom he settled as garrisons in the country. The historicity of these accounts cannot be proved, but it is clear from many papyri and inscriptions found there that from the time of Ptolemy I onwards the number of Jews in Egypt grew considerably. Aristeas reports that Ptolemy II set free those Jews who had been enslaved by his father. Friendly relationships apparently continued through the reigns of at least the first three Ptolemies, the Jewish community being permitted to live 'according to the laws of their fathers' with their own Council of Elders.

Synagogues were built in many towns and villages in various parts of the land and especially in Alexandria, where the Jews, though not forming a completely separate community, settled

[1] See pp. 241 ff.

together in one section of the city close to the seashore. They thus enjoyed a certain autonomy in the ordering of their social and religious affairs and were in the main content to live their lives as members of a distinctly Jewish community. There were not a few among them, however, who were deeply influenced by their Greek environment, and so it is not surprising that in course of time there grew up in Egypt a type of Judaism marked by a fusion of Jewish and Greek ideas, which was to have an immeasurable influence on the life and literature not only of the Dispersion but also of Palestine itself.

During the time of the Ptolemies the city of Alexandria became famous throughout the ancient world as a centre of learning and literature, its great Library attracting scholars and philosophers from near and far. Among the many literary works composed there none can compare with the Greek translation of the Hebrew Scriptures known as 'the Septuagint' (or LXX). A legendary account of its origin is given in the Letter of Aristeas (cf. *Antiquities* XII. ii. 4–15), where it is stated that the translation was made in the time of Ptolemy II (285–246 B.C.) at the request of his librarian Demetrius, who wished to add a copy of the Jewish Laws to his collection of 200,000 books for the benefit of Greek readers. At Demetrius' request Ptolemy sent a letter to Jerusalem to the High Priest Eleazar, who in turn sent seventy-two scholars (later legend says 'seventy', hence the name 'Septuagint') to Alexandria to carry out the task. For seventy-two days they lived together in a house on the island of Pharos and at the end of that time had completed their translation. Whilst legendary features in the story can be disregarded, it may nevertheless be taken as certain that the Torah or Pentateuch was actually translated into Greek in Alexandria, possibly under the patronage of Ptolemy II. The rest of the Hebrew Scriptures would be similarly translated later, most of them before about the year 150 B.C. It is hardly likely, however, that the translation was instigated by Demetrius, who died in exile in 283 B.C., or that it was made for the sake of the learned Greeks in Alexandria; it was rather for the benefit of the Alexandrian Jews who were no longer able to read Hebrew and for whom the translations in the synagogue services were quite inadequate. The actual work of translation was no doubt carried out by Jewish scholars of Alexandria, perhaps with scrolls from Jerusalem, and not by Jerusalem scholars as the story claims. As a bond uniting the Jews of the widely scattered Dispersion and as an instrument for the propagation of Judaism throughout the Greek-speaking world the value of this translation can hardly be overestimated.

But what about the Jews in Palestine during this long period of Ptolemaic supremacy? Relatively little information is available, and what there is is often of a legendary character. It would appear that until near the close of the third century the Jews were left in comparative peace provided that they caused no trouble and paid their taxes regularly to the Ptolemaic government. Despite the removal of many into Egypt in the time of Ptolemy I and the voluntary emigration of many others in subsequent years, Jerusalem remained a fairly populous city in which the priestly class was especially influential. In the time of Ptolemy I the High Priest was Onias I (*c.* 320–290 B.C.), who was succeeded by his son Simon I; he was followed by his uncle Eleazar, and he in turn by his uncle Manasseh. Simon I had a son who was apparently too young at the time of his father's death to accept office; but around 245 B.C. he succeeded Manasseh as Onias II. In due course he was followed by his son Simon II (*c.* 220 B.C.), who is given the title 'the Just' by the Jewish writer Ben Sira (cf. Ecclus. 50): Josephus applies this title to Simon I (cf. *Antiquities* XI. viii. 7; XII. iv. 1), but it is much more likely that it was used of the second High Priest of that name.

Considerable light is cast on administrative and social affairs in Palestine during the reign of Ptolemy II (285–246 B.C.) by a large number of papyri containing the correspondence of one Zeno, an agent of the King's chief minister of finance, Apollonius, discovered in 1915 in the Fayum district of Egypt. These Zeno papyri are supplemented by the so-called Vienna papyri, first published in 1936, which consist of two injunctions from Ptolemy II concerning the regulation of flocks and herds and the unlawful enslavement of certain people in Syria, and which are to be dated in the year 261 B.C. These documents show that there was close contact between Palestine and Egypt and that the country was divided up into small administrative units in the charge of numerous officials appointed by senior officials in Alexandria. Of special importance were the agents of Apollonius who were responsible for commercial and trade relations between the two countries. In 259 B.C. Apollonius sent out a trade mission, perhaps with Zeno at its head, to tour Palestine and the surrounding districts with a view to increasing trade with the local inhabitants. In some of the Zeno papyri reference is made to a Jew named Tobias (Hebrew, Tobiah), a man of considerable substance, who was apparently in charge of a military colony of Ptolemaic soldiers situated in 'the land of the Ammonites' in Transjordan. This name appears again in Aramaic characters in a rock-hewn tomb at 'Araq 'el-Emir in Transjordan, dating from the third century B.C., and no doubt refers to the same man. The district is described in the papyri as 'Tobias' land' and his agents as 'Tobias' people'. He was in close contact with the Egyptian authorities and sent personal letters and gifts to Apollonius and even to Ptolemy himself. There can be little doubt that this Tobias was a descendant of 'Tobiah the Ammonite', the formidable enemy of Nehemiah. It has been argued that the biblical Tobiah was himself a Jew, the designation 'Ammonite' referring to his place of habitation rather than to his nationality, and that he may even have belonged to a priestly family. Whether this is so or not it is reasonable to suppose that the Tobiads, having held responsible office under the Persian kings, continued to serve in like capacity under the Ptolemies.

But the chief interest of this period lies in Tobias' son, Joseph, whose mother was none other than the sister of the High Priest Onias II. When this Onias, who was pro-Seleucid in his sympathies, refused to pay the annual tribute of twenty talents to Ptolemy and was in danger of having his land seized, Joseph offered to negotiate with the King, with the result that Onias was forced to relinquish to his nephew his civil

leadership of the Jews. This was a most significant event and
marks the beginning of a rivalry between the House of Onias and
the House of Tobias which was to have important results in
years to come.

Joseph, as the new civil head, called an assembly of the
Jewish elders and persuaded them to renew their pledge of
loyalty to the Ptolemies. Then, having borrowed money from
friends of his in Samaria, he made his way to Egypt, where he
was able to appease the King and, by means of bribes, to win
friends at court in Alexandria. During this journey (according
to Josephus) or, more probably, some years later Joseph was
able to persuade Ptolemy to appoint him as official tax-collector
for the whole of 'Coele-Syria, Phoenicia, Judaea, and Samaria',
a post which he held for the next twenty-two years. During that
time he became an extremely wealthy man and, as a high
Ptolemaic official, exercised considerable authority over the
people of Syria. When, for example, the cities of Ascalon and
Scythopolis refused to meet his demands for taxes he called in
the help of Ptolemy's soldiers and punished them severely. On
his death Joseph's great wealth passed over to his sons, who
were known henceforth as 'the sons of Tobias'. Favourite
among them was Hyrcanus, the son of his second wife, whose
success in business roused the jealousy and hatred of his seven
half-brothers by Joseph's first wife. In course of time, by the
familiar means of bribery, he won for himself the position of
tax-collector which Joseph himself had held for so long.
Hyrcanus and his half-brothers will appear again in future
relationships between the Jews and their new overlords, the
Seleucids.

From the time of the accession of Ptolemy IV in 221 B.C.
until the conquest of Palestine by Antiochus III the Jewish
people were caught up in the cross-currents of war much more
than in earlier years, and, during the crucial years 202–198
B.C. in particular, when the fate of Palestine was in the balance,
their loyalties were divided, the majority siding with Antiochus III. On the one side stood Hyrcanus, Joseph's son, who,
together with his followers, supported Egypt; on the other side

stood his half-brothers who, together with the High Priest Simon II, supported Syria. To settle the issue a *Gerousia* or Council of the Elders was called, presided over by Simon. A decision was taken to support Antiochus, and when, in 201 B.C., he stood before Jerusalem with his army he was welcomed by Simon and a deputation of elders. That same year the Egyptian general Scopas ousted Antiochus, captured a number of cities in Palestine, and put a garrison in Jerusalem. Two years later, however, Antiochus established his claim on Palestine once and for all and entered Jerusalem in triumph. According to Josephus (cf. *Antiquities* XII. iii. 3 f.) he did not forget the loyalty shown him by the Jews. He gave orders for the restoration of Jerusalem, which had been damaged in the war, put up a considerable sum of money to supply the Temple with sacrificial animals, wine, oil, etc., and imported timber free of duty from the Lebanon and elsewhere to repair the Temple. Moreover, he gave the people the right to live according to their ancestral laws. He exempted all Temple officials from taxation, gave general exemption from taxes for a period of three years, and granted relief of one-third of the required tribute money thereafter. Furthermore, he ordered the return of Jewish refugees, the liberation of those who had been enslaved, and the release of prisoners of war, restoring to them their property. Josephus adds that Antiochus also forbade non-Jews to enter the Temple on pain of death and banned the introduction into Jerusalem of the flesh of unclean beasts. The beginnings of Seleucid rule thus augured well for future relationships; but appearances belied realities, as time was soon to tell.

## 3. *The spread of Hellenism*

The chief means of propagating that form of Greek culture and civilization, known as 'Hellenism', pursued by Alexander and his successors was no doubt the founding of Greek cities, a process begun by Alexander himself and maintained by those who followed him. Of greatest importance was

Alexandria, whose reputation was greatly enhanced by Ptolemy II through the erection there of his famous Library and Museum (or 'Academy'). He and the Ptolemies who succeeded him founded many such cities throughout Asia Minor, Palestine, and the adjacent islands. The Seleucids followed the same policy, sometimes taking over old-established cities and converting them to Greek standards, at other times building new townships altogether and settling in them a 'hard core' of Macedonians and Greeks. Within Palestine itself they were to be found particularly along the Mediterranean coast and in Transjordan. In the time of Pompey mention is made of a league called the 'Decapolis', consisting, as the name implies, of ten cities; these were in existence at a much earlier date than this, even though the league itself did not come into being till much later.

Such cities are called 'Greek', not in the sense that they

Ruins of a colonnaded street in Gerasa (Jerash) whose foundation dates from about the time of Alexander the Great. Situated in Transjordan, about 26 miles north of the present-day Amman, it was one of those cities captured by Alexander Jannaeus in 82 B.C. In the time of Pompey (63 B.C.) it is named as a member of the confederation of cities known as the 'Decapolis' to which reference is made in the New Testament (cf. Matt. 4²⁵; Mark 5²⁰, 7³¹).

were necessarily populated by native Greeks, but rather in the sense that they were organized according to a Greek pattern; for the most part they were inhabited by local people whose political and social life had undergone a complete reorientation. As such these cities were much more than merely 'symbols' of

This bowl from the Cyprus Museum shows a typical *ephebos* or Greek youth, riding bare-back and armed with a lance. Note the wide-brimmed hat, the short skirt, and the flowing cloak. This 'Greek style' was copied by Jewish youths many of whom were fascinated by the whole Greek way of life (see pp. 25 f.).

the Greek way of life; they were living embodiments of it, demonstrating a civilization and culture unlike anything known there before. The method of government by democratic senate, for example, closely resembling the Athenian *Boulē* or *Gerousia*, would no doubt give to the people an entirely new mental outlook. The Gymnasium and the *Ephebeion* (or 'Youth Centre') were typical Greek institutions, to be found in all cities of this kind, which breathed the very spirit of Hellenism. They were educational institutions in which the young men of the day could gain an appreciation not only of literature and poetry and music but also of physical culture, which was of the very essence of Greek civilization. 'They expressed', writes Edwyn Bevan, 'fundamental tendencies of the Greek mind—its craving for harmonius beauty of form, its delight in the body, its unabashed frankness with regard to everything natural.'[1] This delight in beauty, shape, and movement found expression in such things as athletic contests and horse-racing, to which the Greeks applied themselves with the utmost seriousness; these were not merely forms of entertainment, but a precious heritage that both perpetuated and strengthened the age-long Greek tradition. Interest in literature and the arts showed itself in the growth of philosophic schools and in the development of drama as a form of cultural expression. Hence, alongside the senate house there appeared the stadium and the hippodrome as emblems of this all-pervasive culture, and alongside these the theatre, which provided everything from classical tragedies to 'music-hall' comedies. Such buildings would convey not only the air but also the appearance of a truly Greek city, as indeed would the style of dress worn, especially by the young men. Members of the *Ephebeion*, for example, wore distinctive dress to show that they belonged to the city's 'young men's guild'; characteristic of this dress was a wide-brimmed hat, a cloak fastened with brooches at the shoulders and high-laced boots. In a number of cities the local dialect or language would still be spoken by some, but just as it was fashionable to 'dress with the times' and keep up with the cultural trends, so it was essential for all educated men, and indeed for any who had even a modicum of interest in culture, to speak the Greek tongue. This Hellenistic culture, then, opened up for many people entirely new vistas, developed new aesthetic appreciation, and encouraged the study of science, philosophy, and the liberal arts in a quite remarkable way throughout the whole civilized world. Intelligent men belonging to traditions other than that of the Greeks saw how superior the Greek way of life was to their own. There was a charm and a vitality about it

[1] *Jerusalem under the High Priests*, 1920, p. 35.

that carried its own appeal to men of diverse religious, political, and cultural backgrounds.

There was another side to Hellenism, however, that was much less attractive. A great deal of what passed as 'culture' was little more than a degenerate form of religious or social life. The religious rites and ceremonies, for example, with which the athletic contests were invariably associated were regularly accompanied by forms of immorality and vice to which many succumbed. Increased wealth led a section of the people to a life of idleness and ease which affected the moral condition of the people as a whole. Here is how the ancient historian Posidonius describes the situation:

> Life is a continuous series of social festivities. Their gymnasiums they use as baths where they anoint themselves with costly oils and myrrhs. In the *grammateia* (such is the name they give to the public eating-halls) they practically live, filling themselves there for the better part of the day with rich foods and wine; much that they cannot eat they carry away home. They feast to the prevailing music of strings.[1]

Such 'culture' was a far cry from 'the glories that were Greece'.

The influence of Hellenism, however, was not confined to political, social, literary, and aesthetic pursuits. By its very nature it deeply affected the religious life and beliefs of the various cultures it invaded. Although Greek in origin and outlook it was essentially a syncretistic system, incorporating beliefs and legends of different religious traditions from both East and West. When Alexander pressed eastwards through Persia towards India, planting Greek cities and cultivating the Hellenistic outlook through trade, marriage, and the like, he made a breach in the cultural barrier between East and West that deeply affected the countries of the Orient. But the effect was reciprocal, for there came flooding back into the lands of the West ideas and influences completely foreign to the Greek way of thinking and living. The Persian empire which Alexander took over had itself taken over the old Babylonian

[1] Ibid., pp. 41 f.

empire, with its interest in cosmology, astronomy, occultism, demonology, and angelology. Besides these the Zoroastrian religion of the old Iranian or Persian empire was a powerful factor, with its stress on such matters as the determinism of history, the doctrine of the 'two ages', the destruction of the world, the Final Judgement, and so on. This Perso–Babylonian confusion of culture to be found in Alexander's newly-conquered empire, intermingling with the Greek culture from the West, gradually built up a syncretistic system of belief that deeply influenced the Jews scattered throughout the Dispersion.

But what about the Jews in Judaea? It is hardly surprising that they too felt the full impact of this alien culture, exposed as they were on all sides to the influence of Hellenistic life and thought. To the south-west lay Egypt, the most powerful advocate of the Greek way of life; to the south lay Idumaea, whose painted tombs in Marissa, dating from the second half of the third century B.C., show ample evidence of Hellenistic culture; to the east and south-east lay Nabataea, in close contact with Egypt through commerce and trade; to the north lay Samaria with its garrison of Macedonian troops; and to the west and north-west lay Philistia and Phoenicia, with their Greek cities dotting the coastal plain.

New aesthetic horizons had been opened up before the Jews in Jerusalem; old Jewish customs and rites now appeared all too crude when judged by the standards of the 'new enlighten-ment'. In particular the rite of circumcision became a cause of acute embarrassment to the young Jewish athlete who, as was the custom, ran naked on the track; he accordingly took measures to have himself 'uncircumcised' so as to avoid the derision of the crowds. Athletic games, horse-racing, and the theatre became increasingly popular with the Jewish youths, who dressed themselves like the Greeks and were not even averse to sacrificing to foreign deities as part of the ritual expected of every participant. But the true Hellenizers among the Jews were to be found in the ranks of the ruling aristocracy in Jerusalem, which consisted for the most part of wealthy priestly families. The story of Joseph the Tobiad and his son

Hyrcanus shows clearly that to amass wealth and to hold an influential position in the land it was necessary to keep in step with the Greeks. The new culture, on its external side at any rate, implied a certain social standing, which was apparently more important to such people than religious scruples.

There were others in Jerusalem, however, who refused to respond in this way to the wiles of Hellenistic culture. Valuable insights are given here by Joshua ben Sira ('Jesus son of Sirach' in its Greek form), who wrote his great book, called 'Ecclesiasticus' in the Apocrypha, around the year 180 B.C.[1] Ben Sira was undoubtedly influenced by the spirit of the age in which he lived, but refused to yield to the attractions of Hellenism. In his book, which shows the outlook of the traditional Judaism of the scribal schools, he sets himself the task of educating Jewish youths in the tenets of that Hebrew wisdom which is to be found in the fear of the Lord, and finds expression in manners and morality. The time had not yet come for traditional Judaism and Greek culture to clash, but already Ben Sira was aware of the danger, and so set himself to fortify men's faith through his teaching.

During this same period there emerged a company of men called the Hasidim (RSV, Hasidaeans), or Pious Ones, who took a firm stand against Hellenism and, in the years to come, were to play a vitally important part in the religious and national life of the Jewish people. They were to come to the forefront some years later at the time of the Maccabaean Revolt, but even before the opposition to Hellenism came to a head in open rebellion their passionate zeal for the Law, and their eagerness to defend the ways of their fathers, must have been a significant factor in the reaction of the Jewish people to the Hellenistic culture. It was almost inevitable that a clash should come, sooner or later, between these champions of the Law and the wealthy aristocrats whose whole outlook on life and religion was so different from their own. It came at last with the accession of Antiochus IV (Epiphanes) to the throne. The policy of religious toleration adopted by the

[1] See pp. 260 ff.

Ptolemies and earlier Seleucids, which had laid the people wide open to the subtle influence of Hellenism, was now abandoned. The tactics of Antiochus made it clear to many of the faithful in Israel that the antagonism between Hellenism and Judaism was not merely a matter of social standing or culture: where their religion and their Law were concerned it was from now on a matter of life and death.

# III

# ANTIOCHUS IV AND THE JEWS

## 1. *The policy and character of Antiochus IV*

BEFORE coming to the throne Antiochus IV, as we have seen, had for twelve years been a hostage in Rome where he made many friends and came to admire Rome's political institutions and military organization. This first-hand knowledge gave him a healthy respect for Roman power in years to come and taught him to exercise that restraint without which, with his impulsive nature, he would more often have found himself in serious difficulties. In 177 B.C. his nephew Demetrius, second son of Seleucus IV, took his place as a hostage in Rome. Antiochus went at once to Athens, where after a short time he again made many friends and was appointed chief magistrate, an honour he was never to forget and which he sought to repay in later years by lavish gifts. On hearing of the murder of his brother Seleucus IV at the hands of his chief minister, Heliodorus, he set off for home and, with the help of Eumenes II, King of Pergamon, ousted Heliodorus from the regency and established himself as King.

The task which now faced him was not an enviable one. He found himself seriously handicapped in three directions— like his brother Seleucus before him he was in desperate need of money; the empire he had inherited lacked cohesion and was in danger of breaking up; his neighbours the Egyptians, the Romans, and the Parthians were pressing in upon him from every side, ready to take the utmost advantage of Syria's weakness. Antiochus determined to deal with each of these difficulties in his own way.

His financial troubles were met, partly at any rate, by robbing various temples and shrines, including the Temple in Jerusalem, whose treasures, as we shall see, he plundered.

The instability and potential disunity of his kingdom he met with a vigorous policy of Hellenization. Such a policy had, of course, already been pursued by his predecessors, but Antiochus devoted himself to the task with the utmost vigour. In particular he encouraged the cities throughout his dominion to adopt a more radical policy of Hellenization in local government and in the ordering of their community life. Religion, as part of culture, came within the scope of this policy of Hellenization; but it was not his intention to ride rough-shod over local sentiments or to suppress the worship of local deities; indeed he was prepared to recognize these gods and honoured them with offerings and sacrifices. The evidence of coins minted during his reign indicates, however, that he himself was particularly disposed to the worship of the ancient god, Olympian Zeus, whom he set up in place of the god Apollo, the traditional protector of the Seleucid dynasty. But Antiochus was no monotheist, nor did he seek to replace the worship of local deities by the worship of this one 'high god'. Zeus could readily be identified with any of these local deities; nevertheless they were able to retain their separate identity and stand side by side in the pantheon. There are indications that Antiochus may have encouraged the people to worship his own person in the form of the god Zeus, for in certain of his coins the image of Zeus appears with features that closely resemble those of the King himself. For the first five or six years of his reign he was designated simply 'King Antiochus', but around 169 B.C. he assumed the additional title 'Theos Epiphanes', meaning 'God Manifest', and in 166 B.C. he added to this the equally divine epithet 'Nicephorus', meaning 'Victorious'. There was, of course, nothing new in a king's claiming divine prerogatives of this kind; Alexander had done so before him and the claim had been made for several of his predecessors on the Seleucid throne. But this was nothing short of blasphemous in the eyes of the Jews who acknowledged the one true and only God.

At this time the dominant claims of Rome were making themselves increasingly felt, and suspicious eyes were cast in the direction of Antiochus, who was now setting himself the task of drawing Egypt and Syria together under Seleucid rule. Roman policy, as we shall see, was constantly being bedevilled by two disturbing factors—political rivalries at home, affecting national stability, and the danger of enemy attack on the eastern frontier. Antiochus, whose growing power was an obvious menace to the security of these territories, was accordingly bound by treaty with Rome not to attack any of her friends or allies, and, if forced to engage in a defensive war, not to lay permanent claim to any conquered territory. Egypt, however, very conveniently played into his hands by declaring war on him in 169 B.C. But Antiochus took the initiative, marched into Egypt with a strong force (cf. Dan. 11$^{25-28}$; 1 Macc. 1$^{16-19}$), and routed the Egyptian army. A year later he decided to risk the wrath of Rome and invaded Egypt a second time (cf. Dan. 11$^{29-30a}$; 2 Macc. 5$^1$), laying siege to Alexandria. Then, proceeding to Memphis, he had himself crowned King of Egypt, an act which did nothing to alleviate the suspicions of Rome. Just as he was preparing to annex the whole of Egypt, Rome acted, promptly and firmly. An embassy arrived in Alexandria, headed by Popilius Laenas, who handed to Antiochus a decree of the Roman Senate demanding his immediate withdrawal from Egypt. When Antiochus asked for time to deliberate with his counsellors, Popilius dramatically drew a circle round him and bade him decide there and then, and not to leave the circle until his decision was made. Antiochus was forced to comply with Rome's demand; in the words of Polybius, he withdrew to Syria 'in high dudgeon indeed and groaning in spirit, but yielding to the necessities of the time'. Repulsed on his western frontiers, he now set off to the east, where the rapidly increasing power of the Parthians had become a serious menace. In 166 B.C. he made a great show of power at the celebrated Festival of Daphne near Antioch, and the following year crossed the Euphrates, leaving the affairs of his kingdom in the hands of a regent, Lysias, who was appointed guardian of his eight-years-old son, soon to succeed him as Antiochus V (Eupator) (cf. 1 Macc. 3$^{27-37}$). Little is known about this Parthian campaign, in which, apparently, Antiochus won a number of victories before dying, it is said, of consumption in 163 B.C. (cf. 1 Macc. 6¹⁻¹⁶).

The picture of this powerful Seleucid king that emerges is one of vivid contrasts, and defies description. It is clear from the account given of his military exploits that he was a soldier and statesman of no mean ability, whose policies were marked by shrewdness and courage. He showed military skill and prowess in the field of battle and at times rivalled the Romans themselves in the difficult and dangerous game of diplomacy. But there was a tyrannical streak about him and an impulsiveness which made even his friends not a little afraid of him. He made friends easily and could be generous in the extreme to those he liked. But he was completely unreliable and unpredictable. One day he would distribute gifts of silver and gold; the next, for no apparent reason, he would dole out the cheapest of trinkets. One moment he would be talkative and friendly; the next silent and moody. He often acted on the spur of the moment and found himself doing the most strange and even outrageous things. Polybius tells us that he would fraternize with the lowliest workman or take part in carousals with undesirable characters. He liked to frequent the public baths, where on one occasion, it is reported, he poured a jar of perfumed ointment over the heads of the bathers so that they slithered about on the floor, the King among them! He would sometimes join the actors in a theatrical performance on the stage, or would turn up at a drinking party as a member of the orchestra or take part in the dancing. Such practical jokes and undignified behaviour caused many of his people to despise him. But with his frivolity there was a fickleness that warned them not to take too many liberties. His mood of joviality could suddenly change to fearful vindictiveness. It is not without significance that he was nicknamed by some 'Epimanes', meaning 'mad', instead of 'Epiphanes', meaning '(God) manifest', for there are indications that towards the end of his life he showed signs of mental derangement, a condition which his drunken habits only helped to accentuate. It was during the reign of this brilliant and besotted man that the Jewish people suffered indignities few nations have ever been called upon to face.

## 2. *Hellenizers in Jerusalem*

When Antiochus Epiphanes came to the throne in 175 B.C. the High Priest in Jerusalem was Onias III, a religious man and leader of the orthodox, who had succeeded his father Simon the Just. Unlike his father, who sided with the Seleucids, Onias gave his support to the Ptolemies. He was no doubt influenced in this decision by the proximity of the large and influential company of Jews in Egypt who would have easier access to the Jerusalem Temple than the more distant colony in Babylonia for whom pilgrimage through a disrupted Syria would be a hazardous undertaking. His policy of friendship with Egypt was opposed by the elder sons of Joseph the Tobiad, one of whom, Simon, was at this time 'captain of the Temple'. This rivalry came into the open during the reign of Seleucus IV when Onias successfully opposed Simon's attempt to gain control of the market in Jerusalem, which carried with it considerable commercial and financial advantages. Simon sought reprisal by denouncing Onias to the King, alleging that he was in league with the Ptolemaic sympathizer, Hyrcanus (Simon's own half-brother), who had a large sum of money hidden away in the Temple (cf. 2 Macc. 3[11]). On hearing this, Seleucus sent his chief minister Heliodorus to appropriate the Temple treasure. Onias, however, refused to give it up, asserting that it had been subscribed by widows and orphans, though some of it belonged to Hyrcanus. Heliodorus thereupon forced his way into the Temple, but (so the story goes) was terrified by an apparition in which he was flogged by two young men (cf. 2 Macc. 3[10 ff.]). As a consequence he gave up his attempt to take the treasure.

Simon, however, not to be outdone, again accused Onias of plotting against the King. Onias decided to put his case person before Seleucus in Antioch; but just at this time the King was murdered by Heliodorus and succeeded by his brother Antiochus IV. Events in Jerusalem, as we shall see, made it impossible for Onias to return there and so he stayed on in Antioch.[1]

With the High Priest safely out of the way the stage was set for the Tobiads in Jerusalem to assert their authority and to establish themselves even more securely in a position of power. They and their fellow Hellenizers in the aristocratic priestly party were openly pro-Seleucid in their sympathies, and saw in the accession of Antiochus IV an opportunity to further their own ends. Fortunately for them they had a champion in Onias' brother, Jason, who preferred this Greek form of his name to the Hebrew form 'Joshua'. During Onias' absence from Jerusalem, and with the full support of the Tobiads, Jason sought appointment to the High-Priestly office in return for a large sum of money to be paid to Antiochus and the pledge of his wholehearted support in the Hellenization of the Jews (cf. 1 Macc. 1[13-15]; 2 Macc. 4[7-15]). Antiochus at once agreed. To him such an appointment was an astute political move, for, quite apart from the financial advantage gained, Jason was the avowed leader in Jerusalem of the pro-Syrian party. Jason accordingly assumed office (174 B.C.) and set in motion his agreed policy of Hellenization. The King gave him permission to build a gymnasium in Jerusalem and to enrol Jewish youths in it. Games were organized in which the athletes, according to Greek custom, ran naked on the track; even young priests left the altar to take part in the sports. They removed their mark of circumcision; they wore the distinctive cap of Hermes, the patron of Greek sports; they changed their Hebrew names to the Greek style, and conformed in almost every way to Greek custom and fashion. The writer of 2 Maccabees records that Jason sought permission 'to register the Jerusalemites as Antiocheans' (4[9]). Scholars differ

---

[1] According to Josephus he fled to Egypt, where in due course he built a Temple in Leontopolis (cf. *War* VII. x. 2); but elsewhere he more accurately refers this to his son Onias IV (cf. *Antiquities* XII. ix. 7; XIII. iii. 1–3). Another tradition states that Onias III was killed at Daphne near Antioch (cf. 2 Macc. 4[33 ff.])

in their interpretation of these words. Some take them to mean that he sought for the citizens of Jerusalem the rights of citizens of Antioch, the Seleucid capital; others argue that Jerusalem was, in effect, replaced by a new city and renamed 'Antioch', with a new constitution, so that its citizens could truly be called 'Antiocheans'; others again take the words to refer to membership of the gymnasium, which formed a 'corporation' of Hellenized Jews with privileged citizenship rights, the members being called 'Antiocheans' in commemoration of their patron Antiochus IV. The granting of this request (whatever its exact interpretation) meant that the concessions previously granted by Antiochus III, permitting the Jews to live according to their ancestral laws, were now abrogated (cf. 2 Macc. 4[11]). The city was given over to the Greek way of life.

It is not in the least surprising that the orthodox Jews in Jerusalem were greatly incensed at these things. Quite apart from Jason's obnoxious policy of Hellenization, it was to them intolerable that a High Priest should be appointed to this divine office by a Gentile King. Their feelings were tempered only by the fact that he at least belonged to the High-Priestly family, and it is probably for this reason that they took no active measures against him. But Jason's position was far from secure. The Tobiads, although they had supported his appointment to the High Priesthood, now found that his policy of Hellenization was not radical enough, and determined to obtain the office for Menelaus (Hebrew, *Menahem*), one of their own number. The sources disagree about this man's identity; but if, as the writer of 2 Maccabees records (cf. 3[4], 4[23]), he was a Benjamite, then he was not even a member of a priestly family. The opportunity came when Jason sent Menelaus to Antiochus with certain moneys which he owed the King. Menelaus grasped his opportunity, pledging to the King a more thorough policy of Hellenization than Jason's and offering three hundred talents more than his rival had been able to give. Antiochus accepted, and Menelaus returned to Jerusalem as the new High Priest. Fighting broke out in the city, in which Menelaus ultimately gained the upper hand, chiefly through the help of Syrian troops sent to assist him. But all was not well with Menelaus. The greater part of the people in Jerusalem were opposed to him, and, to make matters worse, he was finding difficulty in raising the money promised to Antiochus, who now summoned him to Antioch to give an account of himself. Before leaving Jerusalem, with the help of his brother Lysimachus, who was to act as High Priest in his absence, he took possession of a number of golden vessels from the Temple treasury, some of which he sold and others he gave to Andronicus, the King's deputy in Antioch, as a bribe. According to 2 Maccabees, Onias III, the legitimate High Priest, who was still in Antioch at this time, protested against these measures; Menelaus thereupon persuaded Andronicus to have him put to death (cf. 2 Macc. $4^{33-38}$; Dan. $9^{26}$; $11^{22}$). Some scholars believe that this Onias III was the Teacher of Righteousness of the Dead Sea Scrolls and that Menelaus was his opponent, the Wicked Priest.[1]

Meanwhile trouble was again brewing in Jerusalem, where the issue of 'Judaism versus Hellenism' had become much more clearly defined in the eyes of an increasing number of people. Menelaus' plundering of the Temple was the last straw; severe fighting broke out, in which the mass of the people took up arms against the Hellenizers. Lysimachus mustered an army of three thousand men to quell the riot, but his followers were beaten and he himself was killed (cf. 2 Macc. $4^{39-42}$). At this point the Jewish people sent three of their elders to Antiochus to lodge complaints against Menelaus, but without avail. Menelaus retained his office by offering further bribes (cf. 2 Macc. $4^{43-50}$). Meanwhile Jason, who had taken refuge in Transjordan, was biding his time to strike back. His opportunity came when a false rumour reached Jerusalem that Antiochus had died in Egypt. Attacking Jerusalem with a thousand men he compelled Menelaus to take refuge in the citadel (cf. 2 Macc. $5^5$). Not all the orthodox Jews who opposed Menelaus, however, were for that reason on the side of Jason, and many were alienated still further by his

[1] See p. 167.

senseless massacre of many innocent people (cf. 2 Macc. 1$^8$, 5$^6$). At last he was driven out of the city and took refuge again in Transjordan; after many wanderings he died a fugitive and an outcast from his people (cf. 2 Macc. 5$^{7-10}$).

### 3. The vengeance of Antiochus

During this time Antiochus had been taking part in his first Egyptian campaign, in which he defeated Ptolemy VI's army (169 B.C.). On his way back to Syria he learned of the insurrection in Jerusalem and decided to turn aside and subdue the city (cf. 1 Macc. 1$^{20-29}$; 2 Macc. 5$^{11-17}$). In his eyes the people's refusal to recognize his nominee Menelaus as High Priest was an act of rebellion against his own authority which must be punished. Besides this he could not afford to have a pro-Ptolemaic element asserting itself so close to the Egyptian border. Arriving in Jerusalem he reinstated Menelaus and let loose his soldiers to massacre the people. Then, in company with Menelaus (cf. 2 Macc. 5$^{15}$), he desecrated the Temple, plundering the silver and gold vessels that still remained there together with the sacred furnishings and hidden treasures. He then withdrew, leaving the city in the charge of Philip, one of his commanders (cf. 2 Macc. 5$^{22}$).

The next contact Antiochus had with Jerusalem was after his second campaign against Egypt in 168 B.C. when he was severely snubbed by the Roman legate, Popilius Laenas. On his way home he learned of renewed strife in Jerusalem despite the presence there of his commander, Philip. Antiochus was in no mood to be trifled with; he would not tolerate a repetition of the previous trouble and so sent his general Apollonius, leader of the Mysian mercenaries, to deal with the situation (cf. 1 Macc. 1$^{29-35}$; 2 Macc. 5$^{23-26}$). Arriving in Jerusalem, Apollonius waited until the Sabbath, when he knew that the orthodox Jews would not fight, and, under pretence of friendship and peaceful intent, rushed into the city with his troops and slaughtered many of the people. Women and children were taken as slaves; the city was despoiled and burned with fire;

the houses and the surrounding walls were razed to the ground. Not content with this he fortified the citadel on the western hill opposite the Temple with a strong wall and high towers, making it into a fortress, which was now occupied by foreign troops and by a host of Jewish Hellenizers. From now on the Akra, as the fortress was called, became in effect a Greek 'polis' or 'city' in its own right, with jurisdiction over the defenceless city of Jerusalem, which, with its breached walls, lay as open country round about it. The Hellenizers, consisting for the most part of wealthy priests and nobles together with their families, were able to pursue with vigour their policy of Hellenization; even more than before, the control of Jerusalem found its way into their hands. The imposition of taxes and the confiscation of land widened the already great gulf between them and the mass of the people who lived in Jerusalem and the surrounding countryside. Irresponsible men in the Akra took matters into their own hands and much innocent blood was shed. Life for many of these Jews became too much to bear and a considerable number fled from the city (cf. 1 Macc. 1[38], 3[48]). There was nothing now to keep even the most pious of them there, for the holy Temple itself had come under the control of the Akra. The city had become 'an abode of aliens' inhabited by 'people of pollution' (1 Macc. 1[35-36]) who worshipped foreign gods (cf. Dan. 11[39]). The Syrian soldiers, who worshipped the god Baal Shamen (meaning 'Lord of Heaven') and other deities popular within their syncretistic Hellenistic faith, were not slow to appropriate the Temple for their own use. Within its sacred precincts the worship of the God of Israel was combined with the worship of the gods of the heathen. The Hellenizing Jews were not only conversant with these things, they actually threw in their lot with them. Their leader Menelaus, far from protesting, apparently continued to officiate as High Priest, content that Judaism should continue as a syncretistic cult and that the God of Israel should be worshipped in association with foreign gods.

Up to this point the measures taken by Antiochus to subdue Jerusalem had been political in character and not directed specifically against the Jews' religion, even although in the process their religious institutions had suffered. Now he determined to change his tactics and to exterminate the Jewish religion altogether. His plan was put into operation 'a short time afterwards' (2 Macc. 6¹), in 167 B.C.,[1] with the proclamation of a decree forbidding the people any longer to live according to their ancestral laws (cf. 1 Macc. 1⁴¹⁻⁶⁴; 2 Macc. 6¹⁻¹¹), and a special emissary was sent to see that this order was carried out. The aim was the complete abolition of the Jewish religion throughout Jerusalem and all Judaea. Attention was concentrated on those very features of Judaism which ever since the return from the Exile had been recognized as the distinctive marks of the Jewish faith—the observance of the sacrifices and festivals, the rite of circumcision, and the reading of the Law. The traditional sacrifices were prohibited and the observance of the Sabbath and the customary festivals forbidden; children must no longer be circumcised; copies of the Law were to be destroyed. Sentence of death was decreed for anyone found breaking any of these commands. Idolatrous altars were set up throughout the land (cf. 1 Macc. 1⁴⁷); on pain of death Jews were forced to offer unclean sacrifices and to eat swine's flesh (cf. 2 Macc. 6¹⁸). As a crowning deed of infamy, in December 167 B.C. Antiochus introduced into the Temple in Jerusalem the worship of the Olympian Zeus. An altar with a bearded image of Zeus, probably bearing the features of Antiochus himself, was erected on the altar of burnt offerings and swine's flesh offered on it (cf. 2 Macc. 6²). It is this altar which Daniel calls 'the abomination that makes desolate' (Dan. 11³¹, 12¹¹). The Syrian soldiers and the 'heathen' generally offered forbidden sacrifices and took part in acts of sensuality and drunken orgies. It was impossible to live as Jews in circumstances like these. They were even compelled to take part in the monthly sacrifice offered in commemoration of the King's birthday and to walk in the

[1] Or 168 B.C. The uncertainty is due to the fact that dates for this period are calculated from the 'Seleucid year', which is taken as either 311 or 312 B.C.

procession of the god Bacchus, garlanded with ivy wreaths (cf. 2 Macc. 6³⁻⁷). These measures were enforced on the Jews not only in Jerusalem and Judaea but also in many other places throughout the empire. Even the Samaritan Temple on Mount Gerizim was also dedicated to the god Zeus (cf. 2 Macc. 6²). All who refused to conform to the Greek way of life were to be put to death (cf. 2 Macc. 6⁸⁻⁹).

The High Priest Menelaus and his Hellenizing priests no doubt acquiesced in these measures; others submitted with a less easy conscience because of the dire penalties which might otherwise follow (cf. 1 Macc. 1⁴³⁻⁵²). There were others, however, who 'chose to die rather than to be defiled by food or to profane the holy covenant' (1 Macc. 1⁶³). The accounts given of the persecution of these people are in part legendary (especially in 2 Macc. 6–7), but they give some idea at least of the severity of the punishment meted out to them. An aged scribe, Eleazar, was forced to open his mouth to eat swine's flesh and on refusing was flogged to death (cf. 2 Macc. 6¹⁸⁻³¹). A mother and her seven sons were slaughtered one after the other for refusing to pay homage to an idol (cf. 2 Macc. 7). Copies of the Law were torn in pieces and burned (cf. 1 Macc. 1⁵⁶). Mothers who had circumcised their newly born children were put to death together with members of their families (cf. 1 Macc. 1⁶⁰⁻⁶¹; 2 Macc. 6¹⁰). Many people who had left the cities and crowded out into the villages and the surrounding country were continually molested by Syrian agents determined to stamp out the Jewish faith.

# IV

## THE FIGHT FOR FREEDOM
### (166–142 B.C.)

### 1. *The beginnings of revolt*

THE Jews were stunned by the suddenness and ferocity of these events. Many in Jerusalem and neighbouring cities, as we have seen, fled into the open country, where they took refuge in the villages, the mountains, and the desert. Others no doubt fled much farther afield and swelled the numbers in the Dispersion in different parts of the empire.

There were some, however, who decided that the time had come for drastic action. In the village of Modein, seventeen miles north-west of Jerusalem, there lived an aged priest named Mattathias with his five sons—John, Simon, Judas, Eleazar, and Jonathan—who had apparently moved there from Jerusalem some time before (cf. 1 Macc. 2¹ ᶠᶠ·). Mattathias' grandfather was a man called Asamonaeus (cf. *War* I. i. 3; *Antiquities* XII. vi. 1), and this is the probable origin of the name 'Hasmonaean' which is commonly given to his descendants.[1] One day Antiochus' agents arrived at the village and began to compel the people to renounce their God and to offer unclean sacrifices (cf. 1 Macc. 2¹⁵ᶠᶠ·). Mattathias, as an acknowledged leader of the community, was bidden to show a good example by being first to make his offering; if he did so he and his sons would be rewarded and be counted among 'the Friends of the King'. Instead, he defied the order and publicly pledged his loyalty to the ways of his fathers. When a renegade Jew stepped forward to offer the required sacrifice, Mattathias put words into deeds and slew him on the altar. Then, turning on a Syrian

---

[1] Another explanation is that it comes from the word *Hasmonaim* meaning 'Princes'. See p. 185.

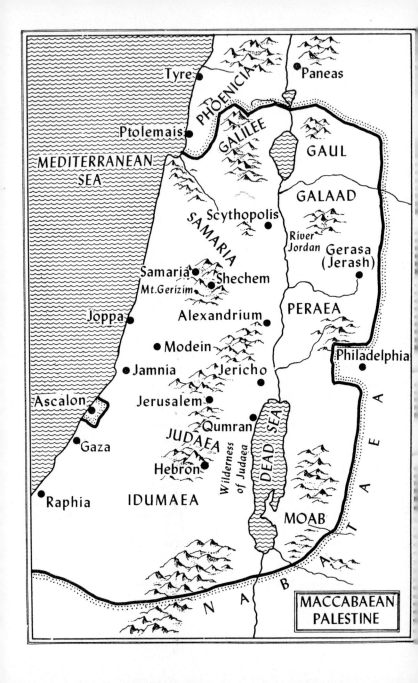

MACCABAEAN
PALESTINE

officer who was standing by, he slew him also, and finally destroyed the altar itself. It was impossible for Mattathias and his
sons to remain in Modein any longer, and so, calling upon all
who were 'zealous for the Law' to follow him, he fled with his
followers to the mountains in the wilderness of Judaea. Whilst
they were hidden there news reached them of a thousand men,
women, and children who had been slain nearby because they
refused to fight on the Sabbath day. Realizing that such a
policy could only spell disaster for their cause, Mattathias and
his companions came to an important decision—Sabbath or
no Sabbath they would fight to the death in defence of the
holy Covenant which God had made with their fathers
(cf. 1 Macc. 2⁴¹).

At this point an important event took place that gave the
movement not only increased numerical strength but also a new
religious standing. Mattathias and his sons were joined by the
Hasidim (Hasidaeans), who, as we have seen, probably came
into existence some time earlier, during the High Priesthood of
Onias III, but are mentioned now by name for the first time
(cf. 1 Macc. 2⁴²; cf. 7¹³; 2 Macc. 14⁶). At a later stage these men
were to find themselves at cross purposes with the Maccabees,
and ultimately they withdrew from them; but at this juncture
their attachment to the resistance movement gave it the inspiration it required. From the beginning they apparently retained
their identity as a distinct group, and the fight for freedom in
those early days owed much to their devotion and zeal.
It has generally been thought, because they were among those
who refused to fight on the Sabbath day (cf. 1 Macc. 2³⁶), that
they formed a pietistic and pacifist group, intent only on
religious reform and avoiding political and national entangle-
ments as much as possible. This is now seen to be a miscon-
ception. They formed a religious group within Judaism whose
passionate devotion to the Law of God was so intense that they
were prepared for its sake to sacrifice their very lives. Most
scholars see in them the ancestors of the Essenes with whom
they would identify the party of the Dead Sea Scrolls.[1]  The

[1] See pp. 165 f.

evidence of the Scrolls supports the picture given of them in 1 and 2 Maccabees as 'mighty warriors of Israel', ready to fight in defence of the Law (cf. 1 Macc. 2⁴²), who 'keep up war and stir up sedition' against the Syrians (cf. 2 Macc. 14⁶), and form an important element in the revolutionary army (cf. 1 Macc. 7¹³). These 'militant believers', filled with a deep piety and aflame with zeal for God's holy Law, had no doubt for some time taken their stand in opposition to the Hellenizers in Jerusalem. Now they came out openly on the side of Mattathias and his sons, their swords unsheathed in the struggle for religious liberty.

In those early days of the Maccabaean Revolt, as the struggle came to be called, the fighting took the form of guerrilla war-fare (cf. 1 Macc. 2⁴⁴⁻⁴⁸). They went from village to village tearing down the altars, forcibly circumcising those children who had not undergone the rite, and slaughtering any they found who had taken part in pagan sacrifices. In this way 'they rescued the law out of the hands of the Gentiles and kings, and they never let the sinner gain the upper hand' (1 Macc. 2⁴⁸). In that same year, 166 B.C., Mattathias died, his place being taken by his third son, Judas, with whom a new stage in the fighting began (cf. 1 Macc. 2⁴⁹⁻⁷⁰; *Antiquities* XII. vi. 3–4).

Not long after these events a book appeared which despite its obscure symbolism casts a great deal of light on the hopes and fears of the faithful Jews living in those days. The Book of Daniel[1] reflects the outlook of the party of the Hasidim. Its author (or authors) expresses his faith in the speedy triumph of God's purpose, and at the same time encourages his fellow Jews in their sufferings to remain true to the Law and the holy Covenant made with their fathers. Little reference is made here to the events associated with the Maccabaean Revolt. Several reasons can perhaps be given for this. The fighting at this time, as we have seen, had not yet developed into full-scale war, but was still at the guerrilla stage; the author is rather doubtful about 'flatterers' who had joined themselves to the movement (11³⁴); above all, his faith was

[1] See pp. 220 ff. The book, as we have it, probably belongs to the period 167–164 B.C.

set not so much in a victory of arms as in the supernatural intervention of God ($2^{23}$, $8^{25}$), who would send his archangel Michael to rescue his people out of all their troubles ($10^{21}$). The true leaders of the nation were, to him, 'the wise' who 'shall make many understand' ($11^{33}$), in whom we are probably to recognize the party of the Hasidim. The resistance movement under Mattathias and Judas was only 'a little help' ($11^{34}$); deliverance could come from God alone.

## 2. *The rise of Judas Maccabaeus: the rededication of the Temple (164 B.C.)*

Judas, the third son of Mattathias, was a natural successor to his father as leader of the revolutionary movement. He is described as 'a mighty warrior from his youth' (1 Macc. $2^{66}$) and 'like a lion in his deeds, like a lion's cub roaring for prey' ($3^4$). He was given the nickname 'Maccabee', meaning 'hammer' or 'hammer-headed', in token, no doubt, of his military exploits. Although this name applies strictly only to Judas himself it is generally used also with reference to his brothers who continued the 'Maccabaean' Revolt. Under his leadership the struggle passed from the guerrilla stage to that of well-planned battles and full-scale war. Judas from the start won a series of victories, including one over Apollonius and another over Seron at Beth-horon (cf. $3^{10-26}$), which enhanced his reputation and gained for him many more volunteers in the fight for freedom. More important was his rout of Gorgias, at Emmaeus near Beth-horon, whom Antiochus' regent Lysias had sent against Judaea (cf. $3^{27}$—$4^{25}$; *Antiquities* XII. vii. 3–4). The following year (164 B.C.) Lysias himself attacked Jerusalem from the south, but he too suffered defeat at Beth-zur and withdrew to Antioch (cf. $4^{26-35}$; *Antiquities* XII. vii. 5).

Now that their enemies were crushed one thing above all others remained to be done—to purify the Temple and rededicate the sanctuary (cf. $4^{36-59}$). Accordingly, in the second half of the same year (164 B.C.) Judas marched on Jerusalem and occupied Mount Zion, shutting up the Syrian troops and their Jewish sympathizers in the Akra. The Temple itself could now be restored. First he selected priests who had remained faithful during the time of persecution; the altar which had been desecrated by offerings made to the Olympian Zeus was pulled down and a new one made of unhewn stones erected in its place; the sanctuary and the interior of the Temple were rebuilt and refurnished with curtains, lamps, and other holy vessels. And so in the month Kislev (i.e. December) 164 B.C., exactly three years after its desecration by Antiochus, the Temple with its altar was rededicated and restored to its former use. The Feast of Dedication (Hebrew, *Ḥanukkah*) which followed was ordered to be kept year after year on the twenty-fifth day of Kislev in commemoration of this joyous event. Thus 'there was very great gladness among the people, and the reproach of the Gentiles was removed' ($4^{58}$). So as to ensure its safety in the future Jerusalem was fortified with high walls and strong towers, and a garrison stationed there to defend it; similar measures were taken at Beth-zur on the borders of Idumaea to the south (cf. $4^{60-61}$).

### 3. *The rule of Judas Maccabaeus: full religious liberty granted (163 B.C.)*

The position of the Jews in Judea was, for the time being at any rate, tolerably secure. The same could not be said, however, of their fellow Jews in the countries around Judaea, surrounded as they were by Hellenistic influence and under the jurisdiction of foreign powers. Partly for the protection of his people and partly to strengthen his own position in Judaea, Judas now set himself to win complete independence for the Jewish nation, to make the whole Palestinian area and not only Judaea itself thoroughly Jewish. Such a policy, in which he was followed by his brothers Jonathan and Simon and their successors in the Hasmonaean House, was in a sense an extension of the policy formerly adopted by Ezra.[1] All

[1] For other illustrations of this policy and the attempt to proselytize by force see pp. 63, 69, 70.

Jews in the surrounding territories must be brought within the scope of their rule. Accordingly Judas carried out a series of successful campaigns against the Idumaeans in the south, the Baeanites in Transjordan, and the Ammonites north-east of the Dead Sea (cf. 1 Macc. 5$^{1-8}$); on receiving reports of persecution from the Jewish communities in Galilee and Gilead, he sent his brother Simon northwards with an army to the help of the one, whilst he himself, supported by his brother Jonathan, crossed the Jordan to the help of the other. Both campaigns were successful, but as they could not keep permanent control over these areas they brought back the Jewish inhabitants to Judaea (cf. 5$^{9-54}$). In subsequent campaigns against Idumaea and Philistia he captured Hebron and Ashdod, returning home with much plunder (cf. 5$^{63-65}$).

One supreme task, however, remained to be done. The Akra—that hated symbol of Syrian domination—was still in the hands of the enemy and served as a constant reminder that Antiochus' decree forbidding the rites and ordinances of the Jewish religion had not yet been rescinded. Judas accordingly laid siege to it, probably in the spring or summer of 163 B.C. During the blockade some Syrian soldiers together with a number of Hellenizing Jews managed to escape and made their way to Antioch, where they put their case before the King (cf. 6$^{18-27}$). The old arch-enemy of the Jews, Antiochus IV, had died the previous year about two months before the rededication of the Temple (cf. 2 Macc. 9$^{1-29}$),[1] and was succeeded by his eight-years-old son Antiochus V (Eupator). Just before he died he appointed Philip regent and guardian of the young King; Lysias, however, who had been given these appointments at an earlier stage, now saw his opportunity and appropriated both responsibilities (cf. 6$^{5-17}$). When the Jews who had escaped from the Akra made their report, Lysias set off for Judaea with a strong army, forced Judas to retreat, and besieged Jerusalem (cf. 6$^{28-54}$). The situation was saved, however, when Lysias received word that Philip was planning to

[1] According to 1 Macc. 6$^{17}$, however, the death of Antiochus appears to have taken place *after* the rededication of the Temple.

take over the reins of government in his absence. Generous terms were offered to Judas, who agreed to surrender the fortifications around the Temple; in return Lysias granted a general amnesty, rescinded the orders issued by Antiochus IV in 167 B.C. when he set up the worship of the Olympian Zeus, deposed the High Priest Menelaus, and had him put to death (cf. 2 Macc. 13³⁻⁸). Thus, though the Jews were still subject to Syrian rule and a Syrian garrison continued to occupy the Akra, religious freedom was at last secured (cf. 1 Macc. 6⁵⁵⁻⁶²).

## 4. *Judas and his nationalist aims (162–160 B.C.)*

The Maccabaean Revolt, which had begun as a protest against religious persecution, had now achieved its aim; the Jewish people were once more free to live according to their ancestral laws. What had begun as a religious revolt soon developed, however, into a strong nationalist movement for political independence, led in turn by Judas and his brothers Jonathan and Simon. These years were marked not only by opposition to the Seleucids, who remained militarily in control, but also, as previously, by a struggle for political power within the Jewish nation itself. The Syrian government saw no reason to trust Judas further and so decided to strengthen their association with the Hellenizers among the Jews. To this end Lysias appointed as High Priest a man called Alcimus (Hebrew *Jakim* or *Jehoiakim*), who, though a member of the High-Priestly family (cf. 1 Macc. 7¹⁴; 2 Macc. 14⁷; *Antiquities* XII. ix. 7, XX. x. 1), was himself a member of the Hellenizing party. This appointment was not at all popular with Judas, who, it would seem, prevented Alcimus from taking up office in Jerusalem (cf. 2 Macc. 14³). Meanwhile the balance of power in Syria had once more been upset. In that same year, 162 B.C., Demetrius, the son of the murdered Seleucus IV and nephew of Antiochus Epiphanes, escaped from Rome, where he had been kept a hostage, brought about the death of Lysias and Antiochus V, and assumed the throne of Syria as Demetrius I (Soter). Alcimus and his fellow Hellenizers lost no time in lodging their complaints against Judas and in pledging their support for the new King. Demetrius confirmed Alcimus in the High Priesthood (161 B.C.) and sent him to Jerusalem with a strong escort under his general Bacchides. At this point it is reported that certain scribes and Hasidim approached Alcimus and Bacchides seeking to establish good relations, no doubt influenced by Alcimus' promises of loyalty to the Jewish religion and by the fact that he himself belonged to the true priestly line of Aaron (cf. 1 Macc. 7[12 ff.]). It has been generally assumed that this incident marks a profound split in the ranks of Judas' followers and that the Hasidim, seeking only religious independence, now withdrew their support from Judas, whose aim was national independence. This assumption, however, is hardly justifiable on the evidence available. The hopes of the Hasidim for peace were rudely shattered, and their confidence in Alcimus completely broken when, despite his promise that no harm would befall them, he treacherously seized sixty of their number and slew them (cf. 1 Macc. 7[15 f.]; *Antiquities* XII. x. 2). Realizing that Judas had been right in his judgement they threw in their lot with him as formerly. This is implied in the report of a second interview that Alcimus now sought with Demetrius, in which he singled out for special mention 'those of the Jews who are called Hasidaeans, whose leader is Judas Maccabaeus, (who) are keeping up war and stirring up sedition, and will not let the kingdom attain tranquillity' (2 Macc. 14[6]). In response to his appeal for help Demetrius decided to send an army under his general Nicanor to capture Judas and to confirm Alcimus in the High Priesthood. Judas, however, was too powerful for him: near the village of Adasa a battle took place (161 B.C.) in which Nicanor was defeated and killed, and his army driven out into the coastal plain (cf. 1 Macc. 7[26-50]). Alcimus, the High Priest, fled to Syria.

At this point Judas did something which underlines his political aspirations—he sent a deputation to Rome, headed by two Jewish leaders named Eupolemus and Jason, 'to establish a treaty of friendship and alliance' (1 Macc. 8[17]).

The result was a declaration of friendship between the Roman Senate and the Jewish nation (cf. 1 Macc. 8). Rome thereupon sent a warning to Demetrius concerning his future dealings with the Jews (cf. 1 Macc. 8$^{31\,f.}$). Demetrius, however, had already taken steps to avenge the defeat of Nicanor, dispatching an army to Judaea under Bacchides, who was accompanied by Alcimus. Seeing the might of the Syrian army many of Judas' followers deserted him, and in the ensuing battle fought at Elasa (160 B.C.), in the neighbourhood of Jerusalem, Judas was slain (cf. 1 Macc. 9$^{1-22}$).

## 5. *Jonathan as leader and High Priest (160–143 B.C.)*

The death of Judas was a great blow to the nationalist party, and control of affairs once more passed over into the hands of the Hellenizers, with Alcimus at their head. The greater part of the people accepted the situation, gratified no doubt that they could at least continue to worship in freedom according to their ancestral laws.

*Jonathan and Bacchides (160–153 B.C.).* Bacchides' policy was clear—to suppress all resistance by force. Certain of Judas' friends were captured, tortured, and put to death; many others escaped into the desert of Judaea, where they went into hiding. By popular acclamation Judas' younger brother Jonathan was now elected leader in his stead, with the purpose of carrying on the war against the enemy (cf. 1 Macc. 9$^{23-31}$). Bacchides prepared against future trouble by holding certain leading Jews as hostages in the Akra and by building a ring of fortifications round Jerusalem (cf. 1 Macc. 9$^{50-53}$). In the spring of that same year (159 B.C.) Alcimus tore down the wall separating the Temple Mount from the inner court that had previously been forbidden to Gentiles; and when, a short time later, he died, the orthodox Jews regarded this as a just retribution. No suitable man was found to take Alcimus' place and the office of High Priest remained vacant for the next seven years (cf. 1 Macc. 9$^{54-57}$). Following the death of Alcimus, Bacchides decided he could safely leave his command in Judaea and so

An aerial view of the Wilderness of Judaea to the east of Jerusalem showing the semi-arid terrain of eroded limestone and desolate plains. Both here and in deserts farther to the south many Jews from time to time sought refuge from their oppressors.

returned to Antioch. Two years later, however, at the request of the Hellenizers he returned to Judaea, where his army suffered a defeat at Beth-basi in the Judaean wilderness. Bacchides at this point showed open displeasure with the Hellenizers who had brought him into this compromising situation, and in a rage slew many of them. Jonathan thereupon made peace proposals, which were at once accepted. The Syrians handed over the prisoners they had taken and agreed to bring hostilities to an end; Bacchides himself returned to Antioch. Jonathan now took up his headquarters at Michmash, about nine miles north of Jerusalem. From there he 'began to judge the people' and punished the Hellenizers among the Jews (cf. 1 Macc. 9[58-73]). For the next five years (157–152 B.C.) Judaea continued at peace, and the power and influence of Jonathan and his followers rapidly increased.

*Jonathan and Alexander Balas (152–145 B.C.)*. In 152 B.C. the authority of Demetrius I was challenged by a pretender, Alexander Balas, who claimed to be the son of Antiochus Epiphanes. In the course of the next few years both men were to court the favour of Jonathan, who was now recognized as the obvious leader of the Jewish people. Demetrius was first to make concessions; the hostages who had been kept prisoner in the Akra were handed over and Jonathan was permitted to muster troops and equip them with arms. Jonathan took immediate steps to exploit the situation thus created. Moving his headquarters from Michmash to Jerusalem he took control of the city and fortified the Temple area, seriously curtailing the power of the garrison in the Akra there (cf. 1 Macc. 10$^{1-11}$). The Syrian troops were now withdrawn from all the places previously fortified by Bacchides, with three exceptions—the Akra itself, Beth-zur (cf. 1 Macc. 10$^{14}$), and Gazara (cf. 1 Macc. 11$^{41}$; 13$^{43}$).

Alexander Balas, not to be outdone, now determined to outbid Demetrius and offered Jonathan even greater benefits than his rival had done. In a cordial letter he appointed Jonathan High Priest—an honour which the Jews themselves were not yet ready to confer upon him—and gave him the title 'the King's Friend' (cf. 1 Macc. 10$^{15-21}$). Thus by a strange twist of fate Jonathan found himself in league with the professed son of the notorious Antiochus Epiphanes.[1] The Hellenizers now found themselves in a most unenviable position. Without the support of the Syrians their opposition to Jonathan fell to the ground and the political influence they had exercised for many years came suddenly to an end. Jonathan had won by diplomacy, and by exploiting the division within the Syrian camp, what Judas had been unable to gain by force of arms.

Demetrius, however, had not even yet given up hope, and offered Jonathan greater favours still. His promises included exemption from taxation, surrender of the Akra, restoration of

[1] For the claim that Jonathan was the Wicked Priest of the Dead Sea Scrolls see p. 167.

ceded territories, the enrolment of Jewish troops in the Syrian army, subsidies for the Temple, and money for the rebuilding of the city walls. But Jonathan was shrewd enough not to accept such promises at their face value and continued his support of Alexander Balas. As things turned out he made the right decision, for in 150 B.C. Demetrius met Balas in battle and was slain (cf. 1 Macc. 10$^{22-50}$). Shortly afterwards Balas invited Jonathan as his guest to Ptolemais (Acco), on the occasion of his marriage to Cleopatra, daughter of Ptolemy VI (Philometor) of Egypt. There the King treated him with great respect, 'made him general and governor' of Judaea 'and enrolled him among his chief Friends' (1 Macc. 10$^{51-66}$). Jonathan thus held office as a servant of the Syrian government responsible to Balas for his actions. But he was at least in control of his own land, a situation that could be exploited by a man of his shrewdness and skill. With an eye on the complete independence of Judaea he now seized every opportunity to strengthen his own position and to extend his territory beyond the narrow limits of the Judaean state.

Further complications developed in Syrian affairs when, in 147 B.C., Balas' position was challenged by the son of Demetrius I, bearing the same name as his father, who now laid claim to the throne. Two years later Balas was defeated in battle and fled to Arabia, where he was assassinated. The way was open for Demetrius II (Nicator) to take over the Syrian throne (cf. 1 Macc. 11$^{1-19}$).

*Jonathan and Demetrius II* (*145–143 B.C.*). Demetrius, however, whose hold on the throne was none too secure, was as yet young and inexperienced in the arts of diplomacy and war. Jonathan, aware of these things, determined to strike a further blow for the independence of the state of Judaea by attacking the Akra, where the Hellenized Jews with a Syrian garrison were still in control. Demetrius at once ordered him to raise the siege and report to him at Ptolemais. On hearing this Jonathan decided on bold action. Ordering his men to continue the siege he set off for Ptolemais, together with a group of elders and priests, with lavish gifts for the King. Demetrius was so impressed by this show of audacity and arrogance that he forthwith made Jonathan a 'King's Friend', confirmed him in the High Priesthood, and, at his request, annexed to Judaea three districts in the southern part of Samaria—Ephraim, Lydda, and Ramathaim—which he now exempted from taxation (cf. 1 Macc. 11$^{20-37}$).

At this juncture Demetrius found himself in serious trouble. His army, openly rebellious at his treatment of them, deserted him. To make things worse one of Balas' generals, Diodotus Tryphon by name, claimed the Syrian throne for Balas' young son Antiochus. Jonathan immediately took advantage of the situation and sent a request to Demetrius to withdraw his garrisons from the Akra, Beth-zur, and Gazara. Demetrius, besieged in his palace in Antioch by his own people, was glad to make any promises in return for Jonathan's help. But when Jonathan attacked Antioch with three thousand men and rescued the King, Demetrius went back on the promise he had made. In such circumstances it is not surprising that, when Tryphon sought his help, Jonathan turned his back on Demetrius and joined his rival, who crowned his young protégé as Antiochus VI. Jonathan was now confirmed in all the honours conferred upon him by Demetrius; Simon his brother was made governor 'from the Ladder of Tyre to the borders of Egypt' (1 Macc. 11$^{30-59}$).

*Jonathan and Tryphon (143 B.C.).* As one of Tryphon's generals Jonathan now took part in a number of successful campaigns, ranging from Gaza and Ascalon in the south-west to Damascus and the Sea of Galilee in the north. At the same time he took independent action by renewing friendly relations with Rome, which his brother Judas had previously encouraged, and sent letters to Sparta and other foreign powers with the same purpose in view (cf. 1 Macc. 12$^{1-23}$). He went even further and built a number of fortifications throughout Judaea; in Jerusalem itself he increased the height of the walls and erected a great mound between the Akra and the rest of the city, thus cutting off its vital supply-line (cf. 1 Macc. 12$^{24-38}$).

Tryphon, not without reason, viewed these happenings with

the gravest apprehension. The increasing power of the Jews was proving an embarrassment to him in his own plans, which were to kill the young Antiochus VI and claim the throne for himself. He decided, however, not to show his hand openly. Instead he inveigled Jonathan, together with a thousand of his men, to go with him to Ptolemais. As soon as they had entered the city the gates were shut, Jonathan was arrested, and his retinue slaughtered (cf. 1 Macc. 12³⁹⁻⁵³). There was consternation in Jerusalem at the news of Tryphon's treachery and Simon was at once appointed Jonathan's successor. Losing no time he strengthened the fortifications around Jerusalem and sent a powerful force to occupy Joppa, whose inhabitants he did not trust (cf. 1 Macc. 13¹¹, 14⁵; *Antiquities* XIII. vi. 6). Tryphon now marched south from Ptolemais, bringing Jonathan with him. At Adida, near Modein, he tried to parley with Simon but broke his promise that, in return for hostages and 100 talents of silver, he would release Jonathan. He then made an attempt to march on Jerusalem, where the Syrian garrison in the Akra was by now desperate for food, but was hindered by a heavy fall of snow. In a fit of temper he finally killed Jonathan at a place called Bascam on the east side of Jordan and returned to his own land (143 B.C. Cf. 1 Macc. 13¹⁻²⁴).

## 6. *Simon and the independence of Judaea (142 B.C)*

Simon now saw his opportunity to achieve the goal which both Judas and Jonathan had set before them—the independence of the Jewish nation from Syrian control. Judas had achieved the goal of religious independence and Jonathan had made himself master in Judaea; Simon now took the final step and demanded complete political independence. Having consolidated his position by building fortresses throughout Judaea, he sent a deputation to Demetrius II, with suitable gifts, to ask for the recognition of Judaea as an independent state by the grant of release from taxation. The price of such independence would be his loyalty to Demetrius, whose rival Tryphon had by this time murdered the young Antiochus VI and

claimed the throne (cf. 1 Macc. 13³¹⁻³⁴). Demetrius was hardly
in a position to refuse, and in a letter addressed to 'Simon the
High Priest and Friend of Kings' and to the Elders of the
Jews he agreed to an amnesty and granted complete exemption
from taxation, i.e. he recognized Judaea as a sovereign and
independent country. Thus 'the yoke of the Gentiles was
removed from Israel' in the year 142 B.C., and 'the people began
to write in their documents and contracts, "In the first year of
Simon the great High Priest and commander and leader of
the Jews" ' (1 Macc. 13³⁵⁻⁴²).

That same year Simon captured the fortress of Gazara,
between Jerusalem and Joppa, replacing its heathen inhabitants with loyal Jews and appointing his son John as governor.
His most memorable act, however, was the capture of the
Akra in Jerusalem, which for more than forty years had been
in the hands of the Hellenizers, a constant reminder of the
Jews' subjection to the Syrian power. The Akra itself was
purified and the adjacent Temple Mount fortified (cf. 1 Macc.
13⁴³⁻⁵³). The Hellenizing party was now completely crushed
and the last stronghold of Syrian domination removed from
the land.

The state which Simon and his brothers had done so much
to establish was yet to pass through many troubled times.
For the next seventy years or so (142–63 B.C.) it enjoyed
independence so hardly won, until another world-power,
greater even than that of the Seleucids, once more brought it
into subjection. But from the beginning the foundations on
which it had been built were none too strong. The victory of the
Jews under the Maccabees was essentially the victory of a
particular party within the nation, even though it included
the greater part of the people. The Hellenizing party ceased to
exist as an organized military and political force after the fall
of the Akra, but Hellenism as a cultural factor continued to
play a vital part in the life of the Jewish people. The Jewish
state, though now politically independent of Syria, was nevertheless part and parcel of the Hellenistic world in which it
had to live its life. As its contacts with other Hellenistic powers

increased it gradually assumed the character of a Hellenistic state whose High-Priestly rulers became almost indistinguishable at times from the princes and kings of neighbouring peoples.

This is illustrated in the case of Simon himself. Even when allowance is made for the idealized picture of his reign given in 1 Maccabees, it is clear that he was regarded by his subjects as a great and wise ruler, essentially a man of peace, who took seriously his High-Priestly office and was devout in his observance of the Law. It is equally clear, however, that he and the members of his family lived in considerable splendour and amassed wealth which dazzled even the envoys of the Syrian king (cf. 1 Macc. 15$^{32}$), Simon himself using much of his private fortune for public benefactions and fitting out the army at his own expense, after the style of a typical Hellenistic king (cf. 1 Macc. 14$^{32}$). These characteristics, and others less attractive, were to become much more pronounced in the lives of his successors and were yet to cause grave concern among the people, some of whom were convinced that the descendants of the Maccabees had betrayed their God-given trust.

# V

# THE RULE OF THE HASMONAEAN[1] HOUSE
## (142–63 B.C.)

### 1. *Simon* (*142–134 B.C.*)

THE author of 1 Maccabees writes in exalted language of the peace and prosperity of Simon's rule, in which 'he extended the boundaries of his nation and gained full control of the country. . . . Each man sat under his vine and his fig tree and there was none to make them afraid' (1 Macc. 14⁶⁻¹⁵). Having struck the decisive blow for the freedom of his people he enhanced his already great prestige by a treaty of friendship with Rome and Sparta. His brother Judas had previously entered into a treaty with Rome (cf. 1 Macc. 8¹⁷), and his other brother, Jonathan, had been engaged in similar negotiations just before his assassination (cf. 1 Macc. 12¹); but the real credit for recognition of the Jews by the Romans must go to Simon, although some scholars (on the basis of evidence in Josephus) would carry this further down still, into the reign of John Hyrcanus. The Romans received the embassy which Simon sent, together with a substantial gift (cf. 1 Macc. 14²⁴ ᶠᶠ·, 15¹⁵ ᶠᶠ·), and guaranteed complete liberty of worship to all Jews throughout their domains.

At this time a momentous decision was taken, which was to affect deeply his own position and that of his children after him. A decree, engraved in bronze, was set up in the Temple, commemorating his services and those of his family to the Jewish nation and declaring him to be appointed 'leader and

---

[1] The name 'Hasmonaean' is here applied to the High-Priestly House beginning with Simon, and continuing until the year 63 B.C. Strictly speaking it should apply to the whole Maccabaean family. The word does not appear in the books of Maccabees but occurs in Josephus and in later Jewish literature.

High Priest for ever [i.e. with hereditary rights], until a trustworthy prophet should arise' (1 Macc. 14⁴¹). Previously the legitimate High Priesthood had belonged to the House of Onias, but this had come to an end. The intervening High Priests—Menelaus, Alcimus, and Jonathan—did not belong to this family; they did not even owe their appointment to the decision of the people but to that of a Syrian king. Now, by an all-important decision of the Council, the High-Priestly office was vested in Simon and his descendants. In the third year of his rule (140 B.C.) he accepted the Council's appointment and agreed to become High Priest, military commander, and official representative of the people (cf. 1 Macc. 14⁴⁷), with the right to pass on his office to his sons. Thus Simon and his descendants, with both priestly and secular power vested in their persons, found themselves with even greater authority than the family of Onias had ever known.

Simon's troubles, however, were not yet over. In 139 B.C. Demetrius II, who had been taken prisoner by the Parthian king Mithridates, was succeeded by his energetic and enterprising brother Antiochus VII (Sidetes) (139–128 B.C.), who now took up the struggle with the usurper Tryphon. In a letter to Simon he invited his co-operation, offering in return to confirm all the rights and privileges already conferred upon him, with the additional right to strike his own coins (cf. 1 Macc. 15⁶). Within a few months, however, when his rival Tryphon was forced to flee and eventually commit suicide, Antiochus' attitude to Simon changed. Permission to mint his own coins was withdrawn[1] and with it his recognition of Judaea as an independent state. He looked with great suspicion on the expansion of Simon's territory and demanded the surrender of Joppa, Gazara, and the Akra in Jerusalem together with tribute received from captured cities outside

[1] A number of coins have been found bearing the name 'Simon'. The claim that these belong to Simon the Hasmonaean has now been discredited; they are to be ascribed rather to another Jewish leader of the same name at a much later period. The first real Jewish coins belong to the reign of John Hyrcanus. See p. 65.

Judaea; in lieu of this he would be prepared to accept an indemnity of one thousand talents. When Simon refused to comply, protesting that all these places were Judaean territory by right, Antiochus sent his general Cendebaeus against him. In the battle which followed, near the village of Modein, Cendebaeus was routed by Simon's two sons, Judas and John, whom he had placed in charge of the Jewish army. The battle was decisive and peace prevailed during the rest of Simon's rule (cf. 1 Macc. $15^{1-14}$, $15^{25}-16^{10}$).

The Hasmonaean leader, however, was not to be allowed to end his days in peace, for in 134 B.C. he and two of his sons, Mattathias and Judas, were treacherously murdered in the stronghold of Dok, near Jericho, by his son-in-law Ptolemy, who had been appointed captain of the plain of Jericho but who obviously had his eye on a much bigger prize. Offering his co-operation to Antiochus he then sent men to Gazara, where John was in residence, with orders to kill him also. John, however, being warned of their coming, captured and slew them (cf. 1 Macc. $16^{11-22}$). The account in 1 Maccabees stops at this point, but the historian Josephus records that John made his way to Jerusalem, where he was well received. Ptolemy pursued him there, but eventually withdrew to the stronghold at Dok, where he was besieged by John. Fearful for the safety of his mother, who was in Ptolemy's hands, John raised the siege—but to no avail. Ptolemy killed his mother and made his escape (cf. *Antiquities* XIII. viii. 1; *War* I. ii. 4).

## 2. *John Hyrcanus (134–104 B.C.)*

In accordance with the ruling of the Council Simon's third surviving son John (commonly known as Hyrcanus I) succeeded his father as High Priest and ruler of the people. Almost at once he ran into trouble. In the very first year of his rule Antiochus VII invaded Judaea, plundered the land, and besieged Jerusalem. When supplies of food were running short in the city Hyrcanus asked for a seven days' truce, which was readily granted by Antiochus, who was no doubt anxious to avoid a prolonged siege. Shortly afterwards an agreement was reached whereby the Jews had to surrender their arms and pay a heavy indemnity for the return of Joppa and other cities bordering on Judaea. They resisted the demand that a Syrian garrison should be stationed in Jerusalem, and instead handed over to Antiochus a number of hostages, including Hyrcanus' brother, and five hundred talents of silver. Antiochus then destroyed the city walls and withdrew (cf. *Antiquities* XIII. viii. 2–3). Hyrcanus was thus made to realize that independence could be maintained only when Syria was either too busy or too weak to intervene. Fortunately for him this was exactly the state of affairs that prevailed within a few years' time. In 128 B.C. Antiochus VII was killed in a campaign against the Parthians, in which Hyrcanus took part as his ally, and was succeeded by Demetrius II, who had been released from imprisonment in Parthia and became King for the second time (129–125 B.C.). From this time onwards, because of internal strife in Syria, Judaea was able to remain completely independent. According to Josephus, Hyrcanus at this point sent an embassy to Rome, with the result that the Senate confirmed him in his independence and warned the Syrians not to harm the Jews. The indemnity which Hyrcanus had paid for Joppa and the other cities ceased and the long struggle with the Seleucids came to an end.

Hyrcanus now saw his opportunity to extend his borders and so embarked on a series of successful military campaigns. In the north he conquered Shechem and destroyed the Samaritan Temple on Mount Gerizim (*c.* 108 B.C.),[1] whilst in the south he invaded Idumaea, circumcising many of the inhabitants by force (cf. *Antiquities* XIII. ix. 1). During the latter part of his reign he sent an army against the Greek city of Samaria and razed it to the ground (cf. *Antiquities* XIII. x. 2–3), occupying the Esdraelon valley all the way to Mount Carmel (cf. *War* I. ii. 7).

Josephus reports that during these campaigns Hyrcanus made use of foreign mercenaries, whose expenses he met out of the money plundered from King David's tomb (cf. *Antiquities*

---

[1] Another suggested date is 128 B.C.

XIII. viii. 4). Such tactics no doubt contributed to the strained relationships which later developed between himself and a section of the people; they at the same time indicate not only his failure to win their confidence, but also his tendency, as with other Hellenistic rulers, to stand over against the people as a prince in his own right. In 109 B.C. he gave expression to his authority by doing something no Jewish ruler had done before him—he minted his own coins bearing his own name. On the obverse side they read, 'John the High Priest, and the Community of the Jews' and displayed on the reverse side a double 'horn of abundance' with a poppy head inside, ancient

---

### GREEK AND ROMAN COINS

1. Gold stater of Lysimachus of Thrace, very early third century B.C. Obverse: head of Alexander the Great, diademed, with horn in his hair. Reverse: seated Athena, with image of Nikē (Victory) in her right hand.

2. Gold stater of Ptolemy I of Egypt, struck in Cyrenaica, late third century B.C. Obverse: Head of the King. Reverse: probably Alexander, deified, with thunderbolt in chariot drawn by elephants.

3. Silver tetradrachm of Alexander the Great struck in Babylon in 324 or 323 B.C. Obverse: Head of Herakles in lion-scalp head-dress. Reverse: Zeus enthroned.

4. Silver tetradrachm of Ptolemy I of Egypt. Obverse: Head of the King. Reverse: Eagle on thunderbolt.

5. Silver tetradrachm of Ptolemy I of Egypt. Obverse: Heracles in elephant-scalp head-dress. Reverse: Zeus enthroned.

6. Silver tetradrachm of Antiochus IV of Syria. Mint: Antioch. Obverse: Head of Zeus, assimilated to the idealized portrait of the King. Reverse: Zeus enthroned, with image of Nikē (Victory) in his right hand. Legend: King Antiochus, god manifest, bearing Victory.

7. Silver denarius of Rome. Moneyer: L. Mussidius Longus, c. 42 B.C. Obverse: Head of Caesar. Reverse: Cornucopiae on globe, etc.

8. Silver tetradrachm, probably of Antioch on the Orontes. Obverse: Head of M. Antonius. Reverse: Head of Cleopatra.

9. Silver denarius. Struck in the East (perhaps Ephesus) in 28 B.C. when Octavian (later, Augustus) was consul for the sixth time. Obverse: Head of Octavian. Reverse: Crocodile, commemorating the conquest of Egypt and the end of Antony and Cleopatra.

10. Bronze sestertius. Struck at Rome in A.D. 71. Obverse: Head of Vespasian. Reverse: Palm-tree with Jewish prisoners, commemorating the Roman suppression of the First Revolt.

Greek symbols of plenty and fertility, indicating no doubt the prosperity of his reign.

It is in the time of Hyrcanus that the names of the Pharisees and Sadducees first come into prominence (cf. *Antiquities* XIII. x. 5–7).[1] The origins of these two parties are obscure,[2] but it is clear that by this period they were both well-established, exercising a considerable influence on the nation as a whole.

At first, it would appear, Hyrcanus was favourably disposed to the Pharisees, but after a while he broke with them and gave his support to the Sadducees. According to Josephus the occasion of this breach was a banquet given by Hyrcanus to which members of both parties were invited. Declaring his allegiance to the Law Hyrcanus asked his guests to correct him if in any way he had done wrong. All those present then praised his virtues—all except one. This man, Eleazar, a Pharisee, rose up and challenged him to give up the High Priesthood and to content himself with the civil government of the people. When asked to explain himself, Eleazar cast aspersions on the High Priest's birth, suggesting that he was not a fit and proper person to hold this office. Hyrcanus was furious and the other Pharisees indignant. A certain Sadducee named Jonathan, however, at once took advantage of the situation, asserting that this slanderous suggestion in fact met with the approval of the Pharisees as a whole. To prove their loyalty the High Priest then asked the Pharisees what punishment should be meted out to Eleazar, and when they decreed stripes and chains rather than the required penalty of death for slander of this kind, Hyrcanus was convinced of their complicity. He thereupon transferred his support to the Sadducees, forbidding under penalty of severe punishment the regulations laid down by the Pharisees, which hitherto he himself had followed.

Josephus gives as the reason for the Pharisees' hostility to Hyrcanus the fact that they were envious of his successes, and

[1] Elsewhere Josephus assumes they were in existence in the time of Jonathan (cf. *Antiquities* XIII. x. 9).

[2] See pp. 155 ff.

adds: 'So great is their influence with the masses that even when they speak against a king or High Priest, they immediately gain credence' (*Antiquities* XIII. x. 5). Some scholars have seen in this an indication that Hyrcanus had assumed the title of King and believe that this was the real cause of the breach. It is perhaps more likely, however, that their hostility was directed against his assumption of the High Priesthood, which they now saw being profaned before their eyes by political ambitions and the thirst for secular and military power. For a long time there had been a growing discontent with the Maccabees and the Hasmonaean House on the part of the Hasidim and the orthodox Jews generally, not least by reason of the increasing worldliness and secularization of the High Priesthood. It is not surprising that the Pharisees, champions of the Law and spiritual descendants of the Hasidim, should at this juncture voice their protest; nor is it any less surprising that the Sadducees, who belonged for the most part to the wealthy priestly aristocracy and whose antagonism to the Pharisees was obvious to all, should take the opposite side. This decision of Hyrcanus to switch his allegiance to the Sadducees not only casts light on his own worldly ambitions, it also indicates the path which his successors in the High Priestly office were soon to follow.

The Pharisees were not the only spiritual descendants of the Hasidim, however, who voiced their disapproval of the happenings at this time and of those in authority over them. The same could be said of the Essenes, who represented one wing of the Hasidic movement as the Pharisees did another. The relation between the Essenes and the Qumran Covenanters will be considered at a later point.[1] Here we observe that those who were to form the Qumran community, on the shores of the Dead Sea, apparently at this very time expressed open criticism of the Hasmonaean House and of the official Jerusalem priesthood as a consequence of which they (unlike the Pharisees) withdrew into the desert, where they lived an ascetic life ordered by strict discipline and obedience to the Law.

[1] See pp. 164 ff.

### 3. *Aristobulus* (*104–103 B.C.*)

According to Josephus (cf. *Antiquities* XIII. xi. 1) Hyrcanus decreed that his widow should succeed him as 'mistress of the realm' and that the oldest of their five sons, Jehuda or Judas (better known by his Greek name Aristobulus), should serve as High Priest. Aristobulus, however, coveting both civil and religious power for himself, imprisoned the members of his family (with the exception of his favourite brother, Antigonus) and allowed his mother to die of hunger. Antigonus' favoured position soon gained him a number of enemies, including Aristobulus' wife, Salome Alexandra. By rumour and false accusation these people stirred up jealousy and suspicion, with the result that Aristobulus had his brother put to death. The remorse which Aristobulus thereafter suffered is said to have hastened his own death within a year's time (cf. *Antiquities* XIII. xi. 1–3; *War* I. iii. 1–6). In this same account mention is made of 'a certain Judas of the Essene group who had never been known to speak falsely in his prophecies', who foretold the murder of Antigonus. This reference is of significance in that it is the first historical allusion to a member of the party of the Essenes.

Josephus records that Aristobulus was the first Hasmonaean to take the title of King (cf. *Antiquities* XIII. xi. 1), adding that he allowed himself to be called 'Philhellene' ('Greek-lover') (cf. *Antiquities* XIII. xi. 3). Neither title, however, appears on the coins issued at this time, their inscription using the Hebrew form of his name and reading simply, 'High Priest Jehuda and the Community of the Jews'. The historian Strabo, moreover, states that it was his successor, Alexander Jannaeus, who first assumed the royal title. It may well be that he did not actually call himself 'king' among his own people because of the opposition this would rouse, but did so in his dealings outside his realm. It is doubtful, too, whether he officially adopted the title 'Philhellene', but no doubt it was given to him by others and for good reason. Josephus describes him as an ambitious and cruel man, intent on gaining power at any price; but this account probably reflects prejudice in the source Josephus was using, for elsewhere he quotes, apparently with some approval, the words of Strabo, who describes Aristobulus as 'a kindly person and very serviceable to the Jews' (*Antiquities* XIII. xi. 3).

Such 'service' is illustrated by his campaign against the Ituraeans to the north of Galilee, 'a good part of (whose) territory' Aristobulus conquered and added to Judaea. Those who did not flee were compelled to accept circumcision and to observe the Jewish Law, just as Idumaeans in the south had been forced to do in the time of John Hyrcanus. This explains why, in subsequent years, the population of Galilee, though predominantly Gentile by race, was Jewish in religion. Such forcible Judaizing of Gentiles shows that Aristobulus, for all his Greek leanings, was nevertheless an ardent Jew, determined, through proselytization and conquest, not only to conserve but also to enlarge the Jewish state.

### 4. *Alexander Jannaeus* (*103-76 B.C.*)

On the death of Aristobulus his widow Salome Alexandra set free his three imprisoned brothers, one of whom, Jonathan or Jannai, she subsequently married. He is generally known by the Greek form of this name, Jannaeus, to which he added the further name 'Alexander'. Alexander Jannaeus succeded his brother as High Priest, and went beyond him by officially claiming the title of King, which he inscribed on certain of his coins. On some of these the traditional inscription appears: 'Jonathan the High Priest and the Community of the Jews', whereas on others there is a bilingual inscription which reads on the obverse side in Hebrew, 'Jonathan the King' and on the reverse side in Greek, 'King Alexander'. The first type shows a double 'horn of plenty' with a poppy head inside, as in the coins of Hyrcanus; the second type shows an anchor, in imitation of coins of Antiochus VII, possibly in commemoration of his own increasing maritime strength. These anchor coins, bearing the title of 'king' and inscribed in Hebrew and Greek, were probably for use beyond his immediate realm.

Jannaeus was a ruthless man whose character was clearly

revealed at an early stage in his career, when he arranged for one of his two surviving brothers, who might have challenged his authority, to be conveniently put to death. His wife, who was yet to play a significant part in Jewish politics, may have aided and abetted him in these plans. Although High Priest he was essentially a soldier who delighted in war. More often than not he was the aggressor, but despite the help of strong mercenary troops he did not always finish on the winning side. The kingdom he had inherited was a considerable one, embracing Judaea, Samaria, and Galilee; this he now proceeded to enlarge by conquest and proselytization until, in the end, it was as extensive as the ancient kingdoms of David and Solomon (cf. *Antiquities* XIII. xv. 4). Despite his use of Greek on his coins he was not a 'lover of the Greeks' in the way that his predecessor is reputed to have been. This is shown, for example, in his attacks on many Greek cities whose inhabitants he forcibly converted to Judaism. The existence of these cities was a constant menace to the Jewish state, and it in turn was a serious danger to their economic survival. This was particularly so in the case of the coastal cities whose maritime power was now being seriously challenged by the Jews. Having established his power all down the coast from Carmel to Gaza, with the sole exception of Ascalon, Jannaeus engaged in a number of successful campaigns in Transjordan and further to the south. There he encountered serious opposition from the Nabataeans, first under their King, Obedas, at whose hands he suffered a severe defeat (cf. *Antiquities* XIII. xiii. 5), and later under King Aretas, who also defeated him in battle and invaded Judaea (cf. *Antiquities* XIII. xv. 2). This period marked the emergence of the Nabataeans as a powerful people; from their Arab kingdom in the deserts of Idumaea they thrust northwards, subduing the land as far as Damascus, and north-westwards round the southern border of Judaea in the direction of the Mediterranean Sea. After a chequered career as a warrior-king Alexander Jannaeus contracted a disease through his drinking habits and died, leaving the control of his affairs in the hands of his widow, Salome Alexandra (cf. *Antiquities* XIII. xv. 5).

The behaviour of Alexander Jannaeus was hardly likely to win him many friends at home, especially among the orthodox Jews and members of the Pharisaic party. His growing unpopularity was matched only by the growing popularity of the Pharisees themselves, who were openly critical of his manner of life. To them it was quite intolerable that a drunkard and profligate like Jannaeus should claim the status either of High Priest or of King; he had wilfully neglected his spiritual office, sacrificing it to that of a rough soldier whose delight was in war; his sympathies, moreover, were with the wealthy and powerful Sadducaean families. The trouble came to a head on the occasion of a celebration of the Feast of Tabernacles at which he was officiating as High Priest. As he was standing in front of the altar and was about to offer the sacrifice, the people pelted him with citrons, which they were carrying for use in the festival, and hurled insults at him, declaring that he was unfit to hold office (cf. *Antiquities* XIII. xiii. 5). The Talmud states that this outburst was occasioned by a contemptuous and stupid action of Jannaeus, who purposely poured a water libation over his own feet instead of on the altar as was required by Pharisaic tradition. The people's reaction so infuriated the High Priest that, according to Josephus, he let loose his mercenaries, who massacred six thousand of them.

Jerusalem after this was seething with unrest, and the people there waited for opportunity of revenge. This came some time later, in 94 B.C., when Jannaeus returned home after fleeing from the Nabataean King Obedas. The Jews, urged on by the Pharisees, broke out in revolt against their ruler. In the civil war which followed and which lasted for six years, Jannaeus, it is reported, slew no fewer than fifty thousand of his own people, with the help of foreign mercenaries (cf. *Antiquities* XIII. xiii. 5). At the end of this period the Pharisees decided to put an end to this indecisive warfare by calling in the help of the Seleucid, Demetrius III (Eukairos). Thus we find successors of the Hasidim[1], in league with the descendants of Antiochus Epiphanes, fighting against the descendants of the Maccabees!

[1] See p. 160.

Jannaeus, with his mercenaries, was defeated at Shechem and fled to the mountains.

Some scholars see a reference to this situation in the commentary on the Book of Nahum found at Qumran, which tells how 'Demetrius sought to enter Jerusalem on the counsel of those who seek smooth things'. If the people mentioned here are to be identified with Demetrius III and the Pharisees we may find in this incident a reason for the curious turn of events which now took place. According to Josephus, Jannaeus whilst in hiding was joined by six thousand Jews who pledged him their support. The people, it would seem, were faced with two possibilities—life under Jannaeus or life under the Seleucids; many of them chose the former as the lesser of two evils!

This move, however, was ill conceived, for no sooner had Jannaeus re-established his authority and forced Demetrius to withdraw than he set about taking vengeance on his enemies the Pharisees. Many of those who had not joined him he pursued and captured and brought back to Jerusalem, where he took terrible vengeance on them. Whilst feasting and carousing with his concubines he ordered eight hundred of the rebels to be crucified and their wives and children to be slaughtered before their eyes (cf. *Antiquities* XIII. xiv. 1–2; *War* I. iv. 5–6). It is no doubt this event which is referred to in the Nahum Commentary: 'He hanged living men on wood . . . which was not formerly done in Israel'. Josephus reports that the rest of his enemies numbering eight thousand fled by night and remained in exile as long as Jannaeus lived, carrying with them a burning hatred of their King and of the whole Sadducaean party, whose members had not lifted a finger to help them in their time of need.

For the greater part of his reign the Pharisaic opposition had been led by one Simeon ben Shetaḥ, reputed to be the brother of the King's wife, Salome Alexandra. Rabbinical stories, for the most part legendary, show him to have been a determined and fiery-tempered man, not afraid to challenge the King openly or even to insult him to his face. When Jannaeus was forced to flee from Jerusalem, Simeon asserted his authority and established himself as president of the Council, thus assuming the chief religious and political position in the state. When, however, shortly afterwards Jannaeus once more took over the reins of government and set about liquidating his enemies, Simeon, like many others, wisely went into hiding.

A number of scholars believe that the flight of Jannaeus' opponents is to be connected with the founding of the Qumran community, and that he is the Wicked Priest whose name frequently occurs in the Dead Sea Scrolls as the persecutor of the Teacher of Righteousness.[1] It is argued that, though the Qumran Covenanters were not Pharisees and cannot be identified with the Pharisaic opposition to Jannaeus, such opposition would by no means be confined to the Pharisaic party; it may have included also such men as the Teacher of Righteousness and his disciples, whose objection to Jannaeus as High Priest would be every bit as strong as that of the Pharisees themselves. At any rate archaeological evidence shows that the community at Qumran was considerably augmented just at this time. With the flight of these opponents of the King peace prevailed within his kingdom throughout the rest of his reign.

Tradition has it that just before his death at the age of 49 he counselled his wife not to follow his own tactics in her relations with the Pharisees, but rather to take them into her confidence and give them a position of authority within the kingdom. By this means she would win the support of the masses and strengthen her hold over the people (cf. *Antiquities* XIII. xv. 5). Whether Jannaeus actually gave her this counsel or not, this is what she decided to do.

## 5. *Salome Alexandra* (*76-67 B.C.*)

Jannaeus' elder son Hyrcanus might have been expected to succeed his father on the throne; but he was a weak and irresolute man who showed few signs that he was fitted for the kingly office. No doubt his mother, Salome Alexandra, shared this view, for on the death of her husband she at once assumed

[1] See p. 167.

the rank of Queen in her own right, ruling over her people for the next nine years. As a woman, however, she was excluded by the Law from the High Priesthood; she accordingly appointed Hyrcanus to this office. These measures did not please her younger son, Aristobulus, an able and energetic young man, whose obvious ambitions the Queen was forced to restrain for the sake of the peace of the realm (cf. *Antiquities* XIII. xvi. 1–2).

The outstanding feature of Queen Alexandra's reign was the revival during this time of Pharisaic influence and the corresponding curtailment of Sadducaean power. Josephus, for example, states that 'she permitted the Pharisees to do as they liked in all matters, and also commanded the people to obey them' (*Antiquities* XIII. xvi. 2). Whether acting from conviction or simply from expediency, she gave them her energetic support to such an extent that her reign is regarded in Pharisaic tradition as a veritable golden age, in which even the earth brought forth crops of miraculous size—grains of wheat as large as kidneys, barley as large as olives, and lentils like golden denarii! The balance of power in the supreme Council of the nation, traditionally an aristocratic body almost completely under the influence of the Sadducees, was radically altered. Under the leadership of the Queen's brother, Simeon ben Shetah, the Pharisees now gained overwhelming control and became quite obviously 'the power behind the throne'. Since the Council possessed legislative as well as judiciary powers, they were at last in a position to enforce their ideas on the entire nation and to override the judgements of their opponents in the Sadducaean party. Without any delay they reintroduced the Pharisaic regulations that John Hyrcanus had forbidden some years earlier, and required that their views, rather than those of the Sadducees, should be observed in the service and ritual of the Temple. Simeon ben Shetah was again an important figure in these transactions. Tradition ascribes to him, no doubt correctly, the founding of the school system in Jerusalem, which rapidly developed in subsequent years and created throughout the whole country an educated class not confined to members of aristocratic families but comprising also the common people. Such education would consist chiefly of the study of the Law; but its scope was much wider than this and provided a comprehensive system of elementary training.

Other developments, however, took place during Alexandra's reign which had a much less peaceable outcome. Taking advantage of their position in the state the Pharisees recalled those of their friends and sympathizers who had been banished from the land and set free others who had been imprisoned. Not content with this, they now sought revenge for past sufferings; seizing a number of leading citizens who had acted as Jannaeus' advisers when he had crucified the eight hundred rebels, they put them to death. The Sadducees and their associates, not unnaturally, were alarmed at these things and at once sent a deputation to the palace to lodge a protest with the Queen and to win her favour. A prominent member of this deputation was her own son, Aristobulus, who now openly sided with the Sadducees against the Pharisees and denounced his mother bitterly. Alexandra, in a great quandary, acceded to their request to be permitted to leave Jerusalem for their own safety, and gave them permission to take control of a number of fortresses in different parts of the land (cf. *Antiquities* XIII. xvi. 2–3; *War* I. v. 2–3). Aristobulus, with the backing of considerable military forces in the pay of the Jewish aristocracy, and with many strategic strongholds now in friendly hands, was in a much stronger position than at any time before to assert his authority. But the time to act was not quite yet.

His ability as a soldier was recognized by his mother when shortly afterwards she sent him with an army against Damascus; this expedition, however, proved uneventful and he returned home. Some time later, towards the end of Alexandra's reign, the safety of Judaea was threatened by Tigranes, King of Armenia, who had already invaded and subdued Syria. The Queen, afraid of invasion, sent envoys with valuable gifts to ask for peace. The situation was saved, however, by the Roman commander Lucullus, who just then attacked the Armenian capital, causing Tigranes to withdraw from Syria (cf. *Antiquities* XIII. xvi. 3–4; *War* I. v. 3).

Not long after these events Alexandra, now 73 years of age, became seriously ill. Aristobulus, realizing that his elder brother Hyrcanus must soon be appointed king, decided to take matters into his own hands. Slipping out of the city by night, he set out for the fortresses which were securely in the hands of his father's friends. There he won the pledge of their support, and within fifteen days had gathered a considerable army and gained control of no fewer than twenty-two of these strongholds. Hyrcanus and the leaders of the Jews, in a panic, sought the Queen's advice. She, however, was too ill to be of any service to them and not long afterwards died. The scene was set for civil war (cf. *Antiquities* XIII. xvi. 5; *War* I. v. 4).

## 6. *Aristobulus II* (*67-63 B.C.*)

On the death of his mother, Hyrcanus, it would seem, assumed the royal office as Hyrcanus II, but his time as King was short. When the two brothers met in battle at Jericho, Hyrcanus' troops deserted him and joined Aristobulus. Hyrcanus himself fled for safety to the fortress called Baris (later to be known as Antonia), to the north-west of the Temple area in Jerusalem, where he was besieged and forced to surrender. An agreement was reached between the two brothers whereby Hyrcanus was to relinquish his offices of King and High Priest to Aristobulus, and retire from public life with no deprivation of property (cf. *Antiquities* XIV. i. 2; *War* I. vi. 1).

All might have gone well if there had not now appeared on the scene a controversial figure whose family was to play a vital part in the affairs of the Jews for many years to come. This was a man named Antipater (shorter form, Antipas), father of the future Herod the Great and son of that Antipater whom Alexander Jannaeus had appointed governor of Idumaea (cf. *Antiquities* XIV. i. 3). Josephus records that he was actually an Idumaean by birth, i.e. a descendant of the Edomites, traditional enemies of the Jews. This is not altogether certain, but even if he was, he would doubtless count himself a Jew and be accepted as such as a result of the forcible Judaizing of the Idumaeans in the time of John Hyrcanus (cf. *Antiquities* XIV. viii. 1). Concerning this enigmatic figure Josephus gives conflicting evidence. On the one hand he describes him as 'by nature a man of action and a trouble-maker' (*Antiquities* XIV. i. 3), capable of bitter hatred and crafty intrigue; on the other hand he portrays him as an outstanding leader and a brave soldier, noted for his good sense and 'distinguished for piety, justice, and devotion to his country' (*Antiquities* XIV. vi. 3, viii. 1, xi. 4). Whatever the true assessment of his character may be, he was already a man of some wealth and standing among the Jews, having won for himself many friends and an influential position within the nation. Envious of the popularity and influence of Aristobulus, he now decided, no doubt with his own advantage in mind, to stir up further trouble between the two brothers and to support the cause of Hyrcanus for whom, it would seem, he had a genuine affection (cf. *War* I. x. 5). By means of intrigues and false accusations he fostered opposition to Aristobulus among the leading Jews and persuaded Hyrcanus that he was in danger of losing his life if he remained where he was. Hyrcanus was at first loath to believe such things about his brother, but finally gave in, leaving Jerusalem secretly by night for Petra, capital of the Nabataean kingdom, in company with Antipater. There Aretas, the Nabataean King, consented to help him regain his position in Jerusalem if he would promise the return of twelve cities and other territory which his father Alexander Jannaeus had confiscated. When Hyrcanus agreed to this proposal Aretas sent an army into Judaea. Aristobulus was defeated and many of his followers deserted him and fled; he himself escaped to Jerusalem where, at the time of the Jewish Passover, the Nabataean army besieged him in the Temple area (65 B.C.) (cf. *Antiquities* XIV. i. 3–4; *War* I. vi. 2). Within the city itself the priests and their followers remained loyal to Aristobulus, whilst the Pharisees and the general populace gave their assistance to the attackers.

A palace tomb in Petra, carved out of the solid sandstone rock. Petra, meaning 'Rock' is perhaps to be identified with the Edomite city called 'Sela' ('Crag') in the Old Testament (cf. Jer. 49$^{16}$). It is situated in an isolated and almost inaccessible position about 60 miles north of Aqabah and is approached (normally on horseback) through a narrow gorge flanked by great cliffs of variegated rock. In the time of the Hasmonaeans it was the powerful capital of the Nabataean kingdom. Hyrcanus II and Herod the Great for a while sought refuge here. It persisted through the Roman period and fell into ruins after the Mohammedan conquest in the seventh century A.D. The Nabataeans adapted the Graeco-Roman styles in architecture to their own medium of rock carving, and there is evidence to prove, from several unfinished façades, that the buildings were cut from the top downwards. The magnificent colourings of the rock formations have given it the name 'a rose-red city half as old as time' (from *Petra* by J. W. Burgon, 1813–88).

In this connexion Josephus refers to a certain Onias whom he describes as 'a righteous man and dear to God' whose prayers for rain in a time of drought had once been wonderfully answered. The followers of Hyrcanus, impressed by his ability in prayer, bade this man place a curse on Aristobulus and his supporters. When he refused he was set in the midst of the mob and forced to speak. Instead of doing what they demanded, however, he prayed that neither side should have its way against the other. The infuriated mob thereupon stoned him to death (cf. *Antiquities* xiv. ii. 1). This incident is of significance in the light of the claim made by some scholars that this Onias may have been the Teacher of Righteousness mentioned in the Dead Sea Scrolls and that either Hyrcanus II or Aristobulus II was the Wicked Priest.[1]

This was the state of affairs prevailing in Judaea when in 65 B.C. the Roman armies appeared in Syria, bent on the greater security of their realm and at the same time seeking opportunity, no doubt, for economic advancement. For some while the whole structure of the Seleucid empire had been crumbling; now it collapsed before the might of Rome. The conquest of Syria was to be but one stage in the extension of Roman authority as far as the river Euphrates. In such circumstances civil war in Judaea was an intolerable embarrassment. Accordingly the Roman general Pompey ordered Scaurus, legate of Syria, to proceed there and effect a speedy settlement. On his arrival in Judaea Scaurus was met by envoys from both Hyrcanus and Aristobulus, each eager to outbid the other for his help. Aristobulus apparently offered the bigger bribe, which was accepted by Scaurus, who now ordered Aretas to raise the siege of Jerusalem and withdraw his army, on pain of being regarded as an enemy of Rome. Before returning to Damascus Scaurus confirmed Aristobulus in office. The latter quickly followed up his advantage by pursuing Aretas' retreating army and inflicting on it a crushing defeat (cf. *Antiquities* xiv. ii. 3).

Aristobulus now sought to win further favour from Pompey

[1] See p. 167.

by sending him a golden vine worth five hundred talents; but, although willing to receive the gift, Pompey was not averse to giving his support to Hyrcanus should the need arise. In 63 B.C., when in Damascus, he received three deputations from the Jews—one led by Aristobulus, who sought to justify his actions by asserting that his brother was incompetent to rule, a second led by Hyrcanus, who insisted that since he was the elder brother he was the legitimate ruler, and a third representing apparently the Pharisaic element among the people which asked for the abolition of the Hasmonaean rule and the reinstatement of the former High-Priestly house. On this occasion, it is reported, Pompey was displeased with Aristobulus' violent manner and decided to withhold his decision until he had settled his affairs with the Nabataeans. Aristobulus, however, was too impatient or too fearful to wait, and set off at once for Judaea. Pompey, fearing the worst, went after him with an army and caught up with him at the fortress of Alexandreion where he had taken refuge. On the advice of friends Aristobulus submitted; but no sooner had he done so than he set off resentfully for Jerusalem, where he began to make preparations for war (cf. *Antiquities* XIV. iii. 1–4). Once again, however, he surrendered himself to Pompey, promising to give him money and to admit him to Jerusalem. When, however, Pompey sent his officer Gabinius to take possession of the city he found the gates securely locked against him. Aristobulus, who was still in Pompey's hands, was put under arrest and the Roman army advanced against Jerusalem.

Within the city loyalties were completely divided. Aristobulus' supporters, determined to put up a strong resistance, took up their position in the fortified Temple area and prepared for a siege. Hyrcanus' supporters decided to capitulate and opened the gates to Pompey's army. For three months those in the Temple area continued to resist, but at last the wall was breached and the Temple itself taken. A terrible massacre followed, in which twelve thousand Jews were done to death, the very priests being killed as they officiated at the altar, preferring to die in the pursuit of their duty rather than neglect any of their holy offices. The Temple was further desecrated when Pompey and certain of his men entered into the Holy of Holies, an act of sacrilege which greatly shocked the whole Jewish population and was never forgotten. He did not plunder the Temple treasures, however, but instead on the following day gave orders for its cleansing and for the resumption of the customary sacrifices. Hyrcanus was reinstated as High Priest and appointed ethnarch,[1] the title of king being now no longer used (cf. *Antiquities* XIV. iv. 1–4). His authority henceforth was to be exercised under that of Scaurus, whom Pompey left behind as legate of Syria. Aristobulus was taken as a prisoner to Rome together with his two daughters and his two sons Alexander and Antigonus, the former of whom managed to escape on the way there (cf. *Antiquities* XIV. iv. 5). Aristobulus was further humiliated when in 61 B.C. he was forced to take part in a victory-procession in Rome, walking in front of Pompey's chariot as part of the spoils of war.

In this way the rule of the Hasmonaean House came to a dismal end. Further attempts were made, as we shall see, to regain lost ground and restore Hasmonaean authority, but for all practical purposes Pompey's victory put an end to their effective rule. Independence, so dearly bought, was now forfeited; the land, deprived of its hard-won conquests, was greatly reduced in size,[2] and the High Priest of the Most High God became once more the vassal of a foreign power.

[1] This title, meaning 'ruler of the people', was second only to that of 'king'.
[2] See below.

# VI

## THE JEWS UNDER THE ROMANS
### (*63–4 B.C.*)

### 1. *Roman measures and Jewish revolts*

As a result of Pompey's conquest the Hasmonaean kingdom became part of the Roman province of Syria, of which Scaurus was governor. This whole area, comprising the western part of the former Seleucid empire, was of the utmost importance to the Romans, not least because it formed a strategic line of defence against the ever-present menace of Parthian invasion from the east. To take the fullest advantage of its strategic position, however, it was necessary to guarantee the unity of the country and to put its control in the hands of the central government. For this purpose certain sweeping administrative reforms were carried through. Whole areas which had been added by conquest to the Hasmonaean kingdom were 'liberated' and placed under the authority of the governor of Syria. These included the city and land of Samaria, a number of Hellenistic cities on the coastal plain, and several others, including Pella and Scythopolis, in Transjordan and the Jordan valley area, which were now incorporated in the territory known as the Decapolis (or 'ten cities'). Territory under Jewish control was thus reduced to Judaea itself together with the districts of Galilee in the north, Idumaea in the south, and 'Peraea' on the east side of Jordan. Over this territory Pompey set up Hyrcanus II as High Priest and ethnarch, but withheld from him the title of king. He was no longer ruler of a kingdom but High Priest of a religious community with its centre of worship in Jerusalem. Hyrcanus was personally responsible to the Roman governor, to whom his people had to pay annual tribute (cf. *Antiquities* xiv. iv. 4; *War* i. vii. 6).

The country remained at peace for six years, until in 57 B.C. an attempt was made by Alexander, the son of Aristobulus, who had escaped on his way to Rome, to gain the mastery over his uncle Hyrcanus. Collecting an army he captured the fortresses at Alexandreion, Hyrcania, and Machaerus. The recently appointed governor of Syria, Gabinius, at once took action; with the help of Mark Antony he defeated Alexander near Jerusalem and caused him to withdraw to Alexandreion, where he surrendered. Alexander was set free, but the fortresses he had taken were demolished (cf. *Antiquities* XIV. v. 2–4; *War* I. viii. 1–5). Gabinius, as a consequence of Alexander's revolt, now carried out further administrative changes which strengthened still more the central government's control over Jewish affairs. Their territory was divided up into five independent districts directly responsible to the provincial governor in matters of government and taxation.

This tightening of control, however, did not prevent still further outbreaks. The Jews as a whole were unhappy about recent government moves and about the continuing High Priesthood of Hyrcanus. This general restlessness was a signal for Aristobulus and his son Antigonus, who had by this time also escaped from the Romans, to raise the standard of revolt (56 B.C.). The rising, however, was short-lived. Forced to withdraw to the fortress of Machaerus, east of the Dead Sea, they surrendered. Aristobulus was carried off to Rome a second time, though Antigonus was set free (cf. *Antiquities* XIV. vi. 1; *War* I. viii. 6). Within a few months of these events, during the absence of Gabinius in Egypt, Antigonus' brother Alexander again took up arms. On his return from Egypt Gabinius, whose army had been helpfully supplied with grain by Antipater, now requested his further help in trying to win over the Jews to a more favourable frame of mind. When these attempts failed, he advanced to meet Alexander's army and routed it near Mount Tabor on the southern border of Galilee. Gabinius then proceeded to Jerusalem, where, says Josephus, 'he reorganized the government in accordance with Antipater's wishes' (*Antiquities* XIV. vi. 3–4; cf. *War* I. viii. 7).

Shortly afterwards (54 B.C.) Gabinius' place in Syria was taken by Crassus, who dealt with the Jews much more severely than his predecessor had done. To finance his projected campaign against the Parthians he ransacked the Jerusalem Temple and stole the treasures which Pompey some years before had left intact. The following year he was defeated in battle by the Parthians near Carrhae and was killed a short time later. From 53 to 51 B.C. Syrian affairs were in the hands of Cassius, who, after the death of Crassus, sought to stem the advance of the Parthians eastwards. Like his predecessor he was favourably impressed by Antipater. It was at his instigation, for example, that he put down a popular rising in Galilee (51 B.C.), selling thirty thousand of his captives into slavery and putting to death one of the ringleaders named Peitholaus, who represented the cause of Aristobulus and his sons against the High Priest Hyrcanus (cf. *Antiquities* XIV. vii. 1–3; *War* I. viii. 8–9).

In the year 49 B.C. the growing rivalry between Pompey and Julius Caesar finally burst into civil war, and soon Caesar found himself master of Rome. In the light of these events Pompey's forces in Syria withdrew eastwards, leaving Antipater and his supporters in a precarious position. Caesar now decided to release Aristobulus and send him to Syria as his champion; before this plan could be implemented, however, Aristobulus was poisoned by Pompey's supporters, and the following year his son Alexander was beheaded on the express orders of Pompey himself. Antipater now decided upon a bold policy. When Pompey was defeated the following year at the battle of Pharsalus and afterwards assassinated, he and Hyrcanus determined to change sides and come out openly in support of Caesar. Their bold move was accepted, and soon Antipater was able to express his friendship in a practical way. During Caesar's campaign in Egypt he went to the help of his armies in a difficult situation; Hyrcanus on his part also showed his willingness to help, by urging the Jews in Egypt to take Caesar's side. Despite the plea of Aristobulus' remaining son Antigonus that he had a right to the High Priesthood rather than

Hyrcanus, Caesar responded to the proffered friendship of Anti-pater and Hyrcanus and rewarded them handsomely for their loyal help. The five administrative districts established by Gabinius were now abolished, and Judaea was once more united under the leadership of Hyrcanus, whom Caesar now confirmed in the hereditary office of High Priest, and appointed ethnarch, also with hereditary rights. Thus Hyrcanus received back that political authority which Gabinius had taken away from him. He and his descendants, moreover, were now named as 'allies' and 'friends' of Rome. Antipater was likewise honoured by being appointed procurator of Judaea and being given Roman citizenship with exemption from taxes. No Roman troops were to be billeted in Judaea during the winter months and no money was to be required from the people for this purpose. Permission was given to rebuild the walls of Jerusalem. The strategic seaport of Joppa was restored to the Jews together with certain other places, including a number of villages in the plain of Jezreel. Josephus further records that the Jews of the Dispersion—in Alexandria and Asia Minor—like-wise received generous preferential treatment, being granted complete freedom in the exercise of their religion (cf. *Antiquities* XIV. viii. 1–5, x. 1–7; *War* I. ix. 1–x. 3). Having received such remarkable concessions it is hardly surprising that the Jews, above all people, mourned the death of Caesar when a few years later he fell by the hands of his assassins.

The events of these days are reflected in an important book, the so-called Psalms of Solomon,[1] written about the middle of the first century B.C. These Psalms, eighteen in all, are generally taken to represent the religious outlook of 'quietist' Pharisaism at this time. Most scholars identify the invader, referred to in Ps. Sol. 2 and 8, with Pompey, and find in the book a commentary on the years 63–48 B.C., i.e. the period between Pompey's capture of Jerusalem and his death. Of greatest significance are Ps. Sol. 17 and 18, where the writer looks away from the faded glories of the Hasmonaean House to the splendour of the messianic age and the glory of the Davidic

[1] See pp. 291 ff.

Messiah. God's anointed one would purge Jerusalem and establish his eternal kingdom; the humble poor of Israel would enter into their inheritance and the nations would come from the ends of the earth to see his glory.

## 2. *The rise of Herod and the reign of Antigonus*

It is quite clear from the events which followed Caesar's decree that the real power in Judaea lay in the hands not of Hyrcanus but of Antipater, who took advantage of the weakness and indolence of his companion to establish his own authority. In particular he appointed his elder son Phasael governor of Jerusalem, with jurisdiction over Judaea and Peraea, and his younger son Herod governor of Galilee (47–46 B.C.). The latter soon made his presence felt by capturing a brigand-chief named Ezekias, who had been troubling Galilee, and putting him to death together with many of his men. Hyrcanus was jealous of the reputation Herod was building up for himself, and the aristocratic families and other members of the supreme Council (to which Josephus now gives the name 'Sanhedrin') were furious because he had thus taken matters into his own hands. Hyrcanus was prevailed upon to summon Herod to appear before the Sanhedrin. This he did, but when Herod appeared in Jerusalem it was with the moral backing of the governor of Syria, Sextus Caesar, and with the military backing of a strongly armed bodyguard! In such circumstances Hyrcanus and the Sanhedrin had little option but to pronounce his acquittal. Herod, however, interpreted these proceedings as a personal insult, and within a short time appeared before Jerusalem with a considerable army, determined to assert his authority. Only the earnest pleading of his father Antipater turned him aside from his purpose. Herod then returned to Galilee, satisfied that he had at least terrified the Jerusalem aristocracy with a display of his power. During these events Sextus Caesar appointed him governor of Coele-Syria and Samaria (cf. *Antiquities* xiv. ix. 1–5; *War* i. x. 4–9).

After the death of Julius Caesar in 44 B.C. the government of

Syria came into the hands of Cassius, who had already served in this capacity during the years 53–51 B.C. He won for himself the hatred of the Jews by exacting from them large sums of money for the support of his army. Their bitterest hatred, however, was reserved for Antipater, who once more changed sides and placed his services, together with those of his son Herod, at the disposal of Cassius, offering to collect the required payments from the Jews. For this service Herod was confirmed in his office as governor of Coele-Syria. Antipater was much less fortunate, however, for he was poisoned (43 B.C.) at the instigation of a rival named Malichus, who was himself shortly afterwards put to death by Herod (cf. *Antiquities* XIV. xi. 2–6; *War* I. xi. 1–8).

A short time later, when Cassius left Syria to join Brutus, outbursts of violence took place in Judaea and in Galilee in which Antigonus was involved. Herod defeated the rebels in battle and banished Antigonus from the country. Hyrcanus was grateful to Herod for this act, for, although he distrusted him, his most dangerous rival was Antigonus himself. Herod at this time won for himself an even more favourable position by becoming engaged to Mariamne, daughter of Antigonus' brother Alexander and of Hyrcanus' daughter Alexandra. But the time had come for Herod, like his father before him, to change sides. In 42 B.C. Cassius and Brutus were defeated at the battle of Philippi by Antony and Octavian. Control of Syria thereafter passed into the hands of Mark Antony, whose goodwill Herod and Phasael at once sought to win. Despite charges brought against him by the Jews, Herod won the approval of Antony who now appointed him and his brother joint tetrarchs, with control over the administration of Judaea. During these proceedings Hyrcanus had stood up for Herod and Phasael; but now he found himself deprived once more of all political power (cf. *Antiquities* XIV. xi. 7–xii. 2, xiii. 1; *War* I. xii. 1–5).

In 40 B.C. Antigonus, who had been biding his time awaiting further opportunity to assert himself, made another determined attempt to win back the throne, with the help of the Parthians

The impressive rocky plateau of Masada where Herod built a palace fortress for the members of his family. Situated near the desolate western shore of the Dead Sea about 10 miles south of En-gedi, it is famous for the stand taken there by the Zealots in the War with Rome, A.D. 66–73. Josephus reports that of its 960 occupants only 7 women and children survived. All the others, rather than surrender, slew one another by mutual consent. Masada has now been excavated by the Government of Israel.

whose support he enlisted in return for suitable bribes. Hyrcanus and Phasael were taken prisoner and subsequently handed over to Antigonus. Antigonus thereupon cut off Hyrcanus' ears, thus making him unfit to hold the High Priestly office (cf. Lev. 21$^{17}$ $^{ff.}$), before handing him back to the Parthians, who carried him off to Babylon. Phasael decided to commit suicide by dashing his head against a rock. The way was now open for Antigonus to realize his great ambition. With the full backing of the Parthians he assumed leadership of the nation as both High Priest and King. Coins struck during his three years' reign (40–37 B.C.) show on the obverse side the inscription, 'King Antigonus' (in Greek), and on the reverse side, 'Mattathias the High Priest and the Community of the Jews' (in Hebrew, with the Hebrew form of his name. Cf. *Antiquities* XIV. xiii. 1–10; *War* I. xiii. 1–11).

Meanwhile Herod, barely escaping capture himself, escorted

his family to the fortress of Masada on the western shores of the Dead Sea and then fled for refuge to the Arab city of Petra. Meeting there with a cold reception, he left for Alexandria and from there set sail for Rome, where after a perilous voyage he was received favourably by Antony and Octavian. As a result of Antony's special pleading and with the approval of Octavian, the Roman Senate to Herod's utter astonishment unanimously elected him King of Judaea (39 B.C.). To be appointed king, however, was one thing; to take possession of his kingdom was another. But Herod was a resolute as well as a ruthless man. Back in Syria the Roman governor Ventidius had driven out the Parthians, but had left Antigonus in possession of his throne on payment of substantial tribute. Herod now landed in Ptolemais, collected an army, captured Joppa, removed his family from the fortress of Masada, where they were undergoing a siege, and advanced against Jerusalem. He was unable, however, to press home his advantage because of lack of support from the available Roman forces, and so withdrew into Galilee, where he spent some months clearing the land of robbers and putting down insurrection. Shortly afterwards, however, having received from Antony a pledge of Roman support, he made himself master of Galilee and then of the whole country. With the passing of winter he laid siege to Jerusalem, helped by the Roman army. Jerusalem fell and a great massacre followed, in which Herod had to buy off his Roman allies with substantial gifts of money. Antigonus was beheaded, and with his death the dwindling influence of the Hasmonaean House came to an end. Herod, who during the siege of Jerusalem had strengthened his position by marrying Mariamne, to whom he had been betrothed for five years, now took possession of his kingdom (37 B.C.) (cf. *Antiquities* xiv. xiv. 1–xvi. 4; *War* i. xiv. 1–xviii. 3).

### 3. *The reign of Herod the Great (37–4 B.C.)*

Herod the Great was a man of overpowering personality who contrived to be 'everything to all men' and was prepared to use every means to gain his own ends. By religion he was a Jew, by race an Idumaean,[1] by cultural sympathies a Greek, and by political allegiance a Roman. To his inferiors he was utterly ruthless; to the members of his own family he could behave in a most cruel manner; to his superiors he adopted a cunning policy of 'playing along with' whichever ruler at that moment found himself in power, and, like his father before him, was ready to change sides at a moment's notice in order to realize his ambitions.

*Home affairs and foreign policy (37-25 B.C.).* In 37 B.C., when he came to the throne, his kingdom was confined to Judaea, Idumaea, Peraea, and Galilee together with the port of Joppa and villages in the plain of Jezreel. Any plans he may have had for consolidation and expansion of this territory suffered a serious set-back in 34 B.C. when Antony transferred to Cleopatra the coastal cities of Phoenicia and Philistia as well as the most fertile part of his kingdom in the region of Jericho, which she proceeded to lease to him for a rent of two hundred talents! On Cleopatra's death, however, in 30 B.C. these were all restored to him by Octavian, and in subsequent years he gradually gained possession of the whole of Palestine apart from the independent cities of the Decapolis and the coastal strip to the north of Caesarea (cf. *Antiquities* xv. vii. 3, x. 1). It speaks highly for his powers of diplomacy that he was able to maintain this extensive kingdom intact until the time of his death.

Herod enjoyed the official title *rex socius* or 'confederate king'. As such he was a vassal king; nevertheless he was a real king, responsible not to the governor of Syria but directly to Caesar and the Roman Senate. Apart from certain restrictions on the issuing of his own coinage he was given full authority within his kingdom and shared all the rights of Roman citizenship. It was not customary for a *rex socius* to appoint his own successor, but in the case of Herod this honour was conferred in the year 22 B.C., only to be withdrawn at a later date when he forfeited the friendship of the Emperor. In the

[1] So Josephus tells us; cf. p. 76 above.

matter of foreign policy he was expected to comply with certain well-defined requirements. For example, he had no right to conclude a treaty with another state or wage war on his own account; moreover, he was under obligation to assist Rome in time of war with men and money, and was responsible for the defence of its frontiers, which in his case meant in particular the border between his own kingdom and those of the Nabataean Arabs to the south and the Parthians to the east.

Despite his endeavours to please he failed to win the confidence and trust of his subjects. The Greeks, for example, were not at all happy about being ruled by a Jew; and the Jews were even less happy, for, if Josephus is right, he was an Idumaean by birth even though his religion was Jewish. In particular, the Jewish aristocracy, both priestly and lay, made it perfectly clear that where they were concerned he was altogether unacceptable. It is not surprising, therefore, that one of his first acts was to despoil the well-to-do of much silver and gold, and to attack the leading members of Antigonus' party, forty-five of whom he put to death. The money thus acquired was used as gifts for Antony and his friends (cf. *Antiquities* xv. i. 2). As his reign advanced the old hereditary aristocracy gave place to a new aristocracy of service, consisting of men who had received their wealth and position from the King, with the result that his policy of administration assumed the nature of a strongly centralized bureaucracy, run on distinctly Hellenistic lines. By these means he dealt a death-blow at the power of the Sanhedrin, which ceased to have any real influence during his reign. Its powers were limited to strictly religious matters, matters of a political character being dealt with by a secular royal Council set up by the King, also on Hellenistic lines.

His attitude to the Pharisees, however, was much more favourable, for he could not forget that it was two of their number, Shemaiah and Pollio (Abtalion), who persuaded their fellow citizens to open the gates to him during his siege of Jerusalem. The fact that they did this not out of any love for Herod but because they saw in him God's instrument of judgement did not alter his attitude towards them. That they chose to adopt a quietist attitude and devote themselves to religious rather than to political affairs suited his purposes admirably; besides this, with them on his side he had a much better chance of winning the approval of the common people. He thus tried every means to appease them and to win their confidence by respecting their religious prejudices, by observing their ritual laws, and even by excusing them from taking an oath of allegiance to his royal person, a concession which the Essenes also shared (cf. *Antiquities* xv. x. 4). One important, if incidental, result of this policy was that during his reign there was a considerable increase in genuine piety among the common people. Despite his obvious desire to please, however, the Pharisees remained suspicious and aloof.

To placate the people still further Herod, near the beginning of his reign, brought back the former High Priest Hyrcanus from Babylon, even offering to share the throne with him. His subsequent treatment of the High-Priestly office, however, soon undid any good he had done in this way. Hyrcanus, because of his mutilated ears, could not serve as High Priest, nor could Herod himself, by reason of his lineage. He thus decided to degrade the office as much as possible by breaking the hereditary principle on which it had been based and by abolishing its lifelong tenure. From now on the High Priest was to be appointed by the King and would be permitted to hold office only so long as it pleased the King. Thus during the period of his reign no fewer than seven High Priests were appointed and then removed from office (cf. *Antiquities* xv. iii. 1, 3, ix. 3, xvii. vi. 4, etc.). The natural successor to Hyrcanus was the young Aristobulus (III), son of Hyrcanus' daughter Alexandra (i.e. Herod's mother-in-law). Herod, however, passed him over and appointed an obscure priest from Babylon named Ananel (cf. *Antiquities* xv. ii. 4). Alexandra took this as a gross insult and appealed to Cleopatra to use her influence with Antony on behalf of her son. Aristobulus' sister Mariamne (Herod's wife) also used her persuasion on her husband, with the result that Ananel was deposed and the sixteen-years-old Aristobulus set up in his place (36 B.C.).

Following this there was at first a show of friendship between Herod and Alexandra, but soon his suspicions were aroused that she was attempting to overthrow the government, and so he had her put under house-arrest. The discovery soon afterwards of her plan for her son and herself to escape to Cleopatra in Egypt in two coffins convinced him all the more of her guilt. Jealousy was added to suspicion when, at the Feast of Pentecost, the young High Priest was given a resounding welcome by the people. Shortly afterwards the King decided upon drastic action. At a reception in Jericho his young men, who had been bathing with Aristobulus, held him under the water until he drowned (cf. *Antiquities* xv. iii. 3). The report of this 'accident' was conveyed to Alexandra, who, from now onwards, sought revenge on her son-in-law Herod.

Once more Alexandra appealed to Cleopatra, with the result that Herod was summoned to appear before Antony. Realizing that he might never return from his interview, he committed Alexandra and his wife Mariamne to the watchful care of his uncle Joseph, who was also the husband of his sister Salome. His secret orders were that Mariamne, whom he loved dearly, should be killed if he himself were sentenced to death. He could not bear the thought of her belonging to anyone else, least of all to Antony who, he suspected, already had designs upon her. When a false report of Herod's death reached Jerusalem, Alexandra put her plans into operation to ensure the royal succession for her family, whilst Joseph divulged to Mariamne Herod's secret orders about her own fate. When Herod returned home safe and well, his mother Cypros and his sister Salome acquainted Herod with Alexandra's plans and insinuated that Mariamne's relations with Joseph left much to be desired. As a result he put Alexandra under arrest and executed Joseph without trial, sparing only his wife Mariamne (35 or 34 B.C.).

Within a few years Herod found himself involved in a crisis of much bigger dimensions. In 32 B.C. civil war broke out between Antony and Octavian, resulting in Octavian's victory at the battle of Actium the following year. It was fortunate for Herod that, prior to this victory, he had been sent at the instigation of Cleopatra and against his own will to fight the Nabataean Arabs, and so had not been directly involved in the war against Octavian. He now resolved on a bold plan—to go to Rhodes in person and throw himself on the mercy of Octavian. Before doing so, however, he decided to safeguard his position at home. Alexandra and Mariamne were again placed under observation, and express instructions given to their guards, another Joseph and Sohemus, to put them to death should he himself not return.[1] More drastic treatment, however, was reserved for the aged Hyrcanus, the only surviving rival claimant to the throne. On the orders of Herod he was brought before the Sanhedrin on a trumped-up charge of treason, duly sentenced, and executed (cf. *Antiquities* xv. vi. 2).

Herod was now ready to present himself before Octavian. With great boldness he confessed his former loyalty to Antony and now pledged his friendship to his rival. Octavian, duly impressed, accepted his offer and confirmed him on the throne, confident that in this audacious and ruthless man he had a ruler who could keep his own people in order and form a strong bulwark on his eastern frontier. Meanwhile, Antony and Cleopatra both having died by their own hands, Octavian transferred Cleopatra's possessions in Palestine to Herod, adding to them extensive territories in Samaria and in the land east of the Jordan, so that his kingdom from now onwards was almost comparable with that of Alexander Jannaeus.

On his return to Judaea in 29 B.C. Herod was again caught up in the domestic intrigues and jealousies that were to play such a big part in his later life. As on the previous occasion, his suspicions were aroused against Mariamne and her guard Sohemus. Further provoked by the insinuations of Salome that his wife intended to poison him, he had Mariamne and her supposed lover put to death. The death of Mariamne was to haunt him for the rest of his days. The following year Alex-

---

[1] The circumstances recorded here are suspiciously like those in the earlier story. The two accounts as given by Josephus reveal a certain confusion.

andra suffered a like fate for taking part in yet another plot against her son-in-law. Finally, three years later, in 25 B.C., his series of executions was brought to a close by the dispatch of one Castobarus, the second husband of Salome, for harbouring 'the sons of Babas', the only survivors of the Hasmonaean family, who were put to death with him. Although Herod was now as deeply hated by the Jews as he ever had been, his position from this point was never again seriously challenged (cf. *Antiquities* xv. vii. 10).

*His policy of Hellenization and programme of building (25–13 B.C.).* This story of plots and intrigues should not blind us to the fact that Herod's reign was a time of peace and prosperity for the nation as a whole. Despite his lavish expenditure on enormous building schemes and the expensive gifts he was constantly making to members of his own family and foreign dignitaries, he managed to keep his coffers full and, indeed, to increase steadily his royal revenue. He was a man of great business ability whose powers of planning and organization raised the country to a peak of prosperity. As examples of this we note especially a new scheme of irrigation he introduced to fertilize the lower Jordan valley, and a new city and port built on the site of Straton's Tower, whose excellent harbour encouraged profitable overseas trade, which he called Caesarea in honour of the Emperor.

In order to maintain this state of affairs he pursued three well-defined policies. One was to encourage good relations with Octavian and to promote that Hellenistic culture of which Rome was now champion; another was to cultivate the confidence and trust of his own people by, for example, reducing their burden of taxation (cf. *Antiquities* xv. x. 4, xvi. ii. 5) and avoiding offence to their religious scruples; the third was to suppress nationalism, which he regarded (not unjustifiably) as a menace to himself and to the security of the state. For this purpose, and as a defence against attacks from enemies outside, he maintained a standing army (composed largely of mercenaries), established military settlements on his northern and eastern borders, and erected a whole series of impregnable fortresses, some of which he fashioned into palaces for the use of the members of his large family.

The erection of these fortresses was but one part of an enormous building programme undertaken by Herod, especially during the middle period of his reign. This included not only magnificent buildings but also entire cities, erected in the Hellenistic style. As a patron of the arts he initiated quinquennial games in honour of the Emperor, with their athletic and gladiatoral contests, and was known as a liberal supporter and 'perpetual manager' of the Olympic games (cf. *Antiquities* XVI. v. 3). In city after city he built theatres, stadiums, hippodromes, gymnasiums, public baths, colonnaded streets, market-places with elegant statues, and innumerable temples. In Jerusalem itself he built a hippodrome south of the Temple area, a theatre just outside the city wall, and an amphitheatre 'in the plain' a little farther beyond (cf. *Antiquities* XV. viii. 1). Outside his kingdom he dedicated altars, shrines, and temples to heathen deities, as also to his benefactor Octavian.

Within Palestine itself two cities in particular call for special mention. In 27 B.C. he began to restore the ancient city of Samaria, calling it Sebaste in honour of Octavian, who only a few months before had been honoured by the Senate with the title 'Augustus' (Greek, *Sebastos*). The old site was now greatly enlarged, fortified with strong walls and impressive gates, and decorated with beautiful colonnades and magnificent buildings, one of the most impressive being the great Temple of Augustus, the ruins of whose monumental flight of steps can be seen to this day (cf. *Antiquities* XV. viii. 5). The second city is Caesarea, formerly (as we have seen) a small township on the coast called Straton's Tower. On this spot he built a truly magnificent city with a costly artificial harbour, a theatre, an amphitheatre, and all the other appurtenances of Hellenistic culture (cf. *Antiquities* XV. ix. 6).

His most notable work, however, was reserved for the city of Jerusalem itself. Among the fine buildings he erected there were two most impressive palaces which served at the same time as strategic and powerful fortresses. During the time of his

The north-west corner of the Temple area showing the site of the fortress Antonia on the left. This fortress, which occupied a commanding position overlooking the Temple, was built by Herod and named after his friend and patron Antony. It housed the Praetorium and the 'Pavement' mentioned in the New Testament (cf. John 18$^{28}$, 19$^{13}$).

friendship with Antony he had erected a citadel near the site of the Hasmonaean 'Baris', overlooking the Temple at the north-west corner of the Temple area and connected with it by under-ground passages and two stairways. This he called the fortress of Antonia, after his friend and patron.[1] Its high walls and four impressive towers dominated all the precincts of the Temple even more effectively than the Baris and that other citadel, the Akra, had done (cf. *Antiquities* xv. viii. 8, xi. 4, 7). The second building, known as 'Herod's palace', built on the western side of the city, was begun in 23 B.C. (cf. *Antiquities* xv. ix. 3). This was a much larger edifice than the Antonia, having three towers called Hippicus (after a friend), Phasael (after his brother), and Mariamne (after his wife), and containing magnificent royal suites. This building, which was on higher ground than the Antonia, dominated the city as effectively as that other citadel dominated the Temple area. But even these magnificent buildings paled into insignificance before another that was to be Herod's crowning glory, the reconstructed Temple (cf. *Antiquities* xv. xi. 2–3), which Josephus describes as 'the most notable of all the things achieved by him . . . great enough to assure his eternal remembrance' (*Antiquities* xv. xi. 1).

This work was begun in 20 B.C., the Temple proper being completed in eighteen months and the outer courts and porti-coes in another eight years—indeed the process of building continued for a much longer period (cf. John 2[20]) and was completed only in the time of the procurator Albinus (A.D. 62–65) a few years before it was destroyed in the Jewish War against the Romans. The old Temple area was doubled in size by means of embankments and flanking walls towering above the valleys far below. Around the whole area ran a continuous wall, with porticoes supported by gleaming white pillars, the one on the south side being of exceptional size and beauty (cf. *Antiquities* xv. xi. 5–7). In all this work, as in so many other respects, Herod was careful not to cause offence to his Jewish

---

[1] It is generally accepted that the Antonia contained the Praetorium and the 'Pavement' from which Jesus was led out to be crucified (cf. John 18[28], 19[13]).

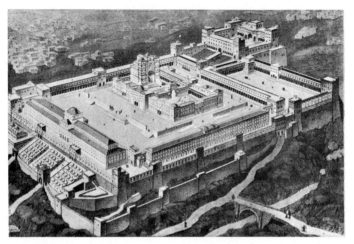

## DIVISIONS OF HEROD'S TEMPLE

*(reconstruction according to the data of Josephus and the Mishnah)*

1 Holy of Holies
2 Sacrificial Altar
3 Nicanor's Gate
4 Women's Court
5 Corinthian Gate
6 Treasury
7 Separation wall between Jews and Gentiles
8 Court of the Gentiles
9 Royal porch
10 Solomon's portico
11 Golden Gate
12 Underground entrances from the south
13 Antonia Fortress

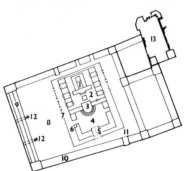

A reconstruction of the magnificent Temple area built by Herod the Great. The complex of buildings in the centre contained the Holy of Holies, the Holy Place, the altar of burnt offering, and the several Courts. The whole area was flanked by a continuous wall constructed with porticoes and supported by gleaming white pillars. The fortress Antonia can be seen in the top right hand corner and the Kidron Valley in the foreground.

subjects. For example, the stones to be used in the building were prepared beforehand by ten thousand workmen so that no noise should be heard there, a thousand of these workmen being priests specially trained as masons and carpenters for work on the most sacred parts of the building (cf. *Antiquities* xv. xi. 2). He was careful, moreover, never to enter the inner Temple himself. In strict observance of the second commandment he refrained from erecting statues in the Temple precincts and even from stamping images on his coins; he did, however, permit a replica of a Roman eagle to be set over the great gate of the Temple, which in due course was to lead to violent reaction on the part of certain Pharisees. In this and in many other ways Herod in fact gave ample cause for offence, despite all his efforts to the contrary.

*Domestic trouble and death (13–4 B.C.).* Herod was a man with many family connexions, which included ten wives, fifteen children, and innumerable grandchildren (cf. *Antiquities* xvii. i. 3). His first wife was the Idumaean, Doris, and his second the greatly loved Mariamne, whom he caused to be put to death. In 23 B.C. he married a second Mariamne, daughter of a Jerusalem priest named Simon, whom he installed in the High-Priestly office so as to make his marriage more fitting to the dignity of a king. Two other wives are deserving of mention because of the part they and their children were to play in forthcoming events—a Samaritan named Malthace and a woman from Jerusalem named Cleopatra.

The last few years of Herod's life tell a sad story of domestic intrigues and family quarrels in which his jealousies and suspicions grew rapidly to the pitch of mania. Goaded on by his scheming sister Salome, he gave free rein to his vindictiveness. The trouble started with the return home in 17 B.C. of his two sons by the first Mariamne, Alexander and Aristobulus, who five years before had been sent to Rome to be educated (cf. *Antiquities* xvi. i. 2). Proud of their royal descent through their Hasmonaean mother, they behaved arrogantly towards the other members of the family, who were mere Idumaeans. Their aunt, Salome, reacted with slanderous allegations that they were plotting to avenge themselves on Herod for the death of their mother (cf. *Antiquities* XVI. iii. 1). As a warning to his two sons Herod brought back from exile their stepbrother Antipater (son of his first wife Doris), whom he now sent to Rome with Agrippa to gain the favour of Augustus (cf. *Antiquities* XVI. iii. 3–4). During his absence his cause was ably supported by his mother Doris, his aunt Salome, and his uncle Pheroras, who continued slanderous attacks on the two brothers. As a result Herod was forced to take action and brought the young men before Augustus for judgement (12 B.C.). A reconciliation was effected, however, and Herod returned home with his two sons (cf. *Antiquities* XVI. iv. 2–4). There, before the Temple, he proclaimed Antipater as his heir and, failing him, the two sons of Mariamne (cf. *Antiquities* XVI. iv. 6). Petty feelings and intrigues continued, however, and members of the court were submitted to blackmail and torture. Alexander and Aristobulus were again charged with treason and summoned before Augustus (cf. *Antiquities* XVI. x. 1–7), who on this occasion allowed Herod to act as he thought best. Sentence of death was passed on the two brothers, who were thereupon taken to Sebaste and executed by strangling (7 B.C.) (cf. *Antiquities* XVI. xi. 1–7).

Antipater's troubles were not yet over, however, for he did not like the attention Herod was now paying to the children of Alexander and Aristobulus, and was afraid of the rival claims of his own half-brothers Archelaus and Antipas (sons of Malthace), Philip (son of Cleopatra), and Herod (son of the second Mariamne) (cf. *Antiquities* XVII. i. 1–3). Becoming suspicious of Antipater's growing impatience, Herod sent him to Rome (5 B.C.), naming him as heir-apparent and Herod as heir presumptive (cf. *Antiquities* XVII. iii. 2). During his absence a plot to poison the King was uncovered, in which Antipater, Doris, and the second Mariamne were all involved. When the unsuspecting Antipater returned home from Rome he was at once arrested, brought to trial, and condemned (cf. *Antiquities* XVII. v. 1–8). Herod now changed his will, naming Antipas (the younger son of Malthace) as his successor.

By this time the King had become seriously ill with a terrible disease, which caused him grievous bodily pain and finally brought him to a state of mental derangement. In spite of this severe handicap he forced himself to deal with a troublesome insurrection caused by certain Pharisees who on receiving a false report of his death, urged their pupils to pull down the golden eagle he had set up over the great gate of the Temple. Forty of them, together with two leading Rabbis named Judas and Matthias, were arrested and put on trial before the dying King. Judgement was passed; the ringleaders were burned alive and the others executed (cf. *Antiquities* XVII. vi. 1–3).

Meanwhile Herod's disease grew worse. A visit to the baths at Callirrhoe, on the eastern shores of the Dead Sea, did not have its desired effect and Herod returned to his palace in Jericho. At this point Josephus narrates an incident which is no doubt apocryphal. Herod, it is said, assembled the chief men of his kingdom and locked them in the hippodrome in Jericho, giving express orders to Salome that they were to be massacred as soon as he himself expired, so that the time of his death would be marked by national mourning (cf. *Antiquities* XVII. vi. 5)! In great physical and mental torment he made an unsuccessful attempt to take his own life, and then gave orders for the condemned Antipater, who lay in prison near by, to be killed and for his body to be buried without ceremony in the fortress of Hyrcania (cf. *Antiquities* XVII. vii. 1). With his own life fast ebbing away he again altered his will. Archelaus he appointed King of Judaea, Antipas tetrarch of Galilee and Transjordan, and Philip tetrarch of Gaulonitis, Trachonitis, and Paneas. Five days after Antipater's death, in the year 4 B.C., Herod himself died. His body, decked in all his royal regalia, was taken with elaborate ceremonial to its last resting-place in the fortress of Herodeion and there was buried (cf. *Antiquities* XVII. viii. 1–3).

# VII

## THE DISPERSION

### 1. *Its extent and causes*

T H E term 'Dispersion' is generally used to describe the scattering and settlement of the Jews outside Palestine during the Persian, Greek, and Roman periods. This process, begun in early pre-exilic days, gained increasing momentum, especially from the beginning of the second century B.C., so that by the time of the Christian era there was hardly a country where the Jews were not to be found. About the middle of the second century B.C. the writer of the Sibylline Oracles, for example, can say of the Jewish people, 'Every land and every sea is filled with thee' (Bk. III, line 271). Barely a century later the geographer Strabo (64 B.C.–A.D. 24) states that in the time of Sulla (*c.* 85 B.C.) 'this people has already made its way into every city, and it is not easy to find any place in the habitable world which has not received this nation and in which it has not made its power felt' (cf. *Antiquities* XIV. vii. 2). Philo (died *c.* A.D. 50) likewise speaks of the widespread dispersal of his people, claiming that 'one country cannot support the Jews, because they are so numerous' (*Flaccus* VII. 45). Later still, towards the end of the first century A.D., Josephus asserts that 'there is not a people in the world which does not contain a portion of our race' (*War* II. xvi. 4, cf. VII. iii. 3; *Against Apion* II. 39 (282)). This is confirmed by two other important passages—1 Macc. 15$^{16-24}$ and Philo's *Embassy to Gaius* XXXVI. 281 f.—which specify the many places throughout Europe, Asia Minor, Babylonia, and beyond where Jewish communities were to be found. Further corroboration is given by the New Testament, which clearly indicates that by that time there was hardly a country or a city to which the Jews had not come (cf. John 7$^{35}$; Acts 2$^{9-11}$; James 1$^{1}$; 1 Peter 1$^{1}$).

Attempts have been made to assess the total population of the Jews in the Roman empire at the beginning of the Christian era, a figure of six to eight millions often being given. The tendency of the sources to give greatly inflated figures makes any such assessment a hazardous undertaking. Josephus, for example, suggests that there were about three million Jews in Galilee alone (cf. *War* III. iii. 2), whilst Philo reckons that there were a million in Alexandria, comprising one-eighth of the total population and occupying two of the five quarters of the city (cf. *Flaccus* VI. 43). There can be little doubt that the Jews, though not as prolific as these figures suggest, were nevertheless very numerous and in certain countries made up a fair proportion of the population.

There was a large Jewish community in *Babylonia* and *Mesopotamia*, for example, tracing back its origins to the deportations from Judaea in 586 B.C. and to the Assyrian conquest of Samaria in 722 B.C. Josephus refers to 'not a few tens of thousands' transported to Babylonia and Hyrcania around the middle of the fourth century B.C. (cf. *Antiquities* XV. iii. 1), who formed a well-organized community in close contact with Palestine. The Book of Esther, whose background is that of the eastern Dispersion,[1] casts valuable light on the thought and temper of the Jewish community in these parts in the pre-Christian era. Relatively little is known about this eastern Dispersion, however, until the emergence of the Babylonian Talmud about the beginning of the sixth century A.D.

In *Syria* too the Jews were numerically strong, especially in Antioch and Damascus. As we have seen, Onias III lived there for a time and, according to one tradition, met his death at Daphne, near Antioch. The Damascus Document suggests, if the reference is to be taken literally, that at some point in the second or first century B.C. members of the Qumran community migrated to Damascus.[2] According to Philo Jews were living 'in every city' not only in Syria, but also in *Phoenicia* and *Asia Minor* where, it would seem, they were less populous (cf. *Embassy to Gaius* XXXIII. 245, 281). From the time (towards the

[1] See pp. 189 ff.          [2] See pp. 167 f.

end of the third century B.C.) when Antiochus the Great deported 2,000 Jewish families to Lydia and Phrygia to serve in his army their numbers grew rapidly.[1] As Philo remarks, 'as far as Bithynia and the remotest parts of Pontus' the Jewish people were to be found (cf. *Embassy to Gaius* XXXVI. 281). In the same passage he tells of Jews living in *Macedonia*, *Greece*, and the *Mediterranean islands*. In *Cyrenaica*, too, and in places much further to the west, Jewish communities had been known from Ptolemaic times. Horace and Cicero indicate, moreover, that across the sea in *Rome* there were Jews to be found during the first century B.C., whilst Philo records that in the time of Augustus there was in that same city a considerable Jewish community of freed-men who possessed their own synagogues (cf. *Embassy to Gaius* XXIII. 155 ff.). Later still, after the death of Herod, it is reported that a Jewish deputation to Rome was met there by more than 8,000 Jews, presumably freed-men (cf. *Antiquities* XVII. xi. 1; *War* II. vi. 1). These references point to a growing and influential population, some of whose members were yet to play an important role in public life, particularly in the later years of the first century A.D.

By far the most important centre of the western Dispersion, however, was *Egypt*, and especially Alexandria. Jer. 44[1] records that a company of Jews migrated there shortly after the fall of Jerusalem in 586 B.C., whilst Aramaic papyri discovered at Elephantine show that a Jewish military colony was stationed there as early as the sixth century B.C. No real cultural or religious significance, however, attaches to this Jewish community until the time of Ptolemy I, who, as we have observed,[2] is said to have transported there 100,000 Jews whom Ptolemy II subsequently set free. Reference has also been made above[3] to the temple at Leontopolis built by Onias IV (or his father Onias III?), which Josephus suggests was meant to provide a religious centre for Egyptian Jewry (cf. *Antiquities* XIII. iii. 1). This, however, is unlikely: its influence was probably limited to a restricted area around Leontopolis right up to the

---

[1] For details see 1 Macc. 15[15-26]; *Antiquities* XIV. x. 8-25.
[2] See p. 18.
[3] See p. 36 n.

time of its capture by the Romans in A.D. 73. Indeed the status of the Onias family is of far greater significance than the influence of the temple, for it would appear that Onias IV and his two sons Chelkias and Ananias, were officers of some distinction in the Ptolemaic army (cf. *Against Apion* II. 5; *Antiquities* XIII. x. 4). Inscriptions and other archaeological evidence show that, whilst they were fairly numerous throughout both Lower and Upper Egypt, it was in Alexandria that most of the Jews lived. Both culturally and religiously Alexandrian Jewry was of the utmost importance and established itself as the recognized centre of the whole western Dispersion.

The causes of this widespread dissemination of Jews throughout the civilized world are many and varied. One important factor was that of *war*, with its accompanying deportations and enslavement not only of prisoners of war but also of entire populations: many thousands of Jews—often whole families together—were uprooted from their homes and sold into slavery. Another factor was that of *emigration* forced upon them by persecution, by the growth of trade, by incentives given to would-be colonizers, and—most important of all—by the natural increase of population in Judaea, which was too small and too poor to maintain its ever-growing community. This underlines a third factor—the *remarkable increase* in the numbers of Jews over the whole area of the Dispersion. It has often been claimed by way of explanation that the Jews were a prolific race because they did not expose their children at birth as certain other peoples did; this, however, should not be over-emphasized, since the documentary evidence available, as in the town of Edfu in Upper Egypt, where the resident Jews had in fact quite small families, does not always confirm such a claim. Again, whereas their numbers were often increased—peaceably or by force—by their absorption of other races, their own religious and racial conservatism prevented their absorption by their neighbours. Pious Jews would not even dine with a pagan, far less take part in those festivities and entertainments that were marks of the alien Hellenistic culture.

Many instances could, of course, be given of Jews who were in fact absorbed by the heathen world; but for the most part they remained loyal to 'the laws of their fathers'. But perhaps most significant of all in this connexion was their strong missionary zeal, evidenced, for example, in the volume of propaganda literature issued at this time. The New Testament itself bears witness to this same fact, recording that the Jews 'compass sea and land to make one proselyte' (Matt. 23[15]), whilst Philo claims that the reason why the Scriptures had in the first place to be translated into Greek was that the heathen might know the laws of God (cf. *Life of Moses* II. 136).

## 2. *Its life and organization*

It is hardly surprising in the light of what has been said above that the Jews of the Dispersion usually dwelt apart from their neighbours in a separate quarter of the city or town, a community within a community. It would be wrong, however, to think of such communities forming completely separate and independent groups, self-contained and self-sufficient, having nothing to do with one another. On the contrary they were deeply conscious of the strong ties which bound them to one another and to their fellow Jews in Palestine. They worshipped the same God, revered the same Book, obeyed the same laws, and shared the same Temple. Moreover, they acknowledged the High Priest in Jerusalem as their legitimate head, and looked to him to speak in their name and to enter into agreements with the secular authorities on their behalf. They paid their annual Temple tax regularly (see below) and took part in pilgrimages to Jerusalem; they received deputations from synagogues elsewhere in the Dispersion and in Palestine itself by means of which views were exchanged and pledges of friendship renewed.

It would be wrong, too, to think of them as living together in ghettos, shut up in their particular section of the town or city, having no contact with the outside world. On the contrary, they shared to a large extent that internationalism which was a mark of both the Greek and the Roman periods. For the most part they pursued the same trades and professions as their neighbours, and in this differed little from the Jews in Palestine itself. Among them were to be found private soldiers and high-ranking officers, policemen, government officials, tax collectors, argicultural labourers, craftsmen, traders, tavern keepers, and singers, as well as doctors, lawyers, preachers, teachers, poets, and writers. The reputation that the Jewish people later came to have in the field of commerce was as yet unknown; most of them, it would appear, occupied themselves with agriculture or followed some trade or profession.

Living in the midst of a Gentile world they were inevitably influenced by its general culture and beliefs. Many were attracted by the Egyptian form of Hellenism, for example, which grew up under the Ptolemies and continued into the Roman period; its philosophical outlook attracted them with its teaching concerning 'wisdom'—an idea already familiar to them in the Old Testament Scriptures and which they now sought to develop along new lines. Others were impressed by ideas to be found in the Syrian form of Hellenism, which was influenced by the Zoroastrian religion of the old Persian empire and by the older Babylonian religion, with its worship of the heavenly luminaries and the planets, which were thought to control the destinies of men and nations.

Although the fundamental tenets of Judaism remained unchanged, this exposure of the Jews to the Gentile world— both in the Dispersion and in Palestine—left a deep impression on their thinking and reveals itself in not a few of the writings of this period. Many of the books issued at this time had a polemic and apologetic aim—they attacked the religions of the heathen and exalted the religion of the God of their fathers. None, however, could compare in influence with the Septuagint translation of the Scriptures, which unlocked the treasures of the Hebrew religion to the whole Gentile world. This, together with the vast network of synagogues in every part of the Dispersion and the many thousands of 'God-fearers' not yet fully committed to the Jewish faith, prepared the way as nothing else could have done for the advancement of Christianity and the remarkable growth of the early Christian Church.

But what about the internal organization of these Jewish communities? Throughout the greater part of the Hellenistic period (the reign of Antiochus Epiphanes being an outstanding exception) they were given freedom to live 'according to the laws of their fathers'; this meant that they could establish their own law-courts, build their own synagogues, set up their own schools, and elect their own officers. The geographer Strabo informs us that in Alexandria, for example, the Jews have at their head an 'ethnarch' appointed by themselves, who 'governs the people and adjudicates suits and supervises contracts and ordinances, just as if he were the head of a sovereign state' (quoted in *Antiquities* XIV. vii. 2). Such organization must have taken different forms in different areas and countries of course. Philo indicates that in the case of Alexandria the ethnarch was replaced in the time of Augustus by a Senate or Council of Elders, called a *Gerousia* (cf. *Flaccus* x. 74 ff.), governed by a number of leading members called 'archons' or 'rulers'. Councils of this kind, with a president and secretary appointed by the rulers, were to be found in many other places throughout the Dispersion: among other things they had the right to levy taxes for communal purposes and to collect contributions for, say, the schools and synagogues. These synagogues, standing at the very centre of the community life, were of the utmost importance, not only as places of prayer, but also as schools of learning and even as courts of justice.[1] There were in addition, however, special law-courts empowered to defend members of the Jewish community in matters of law and in particular to deal with disputes which arose between Jews and Jews.

There was nothing very unusual about this treatment of the Jews during the Greek and Roman periods, for other ethnic groups were regularly treated in the same way. Indeed, every Greek town or city had the right to establish its own municipal

[1] See pp. 124 ff.

and religious institutions and to appoint its own officials in a like manner. Nevertheless the Jews did receive preferential treatment, especially under such rulers as Julius Caesar and Augustus. The Romans no doubt had good reason to cultivate the goodwill of their Jewish subjects. They were well aware, for example, of the strength of world Jewry, and were anxious to maintain good relations in view of the ever-present Parthian menace in the east. Accordingly they offered the Jews a number of privileges in the exercise of their religion which were readily accepted.

One such privilege was the exemption of the Jews from taking part in the cult of Greek and Roman gods. Another, closely related to it, was an alleviation of the requirements in connexion with Emperor-worship. Such worship was still required of them, but ample concessions were made permitting Jews to take part in its ceremonial without necessarily compromising their faith. For example, sacrifices to the Emperor in heathen temples could be replaced by prayers for the Emperor in the synagogues; oaths involving the acknowledgement of the Emperor as divine could be suitably adjusted; the various rites and ceremonies could be re-interpreted so as not to offend religious scruples. Another privilege was the right to observe the Sabbath day and the recognized religious festivals, whilst due recognition was given to the dietary laws. Recognition of the Sabbath, for example, meant that no Jewish soldier could be forced to bear arms on that day; and there is evidence that at certain times at least some Jews were on this ground exempted from military service (cf. *Antiquities* xiv. x. 11). One of the most important of these privileges, however, was the right to collect money and send it to the Temple treasury in Jerusalem. This was all the more significant because such transfer of money from one country to another for commercial purposes was forbidden. Every Jew of twenty years and over was required to pay this annual tax of half a shekel, which together with other gifts was sent as 'sacred money' to Jerusalem, being guaranteed safe passage by the Roman authorities. Theft of such money was regarded as sacrilege and was liable to the death-penalty. In this way very large sums of money indeed found their way to Jerusalem.

It is hardly to be wondered at that their non-Jewish neighbours, who did not share these privileges, resented such preferential treatment. This factor, together with their intolerant attitude to the traditional gods of the Greeks and Romans, led to outbreaks of violence against the Jews in many parts of the Dispersion. Although there is evidence for such opposition in the centuries before the Christian era, it became more open and more frequent in the first century A.D. An examination of these events lies beyond the scope of this book.

PART TWO

# THE RELIGION

---

## VIII

## FOUNDATIONS OF JUDAISM

### 1. *The Torah and the scribes*

THE word 'Torah', usually translated by 'Law', defies simple
definition not only because of its wide range of meaning but
also because of its changing emphases in the post-exilic
period. Basically it signifies 'teaching' or 'instruction' such as
the priest gave in pre-exilic times by means of the sacred oracle.
But in the Hellenistic period especially its meaning is much
more comprehensive than this. G. F. Moore defines it as 'the
comprehensive name for the divine revelation, written and
oral, in which the Jews possessed the sole standard and norm of
their religion.[1]

From the time of Ezra onwards it was believed that this
revelation, derived from Moses himself and formulated under
the inspiration of the Holy Spirit, found its supreme expression
in the written code of Law contained in the Pentateuch; thus
the word 'Torah' came to be used with special reference to the
five 'books of Moses'. In course of time the authoritative
character of these books became more clearly defined, so that
even before the beginning of the Hellenistic period, it would
seem, their 'canonical' status had come to be recognized.

---

[1] *Judaism*, vol. ii, 1927, p. 263.

The prophetic books were likewise believed to be written by the inspiration of the Holy Spirit (as indeed were the rest of the Old Testament books) and were recognized as a closed corpus of sacred writings by about the year 200 B.C. Their authority as 'Torah', however, was not comparable with that of the Pentateuch, whose laws formed the very basis of Judaism. Thus, although 'Torah' meant 'revelation', it came increasingly to be understood in terms of the 'legislation' that characterized the revelation made known through Moses in the five books bearing his name.

It is significant that during this period the idea of 'faithfulness within the *Covenant*' is interpreted increasingly in terms of 'obedience to the *Law*', and that these two words tend to be used almost as synonyms. John Bright goes so far as to say, 'Here law has ceased to be the definition of the requisite response to the gracious acts of God and becomes the means by which men might achieve the divine favour and become worthy of the promises'.[1] Such a judgement is perhaps rather unfair when levelled at the Jewish people as a whole, but it is certainly true of an influential body of opinion within Judaism. An indication of this trend can be seen in the stress which is now laid on outward observances as marks of the religious life. Circumcision, for example, which had been given prominence as a distinctive feature of the Jewish faith in immediately post-exilic days, became of increasing importance as the Hellenistic period advanced; to submit oneself to 'uncircumcision' was to 'forsake the holy covenant' (1 Macc. 1$^{15}$). Similarly, observance of the Sabbath was regarded as of such vital importance that men chose to be slaughtered rather than fight on that sacred day (cf. 1 Macc. 2$^{29-38}$; 2 Macc. 6$^{11}$). Ritual cleanness and obedience to the letter of the Law were believed to be of primary importance. Hence the Jews' fanatical refusal to eat swine's flesh (cf. 1 Macc. 1$^{62f.}$; 2 Macc. 6$^{18}$, 7$^{1}$), their strict observance of dietary laws, fasting, tithing, and other ceremonial requirements (cf. Dan. 1$^{8}$; Judith 12$^{1-4}$; Tob. 1$^{10-11}$; 4 Macc. 5$^{3,\ 14,\ 27}$, etc.); hence, too, their bitter

---

[1] *A History of Israel*, 1960, p. 428.

I

hatred of idolatry of every kind, even if it were but the statue of an eagle over the gate of the Temple (cf. *Antiquities* XVII. vi. 2). It must not be thought, however, that Judaism stood only for legalism and the merely outward observance of the Law. On the contrary, there were many who recognized and responded to its high ethical demand and for whom its observance was a delight (cf. Ecclus. 1[11f.] and several of the Psalms). The literature of this period gives ample proof of the growth of true piety, deep devotion, and a reverence for righteousness. The 'meek' and 'humble' of whom we read in the Psalms and elsewhere belonged as truly to Judaism as the legalists and literalists of their day.

By the beginning of the second century B.C., and indeed some considerable time before this date, Torah religion was truly and firmly based. This is well illustrated by two books written around this time—the Book of Tobit (*c.* 200 B.C.), which lays great stress on the keeping of the Law, and the Wisdom of Ben Sira, or Ecclesiasticus (*c.* 180 B.C.), which likens Torah to Wisdom and refers to it as the supreme gift of God (cf. 24[23]). This reference reminds us that throughout this whole period there was a very close relationship between the practice of the Law and the pursuit of wisdom and that, for some writers, these two words were used as almost synonymous expressions. The teachers of wisdom, who were an active religious force at this time, were also teachers of the Law. The good life, which was the goal of true wisdom, was to be found in obedience to the Law of God. This theme is also found in the Book of Proverbs, for example, and in some of the later Psalms (e.g. Ps. 1, 49, 112, 119). Elsewhere, as in the Book of Jubilees (second century B.C.), the claim is made that the Law is not only perfect but also eternal (cf. 2[23, 31], 15[27], etc.); many of its enactments and institutions, the book claims, date from very ancient times and even from before Creation itself! The different parties in Judaism[1] disagreed, often profoundly, over the precise interpretation of the Law, but behind this disagreement lay a deep loyalty on the part of all of them to the

[1] See pp. 155 ff.

Law itself. Indeeed the belief is expressed that in the glorious Age to Come a new interpretation of the Law will at last be given, when all prevailing difficulties would be done away.

Long before the outbreak of the Maccabaean Revolt, then, the Jews had become 'the people of the Book'. The Temple, as we shall see, continued to be revered; but increasingly their faith found its focus not so much in the Temple as in the Torah, which was recognized by friend and foe alike as *the* symbol of Judaism. It was natural that the Jews of the Dispersion, for example, should turn for consolation to the holy Book, deprived as they were of the holy Temple; the spread of the synagogues and the schools, in both the Dispersion and Palestine, would also enhance its reputation and engender in the hearts of many pious Jews an enthusiastic and even fanatical devotion to the Torah. Thus when the priest Mattathias at Modein summoned the people to resist the orders of Antiochus Epiphanes and to fight in defence of their religion, it was to the Torah that he pointed as the rallying point of revolt: 'Whosoever is zealous for the Torah, and maintaineth the covenant, let him come forth after me' (1 Macc. 2²⁷). The Torah, in the form of the sacred scrolls of the Law, was the outward symbol of that inner faith which they had received from their fathers and which they must never betray. Antiochus Epiphanes readily recognized this fact, for in the persecution which followed we are told that his soldiers 'rent in pieces the books of the Law which they found, and set them on fire. And wheresoever was found with any a book of the covenant, and if any consented to the Law, the king's sentence delivered him unto death' (1 Macc. 1⁵⁶⁻⁵⁷). An assault on the Torah was an assault on the whole Jewish faith.

From an early stage in the development of the written Torah as sacred Scripture the need must have arisen for both definition and interpretation of its contents. For some considerable time after Ezra it was not always self-evident what exactly constituted the Law of God, nor was it clear how particular laws were to be applied in everyday life. To meet this need there emerged a body of men known as *Sôpherîm* or 'scribes', in succession to Ezra (described in Ezra 7[6] as 'a ready scribe in the torah of Moses'), who gradually won for themselves an authoritative place within Judaism. They set themselves the task of collecting, preserving, interpreting, and teaching the Law of God, and it is due chiefly to them that, before the end of the Persian period, the Pentateuch came to be recognized as canonical Scripture. Although they belonged to the priestly caste, being members of priestly or Levitic families (cf. 2 Chron. 34[13]; Neh. 8[7, 13]), their interpretations of Scripture were not confined to cultic laws and regulations, but included ethical teaching. It is these 'wise men' as they are called, who are eulogized, for example, in Ecclesiasticus (cf. 38[24]–39[15]). We are no doubt to see in these Sopherim or their representatives the historical reality behind what Jewish tradition knows as the 'Men of the Great Synagogue', whose founder and first president was believed to be Ezra himself.

Their influence contined throughout the Persian period, but shortly after the beginning of the Greek period it came to an end. The reason for this is no doubt to be found in the radically changed circumstances that now prevailed and for which their particular interpretations of Scripture were no longer adequate. The Greek culture brought with it a flood of new customs and new ideas with which the priestly scribes could not cope. At this point a development took place that was to have the greatest significance in years to come—there arose a class of scribes, chiefly lay, who applied themselves diligently to the task of interpreting and applying the Law in the light of the prevailing circumstances of their own day. This group of men, together with their adherents, exercised a great political and religious influence in subsequent years, and in due course appeared as the party of the Pharisees. The unauthorized teaching of these lay scribes continued until the founding of the Supreme Council or *Gerousia* of the Jews, later to be known as the Sanhedrin, about the beginning of the second century B.C. In this Court, composed of both lay and priestly members, the authority of the scribes was second only to that of the High Priest and his family, the High Priest serving as its president. It continued the work of teaching and interpreting the Law and did much to regulate the life and religion of the Jewish people. The Mishnah tractate *Pirkē 'Abhoth* records that the tradition of the Sopherim in 'the Great Synagogue' was passed on by its last survivor, Simon the Just, to one Antigonus of Socho, and that it was thereafter passed on to a series of scribes, whose names are given in pairs from Jose ben Joezer and Jose ben Joḥanan, in the first half of the second century B.C., right down to Hillel and Shammai in the first century A.D. (cf. $1^{1-12}$).

But what was this 'tradition' which grew up with the Sopherim and developed in succeeding generations under the influence of the lay scribes and their successors? It was a body of 'decisions' or 'judgements' in oral form, explanatory of the written Law and developing alongside it. It is generally referred to as 'the tradition of the elders' or (probably from about the time of Hillel) 'the oral tradition'. It is possible that part of this tradition is to be traced back into pre-exilic times and represents older traditions and collections of laws which may have been lost or destroyed but were preserved in oral form by succeeding generations. Much of it, however, is based rather on custom and usage that grew up in relation to some particular command or ordinance in Scripture. Take as an example the command about doing no work on the Sabbath day. The command itself was clear enough; but what was meant by 'work'? The written law left this undefined. Where Scripture could not help, however, custom could. Certain things were 'done' and other things were 'not done'. Thus custom was able to provide a well-defined code of its own as binding as the written Law, which took its place as oral tradition alongside the word of Scripture. Sometimes laws of this kind could find no real justification in the written Torah; nevertheless they could be justified as forming 'a fence round the Torah' (*Pirkē 'Abhoth* $1^1$) i.e. they gave a danger signal, as it were, which halted a man before he came within reach of breaking the law. For the most part, however, the oral tradition consisted of authoritative regulations arising out of an exegesis of biblical laws of a civil or religious kind. This teaching was called *Halakhah* (Hebrew *halakh*, to walk) because it showed how men should *walk* in obedience to the Law of God in every detail. In practice, however, the scribes were more concerned about safeguarding the legal system built up upon the word of Scripture than in the straightforward exposition of any particular passage or verse. Broadly speaking they followed two methods of interpretation. One was the *midrashic* method, which gave judgements based on and in conjunction with an exposition of Scripture; the second was the *mishnaic* method, which set forth tradition without any attempt to bind it to the text of Scripture. Despite its obvious dangers, especially when divorced from the written Torah, the development of this oral tradition did much to 'democratize' religion and to make the Law of God relevant and real in the lives of the common people. In later years (*c.* A.D. 210) it was classified and codified in the Mishnah, which provided the basis for the Jewish Talmud.

It was inevitable that the question should come to be asked, What is the relation between the oral tradition and the written Torah, and what is their relative authority? The Pharisees were to give a clear answer: Each is of equal antiquity and of equal authority; both together make up the Torah of God, for both have been handed down from Moses through successive generations by faithful men of God. This claim is the likely cause of the breach which emerged in the time of John Hyrcanus between the Pharisees and their Sadducaean opponents in the Sanhedrin who regarded the written Torah as alone the authoritative revelation of God.[1]

## 2. *The Temple and the priests*

Despite the great prominence given to the Torah in the Persian and Hellenistic periods, however, the Temple in Jerusalem continued to occupy a place very much at the centre of the nation's life. Indeed the very prominence given to the Torah meant a more meticulous concern for the proper functioning of the cult, for much of its legislation was directed towards the right performance of the Temple ritual. Information

[1] See pp. 66 f., 161.

A view of the Temple area now known as the Harem esh-Sherif. In the centre stands the famous Mosque of Omar ('the Dome of the Rock') on the site of the original Jewish altar and the Holy of Holies. The Golden Gate can be seen a little to the right of it in the foreground wall. On the extreme left is the Mosque el-Aqsa and on the extreme right, at the north-west corner of the area, the site of the fortress Antonia. (See plan on p. 99.)

concerning the character and content of this ritual is to be found in 1 and 2 Chronicles (c. 350 B.C.), the writer's descriptions reflecting the Temple organization in his own day, and also in the Mishnah, which, though assuming written form only at a later date, nevertheless depicts earlier practice. Such sources indicate that the Temple ceremonies were lively and impressive affairs, accompanied often by choral singing, orchestral music, responsive readings, and colourful processions.

Throughout this period the priests were the acknowledged guardians of the cult and of the whole Temple tradition. Ever since the return from the Exile their status had been jealously guarded and their privileges and responsibilities carefully defined. The authority, however, which they had for long enjoyed as teachers of Torah was greatly diminished by the rise of the lay scribal class, and their responsibilities became increasingly confined to the performance of right ritual and the execution of the required sacrifices. At their head stood the High Priest, who, together with the members of his family, exercised great authority in both religious and political affairs. His office was for life and hereditary in the house of Zadok, and so, according to 1 Chron. 6¹⁻¹⁵, was in direct line of descent from Aaron. The High-Priestly office fell into disrepute at the time of the Maccabaean Revolt, when it was bought and sold to suit the convenience of Antiochus Epiphanes, but regained something of its former authority under the Hasmonaeans, who, though not of the old hereditary Zadokite family, claimed a like authority for themselves. Under the Romans and Herod the Great, however, the influence of the High Priesthood was again seriously impaired. Below the priests in rank were the Levites; in earlier days they had been counted among the priests, but now as 'minor clergy' they were responsible for the more menial tasks associated with the Temple ritual. But, though deprived of priestly responsibilities, they took an active part in the Temple worship, mounting guard at the doors, carrying out the necessary menial tasks, and serving in the orchestras and choirs.

These priests and Levites (who numbered many thousands)

were divided into twenty-four 'courses' or teams (cf. 1 Chron. 24$^{1-19}$), which came up to the Temple in rotation for a week's period of service, each course being further divided into 'fathers' houses' that served on successive days throughout the week. The whole nation was likewise divided into twenty-four groups made up of laymen; representatives of each in turn took part in the Temple worship, though not in the actual sacrificial ritual, as representatives of the whole people. Those who lived in or near Jerusalem were expected to be present in the Temple court during the week when it was the turn of their particular course to function; those who lived at some distance from the city were to meet in their local synagogues for worship four times a day throughout the same week.

The chief feature of the Temple ritual in which these courses were engaged was the offering of the regular daily sacrifices, one in the morning and one in the mid afternoon. These were carried out with careful ceremonial together with other sacrifices of a private character. Priests were chosen by lot for all the different duties to be performed; the *Šema'* (Deut. 6$^{4-9}$ etc.) and the ten commandments were recited; incense was burned on the altar; the priestly blessing was pronounced over the worshipping people; the sacrifice itself was then burned, a meal-offering made, and a drink-offering poured out. To the sound of trumpets and cymbals and other musical accompaniments the Levitic choir then sang the Psalms set for the day,[1] each Psalm being divided into three sections, the people prostrating themselves in worship after each section. The ritual for the Sabbath followed the same pattern, except that there were additional sacrifices and readings from Scripture. A graphic picture of this is given in Ecclus. 50$^{11-21}$, where we see the High Priest in his glorious apparel performing the sacred rites on behalf of the people. It must have been a most impressive service, which captured the imagination as well as the devotion of the worshipping congregation.

Of special interest were the great religious festivals, with their ceremonial and sacrifices. Some of these, like Passover and

[1] See p. 284.

First Fruits, were carried over from the pre-exilic period. Others underwent certain significant changes, such as the great pre-exilic feast of *'Asiph* or Ingathering, at the turn of the year (cf. Exod. 23¹⁶, 34²²), which was now divided into three feasts—*Roš Haššanah* or New Year's Day on the first of Tishri, the Day of Atonement on the tenth, and the Feast of *Sukkôth* or Tabernacles on the fifteenth. Other festivals, unknown in pre-exilic times, now claimed an established place in the Temple ritual, such as the Feast of *Purîm* or Lots (originating in the Dispersion) associated with the Book of Esther,[1] and the Feast of *Ḥanukkah* or Dedication (sometimes called the Feast of Lights) commemorating the rededication of the Temple by Judas Maccabaeus in 164 B.C. All these festivals had their appointed times—Lots in early March, Passover in March–April, First Fruits in May–June, New Year in September–October, Atonement in September–October, Tabernacles in September–October, and Dedication in December.

The post-exilic period also witnessed the growing importance of offerings of an expiatory kind, such as the sin-offering and the guilt-offering, whose purpose was the removal of sin. This sense of sin and the need for forgiveness, arising, no doubt, out of the experience of the Exile and also the stress now laid on the demands of the Law, found its focus in the great Day of Atonement (cf. Lev. 16) on which the High Priest entered the Holy of Holies, seeking the forgiveness of God for himself, the priests, and the people. Part of its ritual was old, but the role played by the High Priest and also the deep sense of need for expiation were new and important factors. Five days later came the joyful Feast of Tabernacles—the Harvest Festival— whose celebrations continued for eight full days. This began at the Harvest full-moon with an all-night festival in which the priests leaped and danced in a torchlight procession, the orchestras played, and the choirs sang. As dawn was about to break, just before the offering of the morning sacrifice, two priests blew on their trumpets, marched across the Temple court to the east gate, then turning with their faces towards

[1] See p. 189.

the Temple pledged themselves and the people to God in these words: 'Our fathers when they were in this place turned with their backs toward the Temple of the Lord and their faces toward the east, and they worshipped the sun toward the east (cf. Ezek. 8[16]); but as for us, our eyes are turned toward the Lord' (*M. Sukkah* 5[4]).

Thus, although the offering of sacrifices played a central part in the Temple ritual, its activities were by no means limited to this expression of worship. The Law and the Prophets were read, the priests pronounced their blessings, and the people responded with shouts of praise or the offering of silent prayer. Of particular significance was the use made of the Psalter,[1] which is sometimes referred to as 'the Hymn Book of the Second Temple'. It is uncertain how many of the Psalms were actually written for cultic use or how many had been previously used in the First Temple; but it is clear that in Persian and Hellenistic times the Psalter was extensively used in this way. It is composed of several collections, some of which are associated with particular 'guilds' or 'choirs' of singers, each with its own choirmaster and each possessing its own hymn book. One such is named after Asaph (cf. 1 Chron. 6[39], 25[1-2, 6, 9]), whose hymn book consisted of Pss. 50 and 73–83, and a second after Korah (cf. 2 Chron. 20[19] etc.), whose collection apparently included Pss. 42, 44–49, 84–85, and 87–88. At a later stage the Korahites are described as merely door-keepers (cf. 1 Chron. 9[19], 26[1, 19]), the Temple singers being arranged in three guilds bearing the names of Asaph, Heman, and Ethan (cf. 1 Chron. 6[33-48]). The singing, as we have seen, was aided by various kinds of musical accompaniments, frequent mention being made of harps, lyres, flutes, trumpets, and other wind and stringed instruments (cf. Ps. 150[3-5]).

Reference has been made above to the use of the Temple as a treasury, not only for the Temple tax[2] and for other gifts given to God but also for the fortunes of private individuals.[3] This reminds us that its outer precincts were used for many 'secular' or 'profane' purposes and resembled at times a busy

[1] See pp. 281 ff.       [2] See p. 110.       [3] See p. 35.

market-place, with constant traffic and the noise and bustle of buying and selling. Here, for example, the money-changers were to be found to whom allusion is made in the Gospels (cf. Matt. 21¹²; Mark 11¹⁵; John 2¹⁴). Thus in many ways the Temple was not only a sacred shrine but also the very centre of public life for Jerusalem and indeed for the whole nation.

## 3. *The Synagogue and its worship*

If the influence of the Temple during the Hellenistic period was great, that of the synagogue was even greater. The survival of Judaism as a vital religion after the destruction of the Temple in A.D. 70 was largely due to the fact that through successive generations the Torah had been nurtured within the synagogue worship and treasured in its 'houses of study'. The history of the synagogue during this period is very difficult to trace and its origins are completely lost in obscurity. It is generally believed, however, that it arose out of the needs of the Babylonian Exile, where the Jews, deprived of their Temple, would gather together on the Sabbath day for instruction in the sacred books, for prayer, and for mutual comfort. Suggestions of this are perhaps to be found in the 'assemblies of elders' mentioned in Ezekiel (cf. 8¹, 14¹, 20¹), and later on in the gatherings in the time of Nehemiah and Ezra (cf. Ezra 8¹⁵; Neh. 8²; Zech. 7⁵). No actual records have come down to us of synagogues in Babylon in those early days; the earliest recorded is that in Nahardea in the third century A.D., which, according to Jewish tradition, owed its origin to the exiled king Jehoiachin, who is said to have built it with stones from the Jerusalem Temple.

Egypt provides much more definite and more plentiful information than Babylon and offers the earliest dated evidence for the existence of a synagogue. This is an inscription from Schedia that records the dedication of a '(house of) prayer' in honour of 'King Ptolemy'. This monarch is generally identified by scholars with Ptolemy III (Euergetes I), whose dates are 247–221 B.C. That is, the inscription dates from a time when

The Wailing Wall in Jerusalem, so called because, before the partition of the city between Jordan and Israel, the Jews used to gather at this spot to lament the destruction of the ancient Temple. The lower sections, which formed part of the western wall of the old Temple area, date from the time of Herod the Great.

the Torah had recently been translated into Greek.[1] There is evidence for the existence of synagogues in at least twelve other places in Egypt during the Greek and Roman periods, the most important being Alexandria, where, in addition to the central synagogue or 'great basilica', there were a number of others in various quarters of the city. This was the picture also in many other parts of the Dispersion. The New Testament, for example, names synagogues in such widely scattered areas as Asia Minor, Syria, Greece, Rome, and Cyprus. We may assume that by the first century A.D. synagogues were to be found wherever there was the necessary quorum of ten males of Jewish birth.

The New Testament also provides evidence of synagogues in Palestine in the first century which had obviously been in existence for some long time. What their earlier history was it is difficult to say. Jewish tradition traces the institution of the synagogue back to the 'Men of the Great Synagogue', i.e. to Ezra and his successors. Many scholars would accept that, although it had its beginnings in Babylon and spread through the Dispersion, it found consolidation in the work of Ezra and was centred in the Law Book of which he himself was 'a ready scribe' (Ezra 7[6]). Concerning its subsequent development in Palestine the Old Testament is strangely silent. Ps 74[8], which refers to the burning of 'all the meeting places of God in the land', is sometimes quoted in this connexion. It is unlikely, however, that these 'meeting places' were in fact synagogues. Moreover, this psalm, which was for long assigned to the Maccabaean period, is now thought by most scholars to belong to a much earlier time.

The expression 'synagogue' represents a Greek word *sunagōgē* meaning 'an assembly' and also 'a place of assembly', i.e. a building where the assembly met. An indication of the character and object of this assembly is given by certain other words used to describe it. In Greek, for example, it is frequently called

[1] Claims have been made for an earlier reference than this, based on a piece of pottery found at Elath and dating probably from the sixth century B.C., which bears the inscription 'house of meeting'.

*Proseuchē* or '(Place of) Prayer' and *Hagios Topos* or 'Holy Place', whilst the word *Sabbateion* or '*Sabbath* (house)' is probably also used with this reference; in Hebrew the expression *Beth Hammidraš* or 'House of Study' is also commonly used in this same connexion. The synagogue was a communal institution whose primary function was the reading and study of the Law within a setting of praise and prayer. As such it readily lent itself to discussion and argument about the right interpretation of Scripture—an exercise dear to the hearts of the scribes, whose 'schools' were closely related to the synagogues or else formed an integral part of them. The synagogue buildings, however, were not restricted to a specifically religious use, but could be used, for example, as courts of justice and for other gatherings of a 'secular' kind. Thus, though the Jewish synagogue had something in common with the Christian Church as a place of prayer and congregational worship, its outlook and emphasis were different; primarily it was a place for the study of the Law of God. It was different from the Christian Church in another respect also, in that it had no 'clergy' in the commonly accepted sense of the word. Its chief officer was a layman called *archisunagōgos* or 'head of the assembly', who presided over its affairs and, for example, called on the members of the congregation to offer prayer and read the Scripture. In some cases a synagogue might have more than one 'head', and in later years the word came to be used as an honorary title. In carrying out his duties he had the assistance of the *hupēretēs* (Hebrew, *ḥazzan*) or 'servant' of the congregation, who seems to have combined the duties of teacher and caretaker. Other officers were the *methurgeman* or 'translator', who, as the word suggests, translated the readings from Scripture into the vernacular, and also the *šaliaḥ* or 'messenger' of the assembly, who led in prayer.

The synagogue service was obviously very different from the Temple service; and yet the two were complementary rather than antagonistic, for 'the religious rhythm of the synagogue coincided more or less with that of the Temple'.[1] An example

[1] C. Guignebert, *The Jewish World in the Time of Jesus* (Eng. tr. by S. H. Hooke), 1951, p. 76.

of this has already been given with reference to the twenty-four 'courses' of laymen, part of whom ministered in the Temple whilst the rest met in their local synagogues to pray and read the Scripture. Synagogal practice varied greatly between Palestine and the Dispersion, and even within a local area or a single city; despite this, however, they shared features which illustrate further the relationship between synagogue worship and that in the Jerusalem Temple. Thus the Sabbath and the great festivals were faithfully observed in both, the same Psalms were sung, and the same kinds of prayers and benedictions used. Moreover, the priests, although holding no post in the synagogue by virtue of their office, nevertheless frequently took a significant part in its life as teachers, and, if present, were expected to pronounce the benediction at the close of each service. Again, prayers were offered three times each day, corresponding to the morning and afternoon sacrifices in the Temple and the burning of the scraps in the evening. Synagogues in the Dispersion were often 'dedicated' to some civic or royal dignitary after the style of local heathen temples; some, such as those early on in Galilee, were erected on the top of a hill, presumably in imitation of the Jerusalem Temple itself; indeed, the Talmud testifies to the fact that early in the first century A.D. there was a synagogue (probably an assembly rather than a building) within the Temple precincts (cf. *M. Yoma* $7^1$ etc.), which was no doubt associated with the 'house of study' there (cf. Luke $2^{46}$). In later years, particularly after the destruction of Jerusalem in A.D. 70, an attempt was made, through architectural construction and interior furnishings, to emphasize this continuity of the synagogue with the Temple—the place of prayer now superseded the place of sacrifice, the fixed synagogue liturgy replaced the ancient Temple ritual.

This synagogue liturgy, though not assuming a fixed form until after the destruction of the Temple, nevertheless contains elements antedating that event by many years. It begins with the recitation of the *Šema'* (Deut. $6^{4-9}$ together with $11^{13-21}$ and Num. $15^{37-41}$) within the framework of three brief prayers

Ruins of a synagogue at Capernaum (the name means 'village of Nahum')
which dates from the third century A.D. but which may well be on the site
of the synagogue where Jesus worshipped (cf. Luke 7⁵).

acknowledging the goodness and love of God. This is followed
by the '*Amidah* or 'Standing (Prayer)', known also as the
*Šemoneh 'Esreh* or 'Eighteen (Benedictions)'. Tradition assigns
these 'benedictions' to the 'Men of the Great Synagogue', i.e.
to the time of Ezra and his successors; but their composition
probably ranges from pre-Maccabaean times down to near
the end of the first century A.D. About A.D. 100 an extra para-
graph against 'apostates' (probably Christians) was inserted
after the eleventh 'benediction', bringing the number up to
nineteen. All the sections within it follow a set pattern, consisting of a brief 'free' prayer followed by an ascription of
blessing to God in terms of the prayer itself. These assumed

a fixed form around A.D. 100 but were not committed to writing until the seventh century. Every Jew was expected to recite them three times each day (cf. *M. Ber.* 3³, 4⁴), except that on the Sabbath, feast days, and the Day of Atonement other brief prayers took the place of numbers 4 to 15.

Occupying a central place in the service was the reading of the Law after the pattern of Ezra himself, who, we are told, 'stood on a wooden pulpit . . . and opened the book in the sight of all the people' (Neh. 8⁴, ⁵). In the years following Ezra such readings from the Law would be associated with the great festivals where it would be read and expounded (cf. Lev. 23), but later on special readings, it would seem, were appointed for the four special Sabbaths in the month Adar (Exod. 30¹¹⁻¹⁶ before the collection of the half-shekel; Deut 25¹⁷⁻¹⁹ before Purim; Num. 19¹⁻²² and Exod. 12¹⁻²⁰ at intervals before Passover); later still Sabbath readings were so arranged that the whole Law was covered in a three years' cycle. At some point before the beginning of the Christian era the custom grew up of introducing, at the Sabbath morning service, a brief reading from the Prophets (called *haphṭarah*, 'conclusion') after the reading of the Law. In due course this developed into a fixed calendar, with readings from the Prophets corresponding to those from the Law; it is not certain whether in New Testament times such readings were determined by a lectionary for the day or were left to the free choice of the reader (cf. Luke 4¹⁶ ᶠᶠ·). Beside the reader stood the *methurgeman*, who gave a *targum* or 'free translation' of the Scripture into the vernacular—Aramaic or Greek as the case might be. It was subsequently required that this translation should be given one verse at a time in the case of the Law and three at a time in the case of the Prophets. It remained oral until the second century, when it assumed written form. This translation was normally followed by a homily or sermon based on the prophetic reading and given by any competent member of the assembly called upon to do so (cf. Luke 4¹⁷; Acts 13¹⁵). These homilies had a prominent place also in the schools and provide the basis for the Midrashim. The service then concluded with a benediction pronounced, as we have seen, by a priest or, in his absence, by a layman.

It is true that this striving in both school and synagogue to discover the right interpretation of the Law in its every detail often led to casuistry of a distressing kind, and fostered the spirit of legalism, which tended to make religion a burden rather than a blessing. But it is important to observe the other side of this picture also. Synagogue worship in particular did much to encourage in many a deep piety that expressed in daily life the sentiments of the Prophets and the Psalms. A reading of the first Mishnah tractate called *Berakhoth* ('Blessings'), for example, with its prescribed blessings and prayers for every aspect of human life, shows how big a part devotion and prayer played in the lives of not a few in the years immediately before and after the birth of Christ. It is worth noting also in this connexion the important part played by the synagogues in fixing the Canon; the use of the Law and the Prophets in synagogue worship, and not the decisions of councils and committees, was perhaps the greatest single factor in determining which books should or should not be acknowledged as authoritative Scripture.

# IX

# RELIGIOUS IDEAS

THE Hellenistic period witnessed the development within Judaism of a number of religious ideas which were to have a significant influence both on Judaism itself and on Christianity in later years. The history of this development can be traced in the apocryphal and 'pseudepigraphical' writings and in the Qumran texts; the New Testament and the rabbinic literature also provide valuable information. Whilst the roots of these several ideas go back into the Old Testament it is quite clear that, in certain respects at least, they were influenced by current Greek and Persian thought; but with that Hebrew genius born of long religious tradition and deep religious faith the Jewish people showed that they could absorb what they received from others without necessarily betraying their own ancestral laws. Space permits only a brief discussion of some of the more important ideas prevalent in Judaism at this time.

## 1. *The ideas of mediation: angels, demons, and other intermediaries*

Post-exilic Judaism was marked by a strong monotheistic faith and by a belief in divine transcendence which tended to remove God farther and farther away from the world he had made. This tendency is noticeable in the literature of the Exile and of the Persian period generally, but in the Hellenistic period it becomes even more clearly marked. One result of this is a growing reluctance to use the divine name and the substitution for it of such high-sounding titles as 'Most High God', 'Ancient of Days', 'Lord of Spirits', etc. But more significant still is the attempt to bridge the gap, as it were, between the awful majesty of God and the world of created things by introducing certain intermediaries, angelic and otherwise, which were to exercise a considerable influence on Jewish and Christian theology alike in years to come. Such intermediaries were, of course, to be found at a much earlier stage in Old Testament thought, and may be described as 'extensions of Yahweh's personality' through which he communicated his mind and will to men; but in the later biblical period they came much more into evidence. Prominent among them are the angels, who as we shall see now assume certain characteristics unknown in Hebrew thought before; alongside these are certain other intermediaries, difficult to define, which represent not so much creatures as personifications of some divine quality or aspect, or else substantial realities[1] alongside God himself, sharing his properties and characteristics (cf. especially Ecclus. 24; Wisd. $7^{22\,\text{ff.}}$). Chief among these are the two ideas of *Wisdom* and *Logos*.

It has sometimes been too readily assumed that the representation or personification of *Wisdom* which we find in the literature of this period is due to either Greek or Persian influence. The word has in fact a long history within the Hebrew tradition and probably has early Canaanite connexions, the figure of Wisdom (a feminine noun in Hebrew) replacing an original goddess figure. In Prov. $8^{22-31}$ it is presented as a female figure standing beside God at the time of Creation, helping him to lay the foundations of the earth. Neither here nor in later references, however, is Wisdom regarded except symbolically as a 'being', far less as a 'divine being' on a par with God himself. Though active in Creation, Wisdom is herself created by God. This same point is brought out by Ben Sira in Ecclus. $1^{1-10}$, where it is specifically stated that the Lord himself created Wisdom first of all created things and has apportioned her to all his works. In a later chapter the writer again stresses her creatureliness alongside her function of mediation in Creation, and points out that her continuing function is to minister to God in his holy Temple (cf. $24^{10}$). But Wisdom is

---

[1] The technical term is *hupostasis*, a Greek word meaning 'basis' or 'foundation' or 'substance'.

associated with God not only in the creation of the universe but also in the revelation of his will, for Wisdom is to be identified with the eternal Law of God: 'All wisdom is the fear of the Lord, and in all wisdom there is the fulfilment of the Law' ($19^{20}$, cf. $21^{11}$, $24^{23}$, $34^{8}$). Another writing of importance in this respect is the Wisdom of Solomon,[1] where the influence of Greek thought is much more obvious. The writer attempts to bring the Old Testament teaching on wisdom into line with Greek speculation, with the result that, even more than Ben Sira, he goes beyond mere personification in his representation of it. Wisdom 'the fashioner of all things' was with God when he made the world, she permeates all things, 'is a breath of the power of God, and a pure emanation of the glory of the Almighty' ($7^{22-25}$). Elsewhere the writer virtually identifies Wisdom with Spirit when he asks, 'Who has learned thy counsel, unless thou hast given wisdom and sent thy holy Spirit from on high?' ($9^{17}$). In these two quotations we are probably to find a reference to the Stoic conception of 'spirit', which, it is said, permeates the universe and orders all things in perfect wisdom.

The influence of the Stoic philosophers is again evident in the use of the expression *Logos* ('word', 'thought', 'reason') in certain Jewish works of this period. Foremost among these are the writings of Philo (*c.* 20 B.C.–*c.* A.D. 50), a Jew of Alexandria, who in an attempt to reconcile Old Testament teaching with Greek philosophy, applied to the Logos all the chief functions of mediation between God and his world, including the work of Creation. This Logos is the world-permeating Reason of God, and as such can be called 'his image' or 'his first-born son' or even 'the second God'. But it can be called this only in a figurative sense, because unlike the Stoics Philo made a definite distinction between the Logos and the personal God. Logos as divine reason does not exhaust man's understanding of the transcendent God, the essence of whose being is unknowable. Alongside Philo's Logos stand certain 'powers' (Greek, *dunameis*), corresponding to Plato's 'ideas', which express the mode of God's action on the universe and through which he is everywhere

[1] See pp. 271 ff.

present. Like these 'ideas' the 'powers' are themselves immaterial and serve as intermediaries between 'the intelligible world' and 'the world of sense or perception'. These 'powers' are the energizing forces in the universe of which the Logos itself is the great artificer and ruler.

The Wisdom of Solomon is of significance in this respect also. Nothing corresponding to Philo's developed doctrine of the Logos is to be found here, but in the thought of the author there is obviously a close relationship between the 'word' (*logos*) of God and the 'wisdom' of God, especially in the work of Creation. For example, just as Wisdom sits on God's throne (9⁴), so it can be said, 'Thy all-powerful Word leaped from heaven, from the royal throne' (18¹⁵). Or, concerning Creation: '(Thou) hast made all things by thy word, and by thy wisdom hast formed man' (9¹⁻²). There are perhaps indications here of the closer identity between these two terms to be found later on in Philo; but care should be taken not to overstate the relationship, for it should be recognized that in the Old Testament the expression 'word' (Hebrew, *dabhar*) of God has a long history, and is to be understood there not so much as a personification as an expression or 'extension' of God's mind and action made known in his dealings with men and the created world (cf. Ps. 33⁶, 107¹⁵, ²⁰; Isa. 55¹¹, etc.). That there was a tendency, even among Palestinian Jews, to personify this 'word' of God is demonstrated, however, in the use in the Targums of the Aramaic expression *Memra* to indicate that idea. But although personal attributes are there given to it, its use is still very different from that of the Greek Logos and expresses rather God's own manifestation of himself.

Much more characteristic of the literature of this period, however, is the function of angels as intermediaries between God and man or between God and his Creation. This, of course, was no new phenomenon, for even in earlier Old Testament writings frequent reference is made to supernatural beings, belief in whom was in no way felt to contradict the fundamental monotheistic faith. During the Hellenistic period, however, this belief in angels and in spirit-beings generally underwent a remarkable development. This was due in part to the desire, already noted, to bridge the gap between the transcendent God and the material world, and in part to an attempt to solve the problem of suffering which was bound up with the much bigger problem of moral evil in the universe. The good angels, obedient to the commands of God, stood over against the fallen angels or demons, who, as evil spirits, indulged in all kinds of wickedness leading men astray and causing sin and suffering on the earth. The spirit-world was thus divided into two vast camps and formed two great armies, God at the head of the one and Satan at the head of the other. Corresponding to these forces in the universe were two spirits in the heart of man—the spirit of truth and the spirit of error—each struggling for the mastery. This, at least, is the teaching of the Testaments of the XII Patriarchs (cf. Test. Jud. 20[1]), and also of the Manual of Discipline among the Dead Sea Scrolls.[1] There can be little doubt that in this development we are to detect the influence of Persian thought, with its teaching concerning the angel hosts under Ahura Mazda and the demon hosts under Angra Mainyu. The dangers to monotheism in such a belief are obvious, and the Jews themselves were not unaware of this. The word 'dualism' has sometimes been used to express the theological outlook of such books as Jubilees, the Testaments of the XII Patriarchs, and 1 Enoch; but care must be taken not to read too much into this expression. The writers of these books were Jews, and as such would deny any betrayal of their traditional monotheistic faith. Their expression of it may have been accommodating and open to misrepresentation; but it in no way contradicted their acceptance of the one, true, and only God to whom all things owed their existence, even the very angels themselves (cf. Jub. 2[2]).

One striking characteristic of this developed angelology is the fact that now the angels are arrayed in descending order of authority, with their officers and 'other ranks' just like soldiers in a great army. Those belonging to the 'officer-class' are given specific duties to perform. It is they, for example, who

[1] See p. 172.

'minister before the Lord continually' (Jub. 30$^{18}$) and guard God's throne (1 Enoch 71$^7$); they also intercede on behalf of men (cf. 1 Enoch 15$^2$, 39$^5$, etc.) and make known to them the divine secrets (cf. 1 Enoch 60$^{11}$; Jub. 4$^{21}$, etc.); besides this they guide men in the right path and report their ways to God (cf. Jub. 4$^6$). Titles are given to them, such as 'Watchers' or 'Wakeful Ones', which indicate their function; but more significant still, they appear now for the first time in Hebrew literature with personal names, i.e. they are identified as individual beings with 'personalities' of their own. Highest in rank are the seven archangels (in another tradition they are four), whose names are given as Uriel, Raphael, Raguel, Michael, Saraqael, Gabriel, and Remiel, each with his specific duties to perform in obedience to the command of God (cf. 1 Enoch 20$^{1-8}$). This practice of naming the angels probably came in from Persia, whilst the number seven as applied to the archangels may be due to Babylonian influence and the worship there of the five planets together with the sun and the moon. Some angels of high rank, it was believed, were set over the nations by God as their 'princes' or 'rulers';[1] not all acted rightly, however, for some led the nations astray (cf. Jub. 15$^{31 f.}$ etc.). Others again, like the *fravashis* in Persian belief, were appointed as guardian angels of individual men (cf. Tobit 5$^{16}$, etc.; Test. Jos. 6$^6$; Matt. 18$^{10}$; Acts 12$^{15}$, etc.). There are, besides these, innumerable inferior angels commissioned to perform a whole variety of tasks. Some of these are in origin simply personifications of the natural elements—spirits of thunder, lightning, sea, hoar-frost, hail, snow, frost, mist, dew, and rain (cf. 1 Enoch 60$^{11-24}$)—whilst others are set over the different seasons of the year (cf. Jub. 2$^2$). Others again are appointed to rule over the stars (cf. 1 Enoch 75$^3$), or else the stars themselves, as in Persian and Babylonian thought, assume the identity of angels (cf. 1 Enoch 86$^{1 ff.}$). According to one tradition it is the angels, in

---

[1] Cf. Dan. 10$^{13 ff.}$ and see commentary *in loc*. For older forms of this belief see Pss. 82$^1$ and 89$^7$, where Yahweh presides over the heavenly council of 'the holy ones', and especially Deut. 32$^8$ (LXX), where he divides the nations among 'the sons of God'.

the shape of fallen stars,[1] which are responsible for the birth of the demons who also inhabit God's universe (cf. 1 Enoch 86[1 ff.]).

In the literature of this period several explanations are given of the origin of evil in the world. One popular explanation, based on the narrative in Gen. 6[1-4], tells how two hundred angels, sometimes called Watchers and at other times identified with the stars, fell down from heaven, took wives from among mortals and begat children by them (cf. 1 Enoch 6 ff.; also Jub. 4). The result was that the whole earth became corrupt and bloodshed and lawlessness were spread abroad (1 Enoch 9[1]). 'The children of the Watchers' are described as great giants who began to commit all kinds of sins and from whose bodies proceeded evil spirits or demons which survived the Flood and continue their evil ways until the day of Final Judgement. In this way evil is credited, not to God, as in the Old Testament, but to the fallen angels whose evil brood now filled the air and planned all kinds of mischief on the earth. Another tradition, found in the Similitudes of Enoch (i.e. 1 Enoch 37–71) and elsewhere, traces the origin of evil not to the fall of the Watchers but rather to a rebellion in heaven on the part of certain angels or evil spirits called 'Satans', ruled over by a chief Satan (cf. 1 Enoch 53[3], 54[6]). The rebellious angels tempt men to do wrong, and also act as angels of punishment, not only for 'the kings and the mighty' whom they cast into 'a deep valley with burning fire', but also for the evil Watchers whom they bind with 'iron chains of immeasurable weight' (1 Enoch 54[3 ff.]).

The word 'Satan' is, of course, found in the pages of the Old Testament itself with reference to a supernatural being in three post-exilic passages—Job 1, Zech. 3[1-9], and 1 Chron. 21[1]. In the first two of these it is written with the definite article and means simply 'the tester' or 'the adversary'; in the third it is used as a proper name and Satan is presented as an adversary of God, enticing King David to act contrary to the

---

[1] Cf. Isa. 14[12 ff.] where the 'Day Star' (AV, Lucifer), representing proud Babylon, falls from heaven and is brought down to Sheol. In Luke 10[18] the same description is given of Satan who, in the Vulgate of Rev. 9[1], is given the name 'Lucifer'.

divine will. In the post-biblical writings, however, he has assumed the character of a demonic prince, leading his mighty army against the Almighty and his heavenly host. Various names are given to him and also to his henchmen, who are sometimes identified with Satan and at other times stand alongside their chief. In the Book of Tobit, for example, he appears as Asmodeus, a name which reflects the *Aeshma daeva* or 'lustful spirit' in the Persian religion; in 1 Enoch reference is made to Semjaza, who is bound by Michael to await the Final Judgement, and to Azazel,[1] whom Raphael binds so as to cast him into the fire (cf. 10[1] ff.); in Jubilees (cf. 10[5] etc.) he is called Mastema; and in the Testaments of the XII Patriarchs and also in the Dead Sea Scrolls he appears as Beliar (or Belial), who in the end will be bound and cast into eternal fire (cf. Test. Jud. 25[3]). The message of writer after writer is that, though these demons and their leaders may array themselves against God in defiance of his will, nevertheless their 'doom is writ'. The 'Day of the Lord' will bring its judgement on men and demons alike.

## 2. *Eschatological expectation*

During the Hellenistic period, especially from the time of the Maccabaean Revolt, eschatological ideas (i.e. ideas relating to 'the End' or 'the last things') were prominent among the Jews. They form the recurring theme of the so-called apocalyptic writings[2] for example, of which many were produced from *c.* 165 B.C. to the close of the first Christian century. Though these books were at first confined to a restricted company of 'the wise' among the people, the ideas they contained belonged to the popular religion, and were no doubt talked about in the synagogues and schools as well as in ordinary conversation. In them the writers recorded 'revelations' (Greek, *apokalupseis*) they had received, from which they foretold the manner of the End and, in not a few cases, tried to calculate the time of its appearing. Though these ideas had their

[1] Cf. Lev. 16[8, 10, 26], where the name is applied either to a scapegoat (so LXX) or to a demon inhabiting the desert.   [2] See pp. 219 ff.

roots in the religion of the Old Testament they were influenced, as we shall see, by foreign notions, and were inspired by the troublous times in which the Jewish people were then living, first under the Seleucids and then under the Romans.

This 'apocalyptic eschatology' was in many respects different from the 'prophetic eschatology' of the Old Testament; nevertheless it claimed to be both a continuation and a fulfilment of it. The prophets believed that the history of their people, and indeed of the whole human race, was in the hands of God, that he had for the world an all-embracing and all-powerful purpose in which they themselves had a glorious part to play. Bound up with this belief was the idea of the Day of the Lord, to be found, with varying emphases and interpretations, in a number of the prophetic writings. The Day would come when God would 'visit' the world in judgement and redeem his people Israel; Israel itself would be judged, but beyond this judgement lay a Golden Age when God's purpose would be fulfilled and his rule of prosperity and peace be ushered in. This future hope is expressed in terms of a coming kingdom, associated more often than not with the restoration of the Davidic line of kings; God's people would be delivered and live in an everlasting kingdom, purged of all enemies and purified of all evil. Even when, as in the writings of Deutero-Isaiah, this coming kingdom assumes transcendent qualities, so that the present world-order is transformed by the miraculous working of God, it is still a kingdom of this world, with Jerusalem as its centre and God's own people as its citizens. 'The latter end of the days' frequently mentioned in the prophets is on the plane of history and within the boundaries of time.

In the apocalyptic books these prophetic ideas underwent certain remarkable developments. The phrase 'the latter end of the days' now indicated not just the end of an historical era, but the end of history itself. Their writers believed that they had been commissioned by God to declare the fulfilment of Old Testament prophecy concerning the nature and time of the End and to describe in detail what the prophets themselves had left only in general terms. In particular they expounded the meaning of the Day of the Lord in terms of the End of the world, when God would intervene either himself or in the person of his Messiah to set right all wrongs and to vindicate his people Israel. Like the prophets before them they too had implicit faith in the all-prevailing purpose of God, embracing past, present, and future, in which the destiny of the whole physical universe as well as that of the whole human race was involved. But in the interpretation and application of this belief they went much further than the prophets. Under the influence of Zoroastrian teaching (which divided up world history into four great epochs of 3,000 years each, culminating in the Golden Age) they too worked it out systematically in elaborate schemes and with complicated systems of measurement, so as to indicate the near approach of the End. Not only so: history thus systematically arranged was also predetermined by God. Its pattern had been fixed beforehand; the duration of each period had been decided in advance; history was moving unerringly and irresistibly to its predetermined goal, the kingdom of God, whose coming would usher in the End.

The historical events marking the divisions of history, it is claimed in these writings, are regulated by the movement of the heavenly bodies (cf· Jub. 4 17, 19 etc.) and have been recorded in heavenly tablets (cf. Jub. 1 29 etc.), whose secrets God has now made known to 'the wise' among the people. The impression of 'foretelling' is strengthened by the writers' adoption, as pseudonyms, of the names of ancient worthies— ranging from Adam to Ezra—to whom the divine secrets, it is said, have been revealed, but which have been kept hidden until now. In this way they are able to relate history in terms of foretelling, and by the calculation of times and seasons to predict the date of the End. Such calculations play a big part in these writings, and make clear not only that the climax of history is at hand but also that there is the closest possible connexion between the events of human history and the working out of the divine purpose, which no one will be able to frustrate or destroy.

It is futile to try to find in these books a systematic doctrine of 'the last things', for among the apocalyptists themselves many diverse beliefs are to be found. In a number of them, such as the Psalms of Solomon, something like the familiar Old Testament picture appears of an earthly kingdom—political, nationalistic and militaristic—over which the promised king of David's line rules in wisdom and righteousness. But for the most part the picture is quite different and the coming kingdom becomes more and more other-wordly, supernatural, and transcendent. Characteristic of this outlook is a belief in the 'two ages'—a familiar idea in Zoroastrianism— in which this present evil age is set over against 'the age to come' when evil will be destroyed for ever. The more restricted outlook of the prophets gives place to a universalistic outlook in which the righteous are saved and the wicked destroyed; the nation, and in particular the Jewish nation, is still the object of God's judgement and salvation, but the righteous individual is also given a share in the coming kingdom by means of resurrection from the dead; God's enemies are no longer simply foreign armies, but the demonic armies of Satan (or Mastema or Beliar), who holds this present evil age in his power; the struggle now assumes cosmic proportions in which not only the Gentile nations but the whole universe itself is involved; deliverance will be wrought by the miraculous intervention of God, who will suddenly appear to rout the armies of Satan. The approach of the End will be marked by a last desperate onslaught of 'the sons of darkness' against 'the sons of light' in which the whole universe is involved. This great Day, like that of the prophetic Day of the Lord, will be preceded by many wonders and signs of a miraculous character—calamity will follow calamity; tribulation will follow tribulation; nation will rise up against nation; the world will be stricken by earthquake, famine, and fire; there will be mysterious portents on the earth and in the heavens, reminding men that the End is near. In the final 'eschatological battle' God and his angels will triumph; evil men will be destroyed; the demons and their masters will be imprisoned; the Creation, now set free from their tyranny, will be re-created and the age of Paradise restored.

The coming of God's kingdom, then, marks the great climax of history. But concerning its nature and duration there is a bewildering expression of opinion. In most of those apocalyptic books written before the Christian era the kingdom is synonymous with 'the age to come' (e.g. Daniel; 1 Enoch 6–36, 83–90; Test. XII Patr.; Sib. Or. Bk. III; Ps. Sol.), whose inauguration marks the beginning of the Golden Age wherein the righteous will receive all kinds of material and spiritual blessings from the hand of God. It is an everlasting earthly kingdom in which the righteous dead will be permitted to share by resurrection, and from which all evil will be removed (cf. Dan. $7^{18, 27}$); as promised of old, nature itself will be transformed and the earth will produce miraculous increase (cf. 1 Enoch $10^{19}$); a renewed Jerusalem will be its centre (cf. 1 Enoch $90^{28\ f\cdot}$); there the dispersed will flock from the ends of the earth; there, too, God's people will dwell in peace around the holy Temple, and men will bring to it their gifts from far-off lands (cf. Sib. Or. Bk. III, lines 667 ff., 702 ff.); over this kingdom a royal prince will rule in righteousness (cf. Ps. Sol. $7^{28\ ff\cdot}$). In other writings, however, the picture is less simple and the tension between 'this-worldly' and 'other-worldly' ideas becomes more clearly marked. The writer of the Similitudes of Enoch (1 Enoch 37–71), for example, sees the kingdom established not only on a transformed earth, but also in a transformed heaven (cf. 1 Enoch $45^{4-5}$), whilst in the Assumption of Moses no earthly kingdom is visualized at all, but only a heavenly kingdom (cf. $10^{9\ f\cdot}$). Some of the apocalyptists, however, strike a compromise by introducing the idea of an interim kingdom here on this earth, followed by 'the age to come' in heaven. This idea is found in a number of writings belonging to the first century A.D., but it appears also in the pre-Christian era in 1 Enoch 91–104 and perhaps also in the Book of Jubilees. The duration of this interim kingdom varies; sometimes it is given as 1,000 years (cf. 2 Enoch $32^2-33^2$; Rev. $20^{4-7}$), at other times 400 years (cf. 2 Esd. $7^{28}$), or else it is for an indefinite period (cf. 2 Bar. $40^3$). In such cases the resurrection and judgement no longer precede the kingdom but come at its close, and introduce the heavenly 'age to come' in which all earthly wrongs will be set right.

## 3. *The messianic hope*

Corresponding to these two complexes of eschatological ideas—the one this-worldly, nationalistic, and political, the other other-worldly, universalistic, and transcendent—there emerge two eschatological figures who act as God's agents in ushering in the kingdom and proclaiming the coming of the End—the Messiah and the Son of Man. But just as there is no clear-cut division between the two eschatologies, so also with the two eschatological figures there is an intermingling of ideas. Despite this, however, the identity of each is never entirely lost: different in origin, they remain distinct also in character.

The word *mašiah* (Greek, *Messias* or *Christos*, Messiah) is used in the Old Testament in a purely non-technical sense to signify one 'anointed' by God for some special task; in pre-exilic times it referred particularly to the King and in post-exilic times, when there was no king on the throne of Judah, to the High Priest. The 'prince' or 'shoot' of the House of David, to whom the prophets point forward, is apparently nowhere called 'the Messiah' in the technical sense of an eschatological figure, until about the middle of the first century b.c. when this identification is first made in Psalms of Solomon 17 [36]. This reminds us that, in both the prophetic and the apocalyptic traditions, the 'Messianic hope' did not necessarily involve a 'messianic figure'. In such apocalyptic works, for example, as the Book of Daniel, the Book of Jubilees, and 1 Enoch 1–36, 91–104, where the future hope is prominent, no reference is made to any such figure. This is perhaps hardly surprising, for during the Persian period the hope of a deliverer of David's line had waned and there seemed little possibility of deliverance coming from that quarter. Men's hopes were set rather on the intervention and kingly rule of God himself than on any earthly representative, and on the keeping of his Law as the primary means of its appearing.

During the time of the Hasmonaeans, however, the hope revived, on the part of some at least, that God would raise up a deliverer who would help to establish the promised kingdom. In the Testaments of the XII Patriarchs, for example, the traditional Davidic leader once more appears (cf. Test. Jud. $17^{5-6}$, $22^{2-3}$, $24^{1-6}$), and alongside him a leader of priestly stock, having precedence over him and demonstrating warlike qualities characteristic rather of the royal prince (cf. Test. Reub. $6^{5 \text{ ff.}}$; Test. Levi $18^{2 \text{ ff.}}$). This priestly figure no doubt reflects the achievements of the Maccabees and the early glories of the Hasmonaean House (cf. 1 Macc. $14^{8 \text{ ff.}}$, where Simon's rule is described in glowing 'messianic' terms). Several considerations indicate, however, that the writer did not have in mind any member of this priestly House which claimed descent from Levi, but another line of priests altogether. A hint of this is given in Test. Levi $8^{14}$: 'A king shall arise in (or 'out of') Judah and shall establish a new priesthood', which, says the writer, is to be called by 'a new name'. T. W. Manson has argued that this 'new name' refers to 'the sons of Zadok', i.e. to the legitimate priesthood displaced from office with the coming of the Hasmonaeans, and this suggestion finds corroboration in the evidence of the Dead Sea Scrolls. Fragments of the Testament of Levi found at Qumran show that this book was highly favoured by the sectaries there; these 'sons of Zadok' (for so they called themselves) would look to their own ranks for this priestly leader and not to the Hasmonaean House which had usurped the true High-Priestly office. Indeed, in the Dead Sea Scrolls themselves the same picture is apparently given of a priestly leader, from 'the sons of Zadok', standing alongside the Davidic leader and having precedence over him in the performance of his priestly functions (cf. *Manual of Discipline*, ix. 11; *Rule of the Congregation*, ii. 18–22) In both the Testaments and the Scrolls, however, it is the Davidic leader who plays the more important part. The expressions 'priestly Messiah' and 'kingly Messiah' have frequently been used in this connexion; but these terms can be misleading. What we have here is an 'anointed priest' alongside of an 'anointed king', who together are to play a leading part in the coming kingdom.

As already noted, however, the most important book for a picture of the Davidic leader is the Psalms of Solomon,[1] which forms a landmark in the development of the messianic hope; for here for the very first time the word 'Messiah' is used as a title of the king of the coming kingdom within an eschatological context (cf. 17[36]). The writer calls him 'the Lord Messiah' and identifies him with 'the son of David' (17[27]), heaping on him 'divine' honours as befits the 'anointed of God'. Nevertheless, he is clearly still a human figure who will rule over an earthly kingdom with its centre in Jerusalem, a military leader who will crush the heathen and make them serve under his yoke (cf. 17[24 ff.]). This same hope of a military Messiah continued into the Christian era, as the evidence of the New Testament (cf. Acts 5[36], 21[38]) and other records (cf. *Antiquities* xx. v. 1, viii. 6) clearly shows.

Alongside of this traditional Messiah, as we have seen, there appears another eschatological figure known as 'the Son of Man' (or simply 'the Man'). These two ideas represent two originally distinct developments within the Jewish eschatological hope, which in course of time and in different writings underwent varying degrees of assimilation. The origin of the 'Son of Man' figure is a subject of much debate among scholars; some argue that it can be adequately explained by reference to the Old Testament where the expression appears frequently, for example, in the Book of Ezekiel, and occasionally elsewhere; others trace its roots back into oriental mythology and find connexions with the Primal or Heavenly Man in Persian and Babylonian tradition.

The first occurrence of the expression in the apocalyptic literature is in Dan. 7[13 ff.], where it is said that he has been given by God 'dominion and glory and a kingdom . . . which shall not be destroyed' (7[14]). A few verses later this 'Son of Man' is identified with the 'saints of the Most High' to whom will be given 'the kingdom and the dominion' (7[27]), i.e. it is a corporate

[1] See pp. 293 f.

figure and is not to be interpreted in terms of a Messiah or indeed of any individual. The final triumph of God's people is an everlasting earthly kingdom in line with popular eschatological expectations.

The next occurrence of the phrase is in the Similitudes of Enoch (1 Enoch 37–71), dating perhaps from the second half of the first century B.C., where the individual reference is more apparent. In these chapters he appears as 'Son of Man', 'Man', 'the Elect One', 'the Righteous One', and even as 'his Anointed'. He is presented as a supernatural angelic being who stands in a special relationship to God, but who at the same time stands as the representative of 'the elect ones', i.e. the faithful among God's people who will one day inherit the kingdom. He was chosen by God before the creation of the world (cf. 46³, 48⁶), when 'his name was named before the Lord of Spirits' (48³), i.e. he had a place in God's purpose from the very beginning. In him righteousness and wisdom dwell (cf. 46³, 49³); with him are hidden the divine secrets of the universe (cf. 62⁶), which he is able to reveal to men (cf. 46³); the greatest secret of all is the Son of Man himself, who will yet be revealed (cf. 48⁶ ᶠ·) and sit on the throne of God's glory as judge both of men and of angels (cf. 55⁴, 69²⁷); in his triumphant rule he will be 'a staff to the righteous' and 'the light of the Gentiles', in fulfilment of ancient prophecy (48⁴; cf. Isa. 42⁶, 49⁶, 61¹⁻²). This same figure appears again, though less prominently, in certain other apocalyptic books of the Christian era—2 Esdras, 2 Baruch, and the Sibylline Oracles Bk. V—the most significant being 2 Esdras, where 'the Man' is once more a transcendent, heavenly being through whom God will yet deliver his creation (cf. 13²⁶).

How, then, are we to interpret this heavenly, transcendent figure, so unlike the traditional figure of the Jewish future hope? We have seen that, in the case of Daniel, the Son of Man is probably to be interpreted symbolically to represent 'the saints of the Most High'. A somewhat similar interpretation is suggested for the Similitudes and 2 Esdras by T. W. Manson and several other scholars, who find the answer to the problem in the Old Testament idea of 'corporate personality', in which the thought moves backwards and forwards between the individual and the group to which the individual belongs. In these writings the Son of Man figure represents on the one hand 'the manifestation of the Kingdom of God on earth in a people wholly devoted to their heavenly King',[1] and on the other hand the leader or ideal representative of the coming kingdom. Dr. Manson goes further than this and hazards the suggestion that this leader is to be identified with the Messiah. Whether this identification can be justified or not, the individual aspect of the Son of Man is clearer in the Similitudes and 2 Esdras than it is in the Book of Daniel.

The relationship between the Son of Man and the Messiah is difficult to define. Some scholars argue that the two terms were not brought together before the time of Jesus and that he was the first to do so. It is important to observe, however, that already in the Similitudes the Son of Man has assumed certain characteristics generally associated with the traditional Jewish deliverer. In 2 Esdras (c. A.D. 90) these characteristics are even more clearly marked (cf. 13[33 ff.]) and he is actually identified with the Messiah (cf. 12[32]); despite this, however, he remains a truly transcendent figure. Thus, although the figure of the Messiah tended to appear in those circles where the traditional hope was cherished, and that of the Son of Man in those where the thought of the transcendent kingdom was uppermost, there seems to have been some degree of 'cross-fertilization' even before the beginning of the Christian era.

## 4. *Resurrection and the life to come*

One of the most remarkable developments during this period was the rise of a belief in life after death conceived in terms of resurrection. Such a belief did not grow up in isolation but rather as part of that complex eschatological pattern described above and in close association with the thought of the Final Judgement when God would reward the righteous and punish

[1] T. W. Manson, *The Teaching of Jesus*, 1931, p. 227.

the wicked. The main lines of this development are fairly clear, but once again there is no consistency of belief, far less is there an established 'doctrine' of the life beyond. For example, in some writings, such as Ecclesiastes, Ecclesiasticus, Judith, Tobit, and 1 Maccabees, the Old Testament belief in Sheol as the realm of the departed still prevails; in others, such as the Wisdom of Solomon (cf. $2^{23}$, $3^4$, etc.), the Book of Jubilees (cf. $23^{31}$, etc.), and 1 Enoch 91–104 (cf. $103^4$, $104^2$ ff., etc.), the writers have in mind something like the Greek notion of the immortality of the soul; but in most, especially those of an apocalyptic character, the belief expressed is that of resurrection from the dead. Again, in a number of the earlier apocryphal books such as Baruch (cf. $2^{30-35}$ etc.) and Tobit (cf. $13^1$ ff., $14^{4-7}$), the future hope is expressed in terms of the nation and not of the individual; in others there is a synthesis of these two eschatologies, the individual being raised in resurrection to take his place as a member of the restored people; whilst in others the idea of individual survival replaces that of the nation.

Ever since the time of the early prophets the Hebrews had been taught that at death a man's shade or ghost went down to Sheol, a land of no-return (cf. 2 Sam. $12^{23}$; Job $7^9$), where, as Ecclesiastes says, 'the dead know nothing, and they have no more reward . . . for there is no work or thought or knowledge or wisdom in Sheol, to which you are going' (Eccles. $9^{5, 10}$). What remained after death was only the shadowy likeness of the once-living man, bereft now of all those qualities which characterized his life upon earth. According to Josephus this ancient belief continued to be held by the Sadducees (cf. also the evidence of the New Testament) and by the Essenes[1] (cf. *War* II. viii. 11, 14) as well as by the apocryphal writers noted above. Evidence for belief in some form of immortality has been claimed by some scholars in the Book of Job (cf. especially $14^{13-15}$, $19^{25-27}$), and in certain of the Psalms (cf. especially 16, 49, 73); but this has been disputed by others.[2] Such a

---

[1] See, however, p. 173.
[2] See further pp. 288 f.

belief, if it is to be found there at all, is at best the uncertain glimmering of hope rather than the firm assertion of faith.[1]

It is of significance that when this assertion came at last to be made it was in the form of belief in resurrection. To the Hebrew mind the body was an essential aspect of personality, and so, according to this understanding, if there was to be a continuation of life after death it had to be in terms of bodily survival. The historical occasion for the rise of such a belief is lost to view, but it may have been the death or martyrdom of certain righteous men in Israel. Great prophets like Jeremiah and Ezekiel had taught the worth of the individual within the nation, and, with others, had asserted that God would reward the righteous and punish the wicked. But what about the righteous dead who had given up their lives for his sake? Surely they must have their place with the living in the coming kingdom! They would be raised to share in the glories yet to be—in an eternal earthly kingdom or an interim kingdom or in 'the age to come', in their physical bodies or in transformed bodies or in 'spiritual' bodies like those of the angels in heaven! What, too, about those wicked men by whose villainy God's name had been dishonoured and his people done to death, but who had died without receiving retribution for their sins? They also would be raised in the last days to receive in their bodies the punishment they so rightly deserved!

These convictions are reflected in two Old Testament passages which provide the first clear indication in this literature of belief in life after death—Isa. 24–27 and Dan. 12. The first of these is a late addition to the prophecy of Isaiah and may be dated around the fourth century B.C.[2] The significant words are in 26¹⁹, which may be translated: 'Thy dead shall live; their bodies shall rise; they that dwell in the dust shall awake and sing; for the dew of light is thy dew, and the

[1] According to early tradition Enoch (cf. Gen. 5²⁴) and Elijah (cf. 2 Kings 2¹¹) were transported bodily from earth to heaven. No generalization, however, can be made concerning the fate of ordinary mortals by reference to the exceptional experience of this 'exclusive spiritual aristocracy'.

[2] See pp. 213 ff.

earth shall give birth to the shades'. Some scholars see in this verse a prophecy concerning the revival of the nation, as in Ezekiel's vision of the valley of dry bones (cf. Ezek. 37); the view taken here is that it refers to actual resurrection.[1] The dead will rise to share in God's final triumph. The second passage, dating from *c.* 165 B.C., is more explicit and refers not only to the very good but also to the very bad, who will be raised together to receive reward or punishment: 'And many of those who sleep in the dust of the earth shall awake, some to everlasting life, and some to shame and everlasting contempt' (Dan. 12[2]). No doubt the writer has in mind those faithful Jews who had laid down their lives in the persecutions leading up to the Maccabaean Revolt, and also those traitors and persecutors who had violated and desecrated the worship of the true God (cf. 2 Macc. 7[9, 14, 23, 35 f.]).

In subsequent writings first the one and then the other of these positions is taken up, with variations on the two themes. The example of the Isaiah passage is followed, for instance, in the Psalms of Solomon and in 1 Enoch 83–90, where it is said that the righteous will 'rise again into life eternal' (Ps. Sol. 3[16]) to 'take their place in the kingdom' (1 Enoch 90[33]), presumably in their physical bodies; in 2 Enoch (first century A.D.), however, they are given heavenly bodies in keeping with their spiritual environment in Paradise (cf. 8[5], 65[10]). But most of the apocalyptic writings follow the lead of Daniel in teaching the resurrection both of the righteous and of the wicked. In 1 Enoch 6–36, for example, it is said that resurrection is reserved for two classes of people—the righteous, or a section of them, who will share in the blessings of the kingdom on a purified earth (cf. 10[17], 25[4 ff.]), and those sinners who, having escaped due punishment in this life, will at last be thrown into the fires of Gehenna (cf. chs. 26–27). Several writers go further still and teach a resurrection of *all* men, to be followed by the judgement. According to the Testaments of the XII Patriarchs, for example, after the resurrection of the patriarchs themselves, and the righteous martyrs, 'then also all men shall rise,

[1] See further pp. 216 f.

some unto glory and some unto shame' (Test. Benj. 10[8]). This same thought is repeated in several later books (cf. Sib. Or. Bk. IV; Apoc. of Moses; 2 Esdras; 2 Baruch): the whole human race is to be raised for judgement when 'recompense shall follow and the reward be made manifest' (2 Esd. 7[35, 37]).

But what is the state of the departed immediately after death and before the resurrection and the great day of judgement? Here we observe a radical change in the familiar Old Testament picture of Sheol. In Isa. 26[19] and Dan. 12[2] the dead are still thought of as 'shades' awaiting the resurrection; but in the extra-biblical writings they are described by the Greek word *psuchē* or its Hebrew equivalent *nepheš*, generally translated 'soul'. In the Old Testament, however, *nepheš* signifies simply a man's 'person' or the 'life principle' in him, with no reference to his condition after death; in the apocalyptic literature on the other hand it implies, among other things, a quality of life in the departed quite unlike that of 'the shade' and points in the direction of the Greek idea of a separable soul. The Hebrew ancestry of this notion, however, is more important than the possible influence of Greek thought upon it, for, as we have seen, the Hebrew awareness of the unity of personality reasserts itself in the union of 'soul' with body in resurrection.

Another significant change is that in Sheol moral distinctions now begin to make their appearance. No longer can it be said that 'one fate comes to all, to the righteous and the wicked' (Eccles. 9[2]): in Sheol the souls of the righteous are separated from those of the wicked, awaiting their resurrection to 'everlasting life' or 'everlasting contempt'. But in a number of books it is more than simply a place of waiting; it has itself become a place of reward and punishment where the souls of men are given a foretaste of the greater joys or sorrows still to come. The writer of 2 Esdras, for example, describes seven degrees of torment which await the wicked (cf. 7[80-87]) and seven degrees of bliss which await the righteous (cf. 7[92-98]), who are kept safe in 'treasuries' (cf. 4[35], 7[32], etc.), guarded by angels (cf. 7[85, 95]) until the Final Judgement comes. But of the wicked it is said, 'And now recline in anguish and rest in torment till thy last time come, in which thou wilt come again, and be tormented still more' (2 Bar. 36¹¹). At a much earlier period than this, however, divisions appear in Sheol which are subsequently to be given distinguishing names like Hell, Gehenna, and Paradise. In I Enoch 22, for example, dating from the first half of the second century B.C., four compartments or 'hollow places' in Sheol are described, graded according to moral judgements. In the first, where there is 'a bright spring of water', the spirits of the righteous dwell; the second is for sinners who have not received in life retribution for their sins; the third is for those righteous who were martyred without receiving their reward; the fourth is for sinners who have already received their punishment during their life upon earth. Here we have the very first allusion in this literature to the idea of the pains of Hell. The spirits of the sinners, we are told, are 'set apart in great pain . . . scourgings and torments of the accursed for ever' (22¹⁰ ᶠ·). Those who have already received punishment for their sins remain where they are in torments, but those who have not so received will be raised thence on the day of judgement in the 'accursed valley' (27¹). The reference here is no doubt to the Valley of Hinnom (Hebrew, *Ge' Hinnom*)—the smouldering garbage heap outside Jerusalem (cf. 2 Chron. 28³; Jer. 7³¹ ᶠ·, etc.)—which appears in apocalyptic lore as Gehenna, the place of eternal fire. Over against 'the furnace of Gehenna' stands 'the Paradise of delight' (2 Esdras 7³⁶), 'the garden of life' (I Enoch 61¹²) where the righteous dwell. Sometimes it is said to be situated on earth, at other times in the third heaven; sometimes it is an intermediate abode, at other times it is the final resting place of bliss, 'where there is no toil, neither grief nor mourning; but peace and exultation and life everlasting' (Test. Abr. 20).

All these speculations point forward with certainty to one thing—the great day of judgement which will surely come. But the manner of its coming is less certain than the fact of its appearing. Sometimes it is seen to be catastrophic, at other times it takes the form of a Great Assize—or else these two elements may be combined, the one representing a preliminary and the other a final judgement. Sometimes, as we have seen, it is the nations which come forward for judgement, at other times it is the souls of men. Sometimes it issues in a world conflagration, at other times it is angels and men who are cast into hell fire. But whatever the destiny of man and his world may be, this at least is certain, that he who created in the beginning will re-create in the End.

# X

## PARTIES WITHIN JUDAISM

THE Judaism of the intertestamental period is a very complex system indeed comprising many religious and political groups (these two ideas can hardly be separated), and a multitude of ordinary Jews who belonged to no identifiable party. Three important parties mentioned by Josephus are the Sadducees, the Pharisees, and the Essenes, to which he adds a fourth, later to be known as the Zealots, which made its appearance around the year A.D. 6 (cf. *Antiquities* XVIII. i. 1–6). Evidence from Qumran, however, as well as from rabbinic sources and the early Church Fathers, makes it clear that there were many other 'splinter' groups besides these, most of them unknown to us even by name. Josephus describes his three groups as 'sects' (Greek, *haireseis*, from which we get the word 'heresy'); this word, however, must not be understood in the sense in which it is normally used in, say, Christian Church history. In pre-Christian times there was no 'normative' Judaism from whose standards of 'orthodoxy' certain sections of the people broke away. Judaism was in fact much less concerned about 'right *belief*' than about 'accepted *practice*'. All sections of the people accepted as a fundamental tenet of their faith that 'the Lord our God is one Lord' (Deut. 6⁴), and upheld the authority of the Torah as the very foundation of their religion. Where they differed was in the interpretation of the Torah and its practical application, a state of affairs which often expressed itself in the most bitter animosity.

## 1. *Sadducees and Pharisees*

According to Josephus (cf. *Antiquities* XIII. v. 9) the Sadducees and Pharisees were in existence in the time of Jonathan

(152–143 B.C.); but it is not until the reign of John Hyrcanus (134–104 B.C.) that we have the first clear historical allusion to them (cf. *Antiquities* XIII. x. 5–6), the occasion being a serious breach between Hyrcanus and the Pharisees.[1] It is clear that by this time Sadducees and Pharisees represented two well-established rival parties within the state, whose religious differences were on occasions so entangled with political differences as to be quite inseparable from them. The exact date of their emergence is unknown, but it is likely that they had closed their ranks and established themselves as organized parties not long after the Maccabaean Revolt.

Many attempts have been made to find in the derivation of the two names 'Sadducees' and 'Pharisees' a clue to their origin and distinctive character. It has been generally assumed that the word Sadducee (Hebrew, *Ṣaddūkîm*) comes from the name Zadok (Hebrew, *Ṣādhok*), High Priest in the time of Solomon, whose successors in the priesthood, the Zadokites, remained in office right down to the period of the Maccabaean Revolt. This suggestion finds support in the description of the Sadducees given by Josephus as a party made up of priestly aristocratic families (cf. *Antiquities* XVIII. i. 4, XX. ix. 1, etc.). There are, however, difficulties about accepting such an explanation. These have been tabulated in a convincing way by T. W. Manson, who offers objections on philological and historical grounds.[2] The Greek form of the word 'Sadducees' (*Saddoukaioi*), as it appears in Josephus for example, presupposes a double 'd' in the Hebrew (or Aramaic) original, whereas there is only one 'd' in the word Zadok; moreover, the natural way in Hebrew to describe the descendants of Zadok is not *Ṣaddūkîm*, but *Benē Ṣādhok* (meaning 'sons of Zadok')—a form which is found in Ecclus. 51 [12] and frequently in the Dead Sea Scrolls. Historically it is strange (if this derivation be accepted) that there is no mention of Sadducees during the time of the

[1] See pp. 66 f.
[2] Cf. *The Servant-Messiah*, 1956, pp. 12 ff.; 'Sadducee and Pharisee: the origin and significance of the names', *Bulletin of the John Rylands Library*, vol. 22, no. 1, April 1938, pp. 3 ff.

Zadokite High Priesthood, but that they make their appearance when this High-Priestly line had virtually ceased to hold office; moreover, although there is evidence for a priestly element within the Sadducaean party, there is also evidence to show that it was by no means limited to members of the priesthood, but probably included a high proportion of wealthy and influential laymen. It is also significant that the Sadducees nowhere claim any connexion with the High Priest Zadok; on the contrary they seem to associate the name *Ṣaddukîm* (Sadducees) with the word *ṣaddiḳîm*, meaning 'righteous ones' (cf. Ass. Mos. 7³). Such a connexion is etymologically impossible (the change from the 'i' to the 'u' cannot be explained), but the pun was too good to miss and no doubt gave them a glow of satisfaction.

Dr. Manson's own suggestion is an interesting one. It is that the meaning of the name is to be found, not in the priestly connexions of the party, but rather in the realm of international politics. He finds its derivation in the Greek word *sundikoi* (Syndics) which can be traced back in Athenian history as far as the fourth century B.C. and is also mentioned in documents from Roman and Byzantine times. These Syndics were civic officials who looked after the fiscal interests of the country, represented the people in legal disputes with foreigners, and were responsible to the community for giving legal advice; in the earlier period in Athens it was apparently their business 'to defend the existing laws against innovation or amendment'.[1] Dr. Manson argues that the word *Saddoukaioi* (Sadducees) is a transliteration of the word *sundikoi* and indicates those civic and political leaders of the Jews who, in the time of the Hasmonaeans, exercised authority through the judicial council known as the *Gerousia*, and subsequently as the *Sanhedrin*. The functions of these Jewish Syndics corresponded closely to those of the Greek officials who bore that name—taxation was closely bound up with the Temple and the priesthood, and so it is reasonable to assume that the priestly Sadducees would have control of the fiscal system; they represented the State in

[1] Ibid., p. 7.

negotiations with foreign powers; they were the official interpreters of the law, a prerogative they jealously guarded.

We can picture them, then, as a small and select group of
influential and wealthy men who exercised considerable power
in the civic and religious life of the nation. The powerful priesthood was represented within this social aristocracy by the
High Priest and his retinue and by other leading priestly
officials. Not all the priests, however, were Sadducees; some
indeed were members of the rival party of the Pharisees.
Nor, as we have seen, were all Sadducees priests, for in the
party were wealthy traders and high-ranking government
officials. They were in fact a company of people, priestly and
lay, who enjoyed the same social standing and were determined
to maintain the existing state of society both in Church and
State. They did not begin, therefore, as a religious party, but
because of their close association with the Temple and the
priesthood, and because politics and religion could not readily
be separated from each other, theirs gradually assumed a religious character over against the party of the Pharisees.

Much of the information which has come down to us about
the Sadducees is obviously biased, for almost everything we
know about them is from sources which have little or no sympathy with their ideals. Josephus alleges that they did not share
the confidence of the mass of the people (cf. *Antiquities* XIII.
x. 6), but rather alienated them by their proud bearing and
the severity of their judgements (cf. *Antiquities* XX. ix. 1; Ps.
Sol. 4² ᶠ·). It is customary to present them as collaborationists,
whose sympathies from before the time of the Maccabaean
Revolt were with those Hellenizers who subverted the pure
Jewish faith. It is true that in the years leading up to the
Maccabaean Revolt the High-Priestly house had lent its
support to the Hellenizers, but it is doubtful whether in the
succeeding years sympathy for the Hellenistic culture was a
distinguishing mark of the Sadducaean party over against, say,
that of their rivals, the Pharisees.

During the rule of the Hasmonaean House the fortunes of
the Sadducees fluctuated, as we have seen; but for the most

part they found its worldly-wise policies to their liking. In politics and in religion they were conservative in outlook, determined at all costs to maintain the *status quo* in both State and Church. As conservatives in politics they stood for the Israelite ideal of a theocratic state under the leadership of the High Priest. For this reason they were suspicious of the popular eschatological faith in the coming of a Messiah: all such teaching was a menace to the existing social and political order and had to be handled with the greatest care. As conservatives in religion they set themselves to preserve all that they believed to be best in their priestly tradition. In particular they championed the observance of the Temple ritual and the prerogative of the priests to interpret the Law, maintaining that their interpretations, together with priestly ordinances and usages arising out of them, were in themselves a sufficient guide for those who sought to obey the commands of God. From an early date their authority as interpreters of the Law met a serious challenge from the Pharisees, who developed their own oral tradition of lay interpretation (see below). The Sadducees rejected this tradition and stoutly defended the Torah as alone authoritative; it is unlikely, however, that they denied the sacredness of the Prophets and the Writings, as some of the Church Fathers, for example, suggest. Certain doctrines which could not be justified by reference to the Torah they rejected; these, as we shall see (p. 163), were simply denials of doctrines expressed positively by the Pharisees.

At long last, some years before the capture of Jerusalem by the Romans in A.D. 70, they were ousted from their stronghold in the Temple, where, indeed, their authority had been challenged many times before. With the fall of the city and its sanctuary they ceased to be of any further significance in the affairs of the nation or in the Judaism of subsequent generations.

Over against the Sadducees stood the Pharisees, who in matters of religion were as progressive as their rivals were conservative. Although priests were to be found in their ranks, theirs was essentially a laymen's movement, whose members, unlike the aristocratic Sadducees, were drawn

largely from the middle class. Although they were first and foremost a religious party they were not averse to political power,
and in the course of the years acquired for themselves an
influential position in the state. It has been customary to
describe them as successors of the Hasidim, who, at the time
of the Maccabaean Revolt, stood firm in their defence of the
Torah. This is true in the sense that, like the Hasidim, they
were above all else zealous for the Torah and showed themselves
valiant champions of Torah religion against the evil influences
of Hellenism. But although they may be said to be *spiritual*
descendants of the Hasidim, it is rather less certain that they
can claim direct lineal descent from them. It is perhaps more
accurate to say that their origin is to be traced to those lay
scribes who, from the beginning of the Greek period, did so
much to 'democratize' religion through their interpretations
of the Torah and its application to everyday life.[1] The exact
relationship between these scribes and the Hasidim is not clear.
A key passage in this connexion is 1 Macc. $7^{12 \text{ ff.}}$, where 'a
company of scribes' is mentioned alongside 'the Hasidim'.
It is generally assumed that these two groups belong together
and that the 'scribes' are in fact the 'scribes of the Hasidim',
in which case it can be said that the Pharisees originated in the
scribal section of the Hasidic movement. The passage, however, is ambiguous, and may suggest that the 'company of
scribes' took independent action and are to be distinguished
from the Hasidim. If this is so, then the Pharisees, though
sharing the Hasidim's zeal for the Torah of God, can hardly
trace their origin back to this group of men.

The Pharisaic party were ably led by learned scribes and,
in the time of the Hasmonaeans, exercised no small authority as
lay members of the *Gerousia* or *Sanhedrin*. Their religious
influence was dominant in the synagogues and schools in
both Jerusalem and the Dispersion, where they were at great
pains to make the Scripture understood by the people. They
cultivated in themselves and in others a spirit of true piety
which showed itself in the homes of the common people

[1] See above, pp. 116 ff.

and won them the support of the masses (cf. *Antiquities* XIII.
x. 6). Though relatively small in numbers, they formed themselves into well-organized 'brotherhoods', and exercised an
influence on Judaism out of all proportion to their size. Their
zeal expressed itself not only in teaching the faithful, but also
in missionary work among the Gentiles (cf. Matt. 23[15]).

The Pharisees differed from the Sadducees in many respects,
but in none more radically than in their understanding and
interpretation of the Torah. Both parties accepted the Torah
as authoritative, but the Pharisees alone accepted the Prophets
and the Writings also as authoritative sacred Scripture, whose
teachings they used in their interpretation of the Torah itself.
From an early date in this period the *priestly* prerogative in
scriptural interpretation had been seriously challenged by a
body of *lay* scribes who developed as their own a system of legal
tradition which was much more broadly based than that of the
priests.[1] This tradition of interpretation was continued by the
scribes of the Pharisees, who, in course of time, built up an
elaborate system of oral laws giving guidance for every aspect
of men's lives. To them religion was a living thing and had
to show itself readily adaptable to the people's diverse and
changing needs. This flexible body of laws stood in marked
contrast to the fixed and rigid priestly laws, with their narrow
application to the Temple and its ritual. But the Pharisees did
not only develop their own tradition of interpretation in
defiance of that of the priests; in course of time they declared
that this 'tradition of the elders' was as authoritative and
binding as the written Torah itself, and so gave it an honoured
place alongside Scripture. Josephus sums up the situation in
these words:

The Pharisees had passed on to the people certain regulations
handed down by former generations and not recorded in the Laws of
Moses, for which reason they are rejected by the Sadducaean group,
who hold that only those regulations should be considered valid which
were written down (in Scripture), and that those which had been
handed down by former generations need not be observed. And

[1] See p. 116.

M

concerning these matters the two parties came to have controversies and serious differences (*Antiquities* XIII. x. 6).

To the Pharisees the Torah had been given in both written and oral form, each of which was equally valid; to the Sadducees the written Torah alone was accepted as the revelation of God's mind and will. It was probably this claim of the Pharisees, as we have seen,[1] which caused the final breach between the two parties in the Sanhedrin during the reign of John Hyrcanus.

The same meticulous care with which the Pharisees sought to interpret the Torah was carried over into the practice of their religion. Every detail was governed by obligatory legal ordinances. They even made 'a fence around the Law'[2] to ensure its observance, and carried out to the very letter the commands of the Levitical code concerning such matters as ritual purification, dietary laws, and tithing. Such strictness in the observance of the Torah in all its minutiae inevitably bred a spirit of exclusivism, which showed itself, for example, in their separation from 'the people of the land' whose non-observance of the Law made them ritually unclean. In such a religion legalism can easily pass over into formalism and formalism into hypocrisy. It is unfair to pass such a judgement on the Pharisaic movement as a whole, but, as the New Testament evidence shows, the danger was always there, and from it some members at least did not escape.

It has been argued that this whole attitude is reflected in the very name by which they were known. The Hebrew word for 'Pharisees' (*Perûšîm*) is generally recognized as a passive form of the verb *paraš*, meaning 'those who are separated' (sc. 'from the people of the land' or 'from unclean things'); these 'separated ones' or 'holy ones' (the two verbal roots are closely connected) are in either case wholly given over to the fulfilment of the Law. Or the expression may refer to their separation from the Sadducaean Sanhedrin, in which case it may have the meaning 'schismatics'. Another suggestion is that the word (in the active form *Parôšîm*) meant originally 'expounder' or

---

[1] See p. 118.    [2] Cf. p. 117.

'interpreter' (sc. 'of the Law'), for the verb *paraš* can mean 'to interpret' as well as 'to separate', and that only subsequently was it made into a passive (*Perûšîm*) and given the sense 'separatists'. This explanation is an attractive one and agrees with the known fact that the Pharisees were 'most accurate interpreters of the Law' (*Antiquities* XVII. ii. 4) who devoted themselves from an early date to the task of biblical exegesis. Yet another solution is offered by T.W. Manson in the works quoted above. He suggests that its derivation is to be found in an Aramaic word meaning 'Persian' and that it indicates innovators in theology, who were given this nickname by their opponents because they derived so many of their ideas from Persian (i.e. Zoroastrian) sources; later on it was given 'an edifying etymology', being linked with the root *paraš*, meaning 'to separate'. This explanation underlines the fact that, despite their strictness in observing the Law, they were much more open to religious innovations than the conservative Sadducees, and in certain instances their beliefs may reflect the influence of Persian ideas, although too much emphasis should not be laid on this fact. One basic belief in which the Pharisees were at variance with the Sadducees was that concerning the life after death. The Pharisees believed in the survival of the soul, the resurrection of the body, and the judgement to come, with its accompanying doctrine of rewards and punishments. The Sadducees could find no justification for these things in the written Torah, and so, in true Hebrew manner, clung to the old belief in Sheol. Again, the Pharisees apparently went far beyond the evidence of Scripture in expressing belief in a highly developed doctrine of angels and demons, which finds expression in many apocalyptic books of this period and no doubt owes much to the influence of Persia. According to Acts 23[8] the Sadducees seem to have denied the existence of angels and spirits. Since, however, reference is made to angels in the Torah, it is likely that what the Sadducees denied was rather the exaggerated form the doctrine assumed in the popular estimation of their day. The Pharisees, moreover, believed that the whole of history was controlled and determined by the divine purpose (which Josephus, in true Stoic fashion, describes as 'Fate', cf. *War* II. viii. 14; *Antiquities* XIII. v. 9); the Sadducees denied this, and maintained man's freedom of choice and his ability to change the course of history. Finally, the Pharisees cherished the hope, fired no doubt by the prophetic promises in Scripture, that God would soon re-establish the House of his servant David in the coming messianic kingdom, in which even the righteous dead would share through resurrection. This hope together with that in a warrior Messiah of David's line finds classic expression in the Psalms of Solomon, a Pharisaic work from the middle of the first century B.C.[1] The Pharisees were not particularly militant in the expression of this hope, but it is significant that, according to Josephus, one of the founders of the revolutionary Zealot party was himself a Pharisee (cf. *Antiquities* XVIII. i. 1), and that at a much later date a prominent member of the party, none other than the celebrated Rabbi Akiba, was deeply involved in the abortive rising under the nationalist leader, Bar Kochba (A.D. 132). The Sadducees, who had everything to lose and nothing to gain by such pursuits, dubbed them as revolutionaries and dangerous innovators in affairs both of Church and of state.

## 2. *Essenes and Qumran Covenanters*

The Essenes were an ascetic sect whose origins can be traced back to the early decades of the second century B.C. and who continued in existence throughout the period of the ministry of Jesus until the Jewish War in A.D. 66–70. From Philo and Josephus we learn that in New Testament times they were about 4,000 strong and were to be found in many villages and towns throughout Palestine as well as in separate communities away from the lawlessness of the cities. They strictly observed the Sabbath and attended their synagogues, where, seated in order of seniority, they studied the Scriptures and cultivated 'love of God, love of goodness, love of man'. They showed great hospitality to fellow members of the sect and had hostels and

[1] See pp. 85, 291 ff.

'wardens' in many towns to provide for their needs. For the most part they lived off the land or else worked at various crafts. It would appear that, although there were varieties of Essenes, they were all inspired by an ascetic ideal which sought separation from the ritual impurities of the world around them. By the first century B.C. they had virtually become a monastic order, made up of priests and laymen, dedicated to the ritual fulfilment of the Torah and to an interpretation of it different in many ways from those of the Sadducees and Pharisees.

The discovery of the Dead Sea Scrolls in 1947 and subsequent years brought a flood of new light on this subject, for there is reason to believe that the people of the Scrolls are of the same lineage as the Essenes themselves. A key to our understanding of the relationship between them is given by the elder Pliny, who tells of a company of Essenes whom he describes as 'a solitary community . . . without women . . . without money . . . and without any company save that of the palm trees', living a little inshore on the western side of the Dead Sea. Further to the south lay the town of Engedi, then the rock fortress of Masada and finally the border of Judaea. This reference gives a valuable hint concerning the identity of these Essenes. About twenty miles north of Engedi and three quarters of a mile from the seashore lie some ancient ruins known as Khirbet ('Ruins') Qumran; nearby are the caves where the Scrolls were discovered. Excavations have shown a direct connexion between these Scrolls and the site, and have demonstrated that Khirbet Qumran was in fact the headquarters for many years of the community about which the Scrolls speak. Moreover, archaeological evidence and internal evidence for the dating of the Scrolls have confirmed the presence of the Qumran community on this spot at the time to which Pliny refers. In the light of these facts it is virtually certain that the members of this community are to be identified with the Essenes of his passage, for it is hardly likely that *two* such communities were situated so closely together at the same period of time in such a barren and inhospitable desert as this was. This conclusion is supported by the evidence of the Scrolls themselves on such matters as the organization and religious beliefs of the Qumran sectaries. Not all that they say tallies with what we know of the Essenes, but the similarities between them are so striking that they cannot be purely accidental.

The derivation of the word 'Essene' is not altogether certain, but it is probably to be taken as the Greek form of an Aramaic word which is the equivalent of the Hebrew *Ḥasidhim*. Indeed it is generally agreed that the Essenes' ancestry is to be found in those 'pious ones' of the Maccabaean and pre-Maccabaean period who resisted the inroads of Hellenism and showed such zeal for the Torah. In the Dead Sea Scrolls themselves there are several indications that seem to support this contention. One of these is in the Damascus Document,[1] which places the beginnings of the movement in 'an age of wrath' 390 years after the fall of Jerusalem in 586 B.C.[2] Some scholars have argued that, although the figure of 390 is probably to be taken only as 'a round number', it may not be very far out and so would point to the year 196 B.C. For another twenty years, we are told, this 'remnant of Israel' was 'like blind men groping for the way', until God raised up for them a leader, the 'Teacher of Righteousness', whom they regarded as their real founder. This takes us to the year 176 B.C., which is approximately the date when Antiochus Epiphanes ascended the throne (175 B.C.) and the Hasidim 'offered (themselves) willingly for the law' (1 Macc. 2[42 ff.]). Other scholars, however, would allow for a margin of error in the reference to the 390 years and bring the appearance of the Hasidim down to the year 175 B.C. ('an age of wrath' indeed), and so the emergence of the Teacher of Righteousness to the year 155 B.C. Others again regard the 390 as a symbolic figure of no real historical value and quite worthless for determining the appearance of the Teacher of Righteousness.

[1] This work, whose existence at Qumran is well attested by many fragments, was already known in two incomplete medieval copies discovered in 1896–7 in an old Cairo synagogue.

[2] With this we may compare Ezek. 4[4 f.] which tells how the prophet Ezekiel was to lie on his left side for 390 days, representing 390 years of captivity for 'the house of Israel'.

It is not at all surprising, in the light of these conflicting interpretations of but one passage in the Scrolls, that many different suggestions have been made concerning the identity of the Teacher of Righteousness, and also of 'the Wicked Priest' who appears there as his chief adversary and persecutor. Some have recognized the Teacher in Onias III, the last legitimate Zadokite High Priest, who was murdered in 171 B.C. (cf. 2 Macc. 4[33 ff.]); in this case the Wicked Priest would be Menelaus and 'the Man of Scorn' (another enemy of the sect), Antiochus Epiphanes. Other scholars, who place the anonymous Teacher of Righteousness twenty years or so later, identify the Wicked Priest with Jonathan the Maccabee. Others again identify this figure with Alexander Jannaeus (103–76 B.C.); in this case 'the Man of Scorn' might refer to the Pharisee, Simeon ben Shetaḥ. On this analysis the Teacher of Righteousness has sometimes been identified with Judah the Essene, who is mentioned just prior to the accession of Jannaeus (cf. *Antiquities* XIII. xi. 2; *War* I. iii. 5). Some have brought down the Teacher's date later still and have found him in one Onias the Just, who was stoned to death in 63 B.C. in the time of Hyrcanus II—who is himself identified with the Wicked Priest (cf. *Antiquities* XIV. ii. 1). Still others maintain that the phrase means simply 'True Teacher', designating the spiritual and judicial head of the community, and that the name may have been applied to a series of men holding the same office.

Quite apart from the identity of the Teacher of Righteousness we do not know the duration of his ministry or at what points in his career the events recorded about him actually happened. But it would seem that near the beginning of his ministry he and his followers, consisting of priests and Levites and faithful laymen, were forced to withdraw from Jerusalem in face of severe opposition. Leaving their priestly offices in the Temple they went into exile to 'the land of Damascus', by which may be meant Transjordan or possibly the Judaean desert, where they entered into 'a new Covenant', pledging their complete obedience to the Law of God. In their 'house of exile', however, they were sought out by the Wicked Priest, a man of considerable authority in Jerusalem who 'built his city of vanity with blood' and 'plotted against the Poor' (another name for the community); this man confronted the Teacher and his followers on their Day of Atonement 'to confuse them and to cause them to stumble', but God would take vengeance upon him and destroy him. His successors, called here 'the last priests of Jerusalem', would in the end be plundered by the Kittim, a foreign foe identified by some scholars with the Seleucids and by others with the Romans.

It is not clear whether this 'land of Damascus' to which the Teacher led the exiles was Qumran or whether certain of his followers subsequently moved there. Much depends on the date ascribed to his emergence as leader and on the length of his ministry, about which no information is given. More solid archaeological evidence is available, however, concerning the occupation of the Qumran site itself, which seems to have taken place during the last third of the second century B.C. A small number of bronze and silver coins dating from the time of John Hyrcanus (134–104 B.C.) suggests the presence there during this period of a rather sparsely populated community. From the reign of Alexander Jannaeus (103–76 B.C.), however, no fewer than 86 coins have been found, indicating a much bigger settlement, caused, we may guess, by an influx of Essenes following the persecutions of Jannaeus. The community, it would appear, continued in strength until about 31 B.C., when a severe earthquake (reported by Josephus) seriously disrupted its life. Many of the Essenes at this point may have sought refuge in Jerusalem, where, by this time, the hated Hasmonaeans had been replaced by Herod. Further evidence from coins shows that on the death of Herod in 4 B.C. the community entered upon a second stage of its life at Qumran, and continued until the second year of the Jewish War in A.D. 68, when their centre was attacked by a contingent of the Roman army and burned to the ground.

Concerning their *organization* and *membership* Josephus tells us that it was a hierarchical system ordered in four grades, and that admission to its ranks was no light matter, but involved three years of hard study and discipline for the 'novice' as he made his way step by step to full initiation. During his first preliminary year he remained outside the sect, being provided with a loin cloth, a white garment, and a trowel (cf. Deut. 23$^{12-13}$). At the end of this period, having given full proof of self-control, he took a ritual bath; then began a further two years' period at the end of which, having proved himself worthy, he was admitted to the communal meal and enrolled among the fully initiated. Although forbidden to take oaths as a general rule, on this occasion he was required to swear most solemn oaths to hold God in reverence, to remain faithful to his comrades, not to communicate their doctrines to others, and to preserve carefully the books of the sect together with the names of the angels. Betrayal of these oaths entailed severe punishments and even banishment from the community. This description finds general confirmation in the Scrolls, which again present the Essenes as a strongly hierarchical organization with graded ranks and officers vested with authority. The required quorum for any community or 'camp' was ten men, each 'camp' having two 'superiors', of whom one must be a priest. This ruling applied also to the sect as a whole. It is clear that what we have here is essentially a priestly hierarchy in which 'the sons of Zadok' wielded considerable authority.

There is conflicting evidence in our sources concerning the Essenes' attitude to *marriage*. Philo, for example, describes them as a celibate community. Josephus simply says that 'they hold marriage in little esteem' and adopt the children of others, whom they rear and train, although there is one order of Essenes which accepts the principle of marriage on the basis of a three-years' trial period. Some of the more important of the Scrolls assume the presence within the community of married members and their families, though restricting marriage to full members. The discovery of a number of female skeletons in the large cemetery adjoining the Qumran site is of significance in this connexion. It is clear, however, that these Essenes were strict in their interpretation of the traditional marriage laws and regarded highly the virtues of continence. In this as in other respects they had much in common with the Israelite warriors of ancient times, who had to set themselves apart from all such ritual impurity in time of war.

Concerning the *property* of the Essenes and the ordering of their communal life there is also a certain amount of ambiguity. Philo, for example, tells us that they relinquished all claims on private income and possessions, kept no slaves and made provision out of a common fund for those of their number who were unable to work by reason of old age or sickness. Josephus likewise states that they despised wealth, and refers to their communal ownership of possessions and to overseers elected by the whole community to manage the common fund. Pliny also describes them as men 'without money'. The evidence of the Scrolls on this matter is difficult to interpret, but they seem to indicate not a total sharing of wealth and property, but rather a compulsory contribution to a central fund out of which the many social needs of the community were met and from which, as in ancient Israel, the priests and the Levites were supported. Because of the danger of ritual contamination through contact with outsiders and their possessions a new member must wait for two years before transacting business with his fellow sectaries; for the same reason business transactions between members and outsiders were strictly limited or even forbidden.

The Essenes' devotion to *the study of the Scriptures* is commented upon by Josephus, who adds that some of them professed to foretell the future by reference to the holy books. Philo likewise tells how they studied the sacred writings for symbolic meanings. These references find verification and clarification in the Scrolls. We are told, for example, that when the full members of the community met together in groups of ten, one of their number was always engaged in the study or exposition of Scripture, whilst ordinary members were required to devote the first third of every night in a similar way, responding at intervals with appropriate blessings. As 'men of the Covenant' they were pledged to a life of obedience to the Law and the

Prophets in accordance with the interpretation given to them by 'the sons of Zadok'. In their interpretation of the Law they showed themselves in several respects to be much more strict than the other religious parties, and in their interpretation of the Prophets developed their own peculiar exegesis.[1] God, they believed, had given to the Teacher of Righteousness the true interpretation (Hebrew, *pēšer*) of the mystery (Hebrew, *raz*) contained in these books. Even the prophets themselves did not understand the true meaning of what they wrote; the Teacher of Righteousness, in his interpretation, demonstrated that they had in fact been writing about 'the last times' in which they, the Essenes, were then living.

The Qumran Scrolls, moreover, bring into clearer focus what we already know from Josephus concerning their early morning acts of *worship*. Their habit of offering prayer at sunrise, for example, is no doubt the truth which lies behind his strange claim that they worshipped the sun! Like the writers of the Book of Jubilees and 1 Enoch they adhered to a solar calendar, different from that followed in Jerusalem, by which they ordered their festivals, a fact which explains why the Wicked Priest, for example, was able to come upon the Essenes 'on their Day of Atonement', which would not be a holy day to him. The most memorable of their feasts, however, was no doubt at Pentecost, when, for the renewal of the Covenant, Essenes from all over Palestine would gather at Qumran and pledge their obedience to God and their loyalty to one another.

Contradictory reports are again given in our sources concerning the Essenes' attitude to *the Temple and sacrifice*. Philo, for example, states that they offered no sacrifices, whereas Josephus records that they sent their gifts to the Temple and offered their sacrifices there under special conditions of purity. For fear of ritual contamination they would not use 'the common court of the Temple' where non-Essenes were gathered, but approached the Temple by some other way. This may well explain the reference to 'the Essene gate' elswhere in Josephus (cf. *War* v.

[1] For a list of their exegetical works see p. 182.

iv. 2). Josephus' account is confirmed by the Scrolls, which tell how offerings were to be brought to the Jerusalem Temple, though never on a Sabbath day or by anyone in a state of ritual impurity. More important than the offering of sacrifices, however, was their responsibility to offer themselves, for they firmly believed that it was their destiny, by submission and suffering, to make expiation for the sins of the people in the manner of the Suffering Servant of the Lord.

Two important ceremonies among the Essenes, already noted by Josephus, were *ritual washings* and *the sacred meal*. As we have seen, admission to membership of the community was marked at the close of the preliminary year by a ritual bath, probably on the Day of Pentecost and in the presence of the whole assembled congregation. The new member, on repentance of his sins, entered one of the large baptisteries still visible at Qumran, was immersed in the waters, and so entered into the fellowship of the Covenant. It would appear that this rite was repeated by fully initiated members of the sect each Day of Pentecost, when, in order of rank, they renewed their Covenant vows. The second type of ceremony, whose origins are probably to be traced back to ancient Temple usage, was the sacred meal, presided over by the priest. This was reserved for those who had completed their one preliminary year and two probationary years and so were fully initiated members. It was not, however, simply a relic of the past; above all it was an anticipation of the Messianic Banquet (cf. Isa. 25[6]) to be celebrated in the coming kingdom, to which reference is made also in the apocryphal and rabbinic literature and in the New Testament (cf. Luke 13[28 f.], 22[30 ff.]; Rev. 19[9]).

Characteristic of the teaching of the Scrolls is the expressed belief in a developed *angelology* in which 'the prince of light' battles against 'the angel of darkness' for control of the universe, and 'the spirit of truth' struggles with 'the spirit of error' for control of the heart of man. But such 'ethical dualism' does not go beyond the bounds of biblical monotheism, nor could it, for the Essenes in this respect stood in the true Hebrew tradition. Their attitude to *idolatry*, for example, was one of vehement opposition. The Christian bishop Hippolytus tells us that they would not even handle a coin with the imprint of an image on it or pass through a city gate surmounted by a statue.

Like many of their fellow Jews, moreover, they believed in a *life after death*. Josephus states that they expressed this in terms of the immortality of the soul, but Hippolytus claims that they believed also in the resurrection of the body. The evidence of the Scrolls is once more very clear, but seems to indicate that they accepted a doctrine of resurrection. This conclusion finds some support in the alignment of the graves in the cemetery at Qumran, at which, contrary to common Jewish practice, the dead were buried with their heads to the south so that, presumably, they would rise facing the north, where, it was believed, Paradise was situated. Fragments of the Book of Daniel found at Qumran show that the Essenes there must have been at least familiar with the resurrection belief.

It is in the expression of their *eschatological beliefs*, however, that the Scrolls are of the greatest interest. Their teaching concerning the messianic hope is, as we have seen, a very debatable point.[1] Three 'messianic' figures appear prominently there—the Prophet (cf. Deut. 18[18 f.]), 'the anointed one' of Aaron, and 'the anointed one' of Israel—the last-named being the promised deliverer of popular Jewish expectation at whose side the anointed priest would stand in the last days. According to the Damascus Document the messianic age would appear forty years after the death of the Teacher of Righteousness and would be accompanied by fearful portents already familiar to us from the apocalyptic literature of this period. Its coming would be the signal for the beginning of a forty years' war (described in great detail in the War Scroll), in which at length 'the sons of light' (the faithful Israel, i.e. presumably the Essenes) would overcome 'the sons of darkness' and receive salvation in the new age soon to dawn.

A study of these three leading parties in the pre-Christian era demonstrates how heterogenous the Judaism of that period was. The day was to come when, after the fall of Jerusalem in

[1] See pp. 145 f.

A.D. 70, 'normative' Judaism would establish itself under the authority of the Pharisees, who, alone of all the major parties, survived the destruction of the state. But that day was not yet. Meanwhile, within the divided ranks of Judaism there were many who waited and watched and prayed.

## PART III

# THE LITERATURE

## XI

## CANONICAL AND EXTRA-CANONICAL BOOKS

THE period from Alexander the Great to Herod the Great was a time of remarkable literary activity, in which the Jews of both Palestine and the Dispersion had a significant part to play. The writer of Ecclesiastes no doubt had in mind the voluminous literary output of the Greek world towards the end of the third century B.C. when he said, 'Of making many books there is no end, and much study is a weariness of the flesh' ($12^{12}$); but his words could have applied almost equally well to Jewish literature also, particularly in the two centuries or so which followed. Many of these works are known to us only by their titles or by brief reference or quotation in other literature. Those that have survived are of diverse kinds, ranging from history to legend, from philosophy to fiction, from poetry to propaganda tracts. Apart from the so-called 'oral tradition',[1] which did not assume written form until about A.D. 210 and can be left out of account for our purpose, those Jewish writings which had any claims to sacredness came to be divided into two classes. Some acquired canonical status, i.e. were regarded as authoritative in matters of religion; others, though recognized as sacred, were

---

[1] See pp. 117 f.

not given the same position of authority. These extra-canonical writings, to which the name 'apocryphal' is often given, were called by the Rabbis 'the outside books'.

## 1. *The canonical Scriptures*

If it is difficult to trace the history of the Old Testament literature, it is much more difficult to trace the idea of canonicity that applied to it. It is clear, however, that the Old Testament Canon did not emerge at some fixed point in time by the vote of a council or committee; rather, it was a growing thing whose roots went far back into Israel's history, to codes, laws, and oracles which, by virtue of their place in ancient tradition as well as their own intrinsic worth, assumed a distinct authority. This authority was confirmed by their use through successive generations in the Temple and synagogue liturgies and in the private devotions of ordinary men and women. During this period those books which ultimately achieved full canonical authority found their own level, as it were, on three distinct planes, representing the three sections into which the Old Testament came to be divided—the Law, the Prophets, and the Writings, the first of which held the highest place in the esteem of the people.

The acceptance as authoritative of the Law book found in Josiah's reign, and of the one read later by Ezra (397 B.C.?), provide examples of the way in which a written work could become in a real sense 'canonical'. But the process must be much more ancient than this. The divine word carried with it an authority which, when such works were collected, would tend to give a special place to the document so formed. An important landmark in the recognition of the authoritative character of the Law is the Samaritan schism (*c.* 350 B.C.). For Jews and Samaritans alike the Law held a central place; but the significant fact here is that the Samaritan version of the Law is substantially the same as that of the Jews. This indicates that it must have been taken over by the Samaritans *before* the final breach, by which time it already had a fixed form and a real measure of authority. This claim to authority no doubt became more firmly established in the succeeding century and a half, so that by the beginning of the second century B.C. testimony to its canonical authority is clearly given in such books as Tobit (*c.* 200 B.C.), which holds the Law in great reverence, and Ben Sira (*c.* 180 B.C.), which likens the Law to Wisdom itself (cf. 24²³, ²⁵).

The canonicity of the Prophets is even more difficult to trace. From earliest times the spoken words of the prophets were acknowledged as authoritative utterances; but the first indication of an authoritative *body* of prophetic writings is given by Ben Sira. In his book he clearly shows a knowledge of most of the Old Testament as we know it, including 'the Former Prophets' (Joshua, Judges, Samuel, Kings) and the three major prophets (Isaiah, Jeremiah, Ezekiel), and actually refers (cf. 49¹⁰) to 'the twelve (minor) prophets' as a distinct collection (cf. Chs. 44–49). These facts indicate clearly that by this time the prophetic corpus was closed and was acknowledged as canonical. They explain, too, why Daniel was not included within the prophetic Canon as might have been expected, for it was not written until about fifteen years after Ben Sira's work. Indeed we note that Daniel itself refers back to the prophecy of Jeremiah as sacred Scripture (cf. Dan. 9²). Several factors no doubt determined the fixing of the prophetic Canon around 200 B.C., one of the most significant being the belief which arose during this period that prophetic inspiration had ceased in the days of Ezra and that the voice of prophecy was now dumb (cf. 1 Macc. 4⁴⁶, 9²⁷, 14⁴¹; Ps. 74⁹; *Against Apion* I. 8; *Antiquities* XI. vi. 1).

Despite this theory, however, it would appear that prophecy did in fact continue even after the time of Ezra, and that certain oracles or collections of oracles have been preserved and incorporated in the writings of other canonical prophets. It is possible that two such collections are represented by Zech. 9–14 and Isa. 24–27, which may have been composed as late as the Hellenistic period.[1]

[1] See pp. 200 ff., 213 ff.

Another landmark in tracing this idea of canonicity is provided by Ben Sira's grandson, who translated his grandfather's book into Greek and added his own prologue (*c.* 132 B.C.). There he refers to 'the law and the prophets and the others that followed them', 'the law and the prophets and the other books of our fathers', and 'the law itself, the prophecies, and the rest of the books'. This reference confirms that the Law and the Prophets were by this time fixed canonical literature, and indicates that there was a third class of books of religious value which was as yet quite fluid and had not acquired a name of its own. Not until New Testament times did this third section of the Canon become clearly determined, and even then some doubt remained over certain books. In Luke 24⁴⁴ we read of 'the law of Moses, and the prophets, and the psalms'. This last expression may indicate that the third section was still undetermined; on the other hand 'the psalms', being the first and most significant book in the Writings, may stand here for the whole collection or perhaps Luke is simply referring to the synagogue use of these three portions of Scripture. Further evidence is given by the writer of 2 Esdras (*c.* A.D. 90), who alludes to the twenty-four books of the Old Testament Canon (cf. 14⁴⁴ ᶠᶠ·), which, by a different division, appear in the English versions as thirty-nine; and also by Josephus, who gives the number as twenty-two (cf. *Against Apion* I. 7 f.), which may represent a different grouping or else indicates that he omitted two of the disputed books.

The canonical authority of three books in particular (Song of Songs, Ecclesiastes, and Esther) was for some time seriously challenged by a number of Rabbis, although the third of these enjoyed no small popularity. In course of time, however, the need came to be felt for a more definitive position and so at the Council of Jamnia (*c.* A.D. 90) confirmation was given to the books contained in the third section of the Canon. By this date the belief had emerged that the canonicity of a book depended upon whether it had been written between Moses and the death of Artaxerxes in 424 B.C. (cf. *Against Apion* I. 8). This did not exclude such works as Esther and Daniel, as might be imagined, for in each case the date of the book was presumed to be that of the events recorded in the story. The assumption of this theory that prophecy had ceased from the time of the Persian period, together with the claim that only those books which were originally written in Hebrew were acceptable, explains the exclusion of certain other sacred writings which might otherwise have aspired to a position of canonical authority.

## 2. *The apocryphal books*

By about the year 250 B.C. the Law had been translated into Greek, and a hundred or so years later the Prophets were likewise available, as the Prologue to Ben Sira testifies (*c.* 132 B.C.). It is much less certain when the translation of the Writings took place and at what point they were accepted by the Jews of the Dispersion as canonical Scripture. In Alexandria, as in Palestine, there was no acknowledged list of such books, at least in pre-Christian times. The Greek version differed from the Hebrew in two respects—the books outside the Law were arranged in a different order, and it included a number of books and parts of books not found in its Hebrew counterpart. It is misleading, however, to speak of 'the Greek (or Alexandrian) Canon' over against 'the Hebrew Canon'. There was in reality only one Canon, that of the Hebrew Scriptures, by which was meant virtually the Law and (to a lesser degree) the Prophets. In the Greek version no recognizable distinction was made between those books which came to be known as 'the Writings' and those others which were accepted alongside them. It is these additional books, found in the Greek version, which for the most part comprise what we know as 'the Apocrypha'. In the Authorized Version they are twelve in number, one of which (2 Esdras) is not found in the Greek version but appears in the Latin Vulgate.

Only a small proportion of these was originally composed in Greek, viz. the Wisdom of Solomon, the decree of Ahasuerus in Esther $13^{1-7}$ and $16^{1-24}$, and 2 Macc. $2^{19}-15^{39}$. The rest,

though gaining popularity in their Greek version, were originally written in either Hebrew or Aramaic in Palestine. Apart
from 1 Esdras (before 200 B.C.) and 2 Esdras (c. A.D. 90) the
books of the Apocrypha were composed during the last two
centuries B.C.

This list, however, does not exhaust those works which the
Rabbis called 'the outside books' and to which the designation
'apocryphal' can be given. There were many others, lying outside both the Old Testament Canon and the Apocrypha, which
were nevertheless regarded by many as sacred writings. They
are generally, if not altogether accurately, referred to as 'the
pseudepigrapha', most of them being classified as 'apocalypses'
or, at any rate, as containing apocalyptic elements. There is no
agreed list of these 'extra-apocryphal' books, but those generally
classified as such are as follows.

*With a Palestinian origin*:

    i. 1 Enoch 1–36, 37–71, 72–82, 83–90, 91–108 (from c. 164
        B.C. onwards).
    ii. The Book of Jubilees (c. 150 B.C.).
    iii. The Testaments of the Twelve Patriarchs (latter part of
        second century B.C.?).
    iv. The Psalms of Solomon (near middle of first century B.C.).
    v. The Testament of Job (first century B.C.).
    vi. The Assumption of Moses (A.D. 6–30).
    vii. The Life of Adam and Eve or the Apocalypse of Moses
        (shortly before A.D. 70).
    viii. The Lives of the Prophets (first century A.D.).
    ix. The Testament of Abraham (first century A.D.).
    x. The Apocalypse of Abraham 9–32 (A.D. 70–100).
    xi. 2 Baruch or The Apocalypse of Baruch (after A.D. 90).

*With a Hellenistic origin*:

    xii. The Sibylline Oracles: Book III (from c. 150 B.C. onwards).
                            Book IV (c. A.D. 80).
                            Book V (before A.D. 130).
    xiii. The Letter of Aristeas (near beginning of first century B.C.?)
    xiv. 3 Maccabees (near end of first century B.C.).
    xv. 4 Maccabees (near beginning of first century A.D.).

A view of the Wadi Qumran looking towards the south, with the Dead Sea in the distance. An opening to Cave 4 can be seen in the cliff-face near the centre of the picture. The ancient ruins of Khirbet Qumran, situated on a plateau off-picture to the left, mark the headquarters of the community who stored away their scrolls in the surrounding caves probably in the year A.D. 68, when about to be attacked by a contingent of the Roman army.

    xvi. 2 Enoch or The Book of the Secrets of Enoch (first century A.D.?).

    xvii. 3 Baruch (A.D. 100–75).

## 3. *The Qumran literature*

The literature of this period has been greatly augmented by the discovery of the Dead Sea Scrolls, the contents of the Essene library hidden away for safety in the Qumran caves in the first century A.D. The Qumran sectaries were keen students of the Scriptures, as the presence of many biblical fragments and scrolls shows, and clearly regarded the Law and the Prophets as authoritative. It is equally clear that the apocryphal and 'pseudepigraphical' types of books were also very popular among them, especially those books of an apocalyptic character.

For example, fragments have been found of Ben Sira, Tobit, 1 Enoch, the Testament of Levi, and Jubilees as well as of the canonical apocalypse, the Book of Daniel. Other fragments indicate that they were familiar with a much wider range of writings than these, of an esoteric and eschatological kind. Among them are the so-called Book of Mysteries, a Midrash (Commentary) on the Last Days, a Description of the New Jerusalem, an Angelic Liturgy, and two works belonging to the Danielic cycle of tradition, viz. the Prayer of Nabonidus and a Pseudo-Daniel Apocalypse.

Not all the books found at Qumran, of course, were necessarily written by the sectaries or even represented their beliefs. Nevertheless, certain of them are clearly 'sectarian documents' whose religious outlook shows a close affinity with that of the known apocalyptic writings, especially in their teaching concerning the messianic hope and 'the last things'. The following is a list of the more important of them, the dates of which probably range from the second century B.C. to the first century A.D.

i. Commentaries on Isaiah, Hosea, Micah, Nahum, Habakkuk, Zephaniah, and Ps. 37 together with a Genesis Apocryphon.
ii. The Zadokite Document or the The Damascus Document.
iii. The Manual of Discipline or The Rule of the Community.
iv. The Rule of the Congregation.
v. A Scroll of Benedictions.
vi. A Messianic Anthology or The Testimonies Scroll.
vii. Psalms (or Hymns) of Thanksgiving.
viii. The War of the Sons of Light against the Sons of Darkness or The Rule for the Final War.

It is clear from an examination of the Judaism of this period that there was no fixed standard of 'orthodoxy' or any consensus of opinion concerning the scope of authoritative Scripture. On the contrary, widely divergent views were held. The Qumran sectaries, as we have seen, valued highly certain sacred writings which had a particular interest or appeal to themselves, and the same must have been true of other groups or parties within Judaism. Josephus informs us that the Essenes,

Jars from Qumran, used for storing the Dead Sea Scrolls hidden away in the surrounding caves. The jars are contemporary with the date when the scrolls were hidden in the caves, probably during the period A.D. 60–73 when the Jews revolted against the rule of Rome. They are similar in style to the domestic jars in use at that time for storing honey, wine, and grain.

for example, took a solemn oath 'to preserve carefully the books of the sect' (*War* II. viii. 7). Thus, although the need was felt for an authoritative Canon and such recognition was given early on to the Torah and the Prophets, this did not automatically involve precise definition of what was or was not sacred Scripture. This stage was reached only at the end of the process, when the late-first-century Rabbis, in the light of their changed circumstances after the fall of Jerusalem, set themselves to define more precisely the nature and basis of their religious faith. Hence the significance of the Council of Jamnia about the year A.D. 90.

In the following pages a few of the books noted above—canonical, apocryphal, and 'sectarian'—will, where possible, be examined against the historical and religious background of the age in which they were written.

# XII

## HISTORY AND ROMANCE

### 1. *1 and 2 Maccabees*

THE First Book of Maccabees, as it is called in the AV, RV, and RSV, is a valuable historical source for the period between the accession of Antiochus Epiphanes in 175 B.C. and the death of Simon in 134 B.C. There is reason to believe that its original title may have been 'The Book of the House of the Hasmonaeans' or perhaps 'The Book of the House of the Princes of God'. If, as has been argued,[1] the word 'Hasmonaeans' means 'princes' and does not derive from the name of Judas' ancestor Asamonaeus, as has been generally believed, then these two titles have the same meaning. There can be little doubt that the Greek version which has survived is based on a Hebrew original, and that the author was a Palestinian Jew whose sympathies were with the Hasmonaean House. Towards the end of the book he refers to 'the chronicles of (the) high priesthood' of John Hyrcanus, which suggests that it may have been written during the latter part of Hyrcanus' reign or in the years following his death. No reference is made by Josephus to the last three chapters of the book, and for this reason a number of scholars conclude that they were added by another hand at a later date.

The book begins with a brief account of Alexander's conquests and the subsequent division of his kingdom (cf. 1¹⁻⁹), then outlines the causes of the Maccabaean Revolt against Antiochus Epiphanes (cf. 1¹⁰⁻⁶⁴) and its beginnings under Mattathias and his sons (cf. 2¹⁻⁷⁰). A fairly detailed account is next given of the events which took place under the leadership of Judas (cf. 3¹⁻9²²), Jonathan (cf. 9²³⁻12⁵³), and Simon (cf. 13¹⁻16¹⁷). The book closes with a brief reference to the rule of

[1] Cf. S. Tedesche, *The First Book of Maccabees*, 1950, pp. 247 ff.

John Hyrcanus (cf. 16$^{18-24}$). The writer alludes to a number of written documents of a diplomatic character, from some of which he quotes; he may have had access to these in the Temple archives, where, it seems likely, official documents and letters of state were preserved. His detailed account of the exploits of Judas indicates that he was familiar with a 'Judas tradition', either in written or in oral form. As already noted, he refers to the 'chronicles' of John Hyrcanus (16$^{23}$ f.); if Hyrcanus' predecessors in the High Priesthood also kept such chronicles, as seems likely, then these too would prove a valuable source of information. At times, however, so vivid are his descriptions of places and events that much of what he writes must surely have been derived from actual eye-witnesses or, in the case of the later events, from his personal experience. There are certain inaccuracies in his references, but these do not cast any serious doubt on his general trustworthiness. Over against pagan writers like Polybius, Pompeius Trogus, Livy, and Appian, whose writings cast broken and fragmentary shafts of light on this period, the author of 1 Maccabees shows himself to be an accurate and largely unbiased historian; his book provides an invaluable source for a period which would otherwise remain for the most part obscure.

It has generally been agreed that the author was a man with Sadducaean sympathies. For example, he makes no reference to angels and spirits or to belief in the resurrection where mention might readily have been made (cf. 2$^{51}$, 3$^{59}$, 9$^{9}$ f.); he is less strict than the Pharisees in his interpretation of Sabbath observance (cf. 2$^{41}$, 9$^{43}$ ff.); he shows great interest in the Law of Moses and in the Temple worship, and speaks highly of the High Priest (cf. 5$^{62}$, 13$^{3}$, 14$^{25}$, 16$^{2}$). This identification, however, must not be pressed, for there is no hint here of a critical attitude to the Pharisees, such as might be expected from a member of the Sadducaean party. Indeed, the author may have written his book prior to the final breach between the two parties which took place probably towards the end of John Hyrcanus' reign and may have belonged to neither. What is clear is that he was a deeply pious Jew who, for all his dependence on the might of the Maccabees, set his trust in God and expressed his reliance on intercessory prayer. He was, moreover, steeped in the sacred Scriptures, holding in great reverence not only the Law (cf. $1^{56\,f.}$), but also the Prophets (cf. $9^{54}$). The period of prophetic inspiration was past, but the time would come when God would raise up a true prophet, to whose word the people would at last pay heed (cf. $4^{46}$, $9^{27}$, $14^{41}$). He sees in the glories of Simon's reign an earnest of the great messianic age in which God's people would receive the reward of loyalty and faithfulness in the face of tyranny and oppression (cf. $14^{4-15}$).

The Second Book of Maccabees differs from the first in two respects, its range and its aim. First, the period it covers is much shorter, extending from just before the accession of Antiochus Epiphanes in 175 B.C. to the defeat of Nicanor in 160 B.C., i.e. it covers roughly the same ground as 1 Macc. 1–7. Second, its aim is not so much to write an impartial history as to demonstrate God's deliverance of his people in time of adversity, i.e. its purpose is apologetic rather than historical. Apart from the two letters at the beginning, which probably represent Hebrew originals, the book was no doubt written in Greek by a Jew of the Dispersion, possibly of Alexandria. Its writer is generally referred to as 'the epitomist', for the greater part of the book, we are told, is an epitome or abridgement of five volumes by a certain Jason of Cyrene (cf. $2^{19-23}$). It is not known who this Jason was or when he wrote his books. The date of 2 Maccabees itself is almost equally uncertain, but perhaps it is to be placed some time early in the first century B.C. There are several indications in the book that the epitomist belonged to the Hasidic tradition, from which the Pharisees and Essenes both emerged, which was at this time critical of the Hasmonaean House. For example, Judas is portrayed as the leader of the Hasidim (cf. $14^6$); approval is given to the decision not to fight on the Sabbath day (cf. $6^{11}$, $8^{25\,ff.}$, $12^{38}$, $15^{1\,f.}$), and any allusion to such fighting is omitted (cf. 1 Macc. $2^{41}$); and belief is expressed in the resurrection of the dead (cf. $7^{9,\,14,\,23,\,36}$, $12^{43}$).

The prevailing theme of the book is the glory and honour of the Jerusalem Temple, a fact which may reflect hostility on the part of the writer towards the Jewish temple in Leontopolis in Egypt. Pride of place is given to the Feast of Hanukkah or Dedication, to be celebrated on Kislev 25th, which commemorated the purification of the Temple by Judas after its pollution at the hands of Antiochus Epiphanes. According to 1 Maccabees the period of desecration was three years (cf. $1^{54-59}$, $4^{52}$), whereas according to 2 Maccabees it was two years (cf. $10^3$). Another disparity between the two books is that in 1 Maccabees Antiochus Epiphanes dies after the rededication of the Temple (cf. $6^{17}$), whereas in 2 Maccabees it is before that event (cf. $1^{11-18}$, $9^1-10^9$). Such discrepancies are bound up with the apparent difference in chronology between the two books, 2 Maccabees consistently counting one year in advance of 1 Maccabees. Both make use of the Syrian calendar, which calculates the beginning of the Seleucid era from the year 312/11 B.C. Towards the end of the book mention is made of a second joyful feast, known as Nicanor's Day, to be celebrated annually on Adar 13th in commemoration of a great Jewish victory over the Syrian general of that name (cf. $15^{27-35}$). This feast, we are told (cf. $15^{36}$), was the day before the Feast of Purim, celebrating Mordecai's victory over his enemies as recorded in the Book of Esther.

The epitomist, however, is not concerned simply with the exploits of the Jews celebrated in the great Feasts of Hanukkah and Nicanor's Day; he is much more concerned to demonstrate the sovereign power of God in saving his people. For this purpose he makes use of colourful legend (cf. the stories of the martyrdom of the aged Eleazar and the Jewish mother and her seven sons in $6^1-7^{42}$) and of graphic stories in which God intervenes in miraculous ways to effect deliverance. Here we read of 'appearances which come from heaven' ($2^{21}$), of angel warriors reinforcing the Jewish armies (cf. $11^{6, 8}$, $15^{23}$), and of visions and dreams ($15^{11}$) and apparitions in the sky of supernatural horsemen clad in gold and mounted on magnificent steeds (cf. $3^{25}$, $10^{29}$ ff., $11^8$). But God manifests himself not only in power, but also in justice. Men will receive just retribution for their sins; as they made others to suffer so they themselves will suffer (cf. $4^{38}$, $5^{10}$, $9^{5 \text{ f.}}$, $13^{4-8}$). Those who appear to escape punishment now will in the end receive it in good measure (cf. $6^{12 \text{ ff.}}$). Israel is God's people and will not escape punishment by reason of her apostasy (cf. $5^{17-40}$, $12^{40}$); but those who have died for his laws will be raised in resurrection to inherit the kingdom (cf. $7^{9 \text{ ff.}}$, $12^{43}$).

## 2. *Esther*

The story of the Book of Esther is set in Susa during the reign of Ahasuerus (i.e. Xerxes I, 486–465 B.C.), King of Persia and Media. It describes the fortunes of the Jews in that part of the eastern Dispersion and tells how Queen Vashti was replaced by a beautiful Jewish maiden, Esther, whose cousin and guardian, Mordecai, was opposed by the King's grand vizier Haman. Haman persuaded the King to sign a decree confirming the slaughter of all Jews in his realm, which was to take place on the 13th day of Adar (February–March). With Esther's help the order was revoked and Haman was hanged on the gallows he had prepared for Mordecai. On the very day decreed for their own slaughter the Jews slew no fewer than 75,000 of their enemies in the provinces, and continued their work of vengeance throughout the following day in the capital, where another 810 were slain. The two days following this massacre, 14th and 15th Adar, were to be observed henceforth as the Feast of Purim, so called because Haman had determined their destruction by 'lot' (Hebrew, *pûr*).

The book purports to be an historical record in keeping with the historical books of the Old Testament; like Kings and Chronicles it refers the reader to certain 'chronicles' (cf. $10^2$) for verification of the facts it records. The author shows an intimate knowledge of Persian customs and the ways of the Persian court with which his story deals; his characters have the appearance of real people; indeed the name of his chief character, Mordecai, is actually mentioned elsewhere in the

Old Testament as one of the exiles carried off by Nebuchad-nezzar (cf. Ezra 2²; Neh. 7⁷), and appears again in a cuneiform tablet with reference to a Persian official in Susa during the reign of Xerxes I. Despite all these appearances, however, the book is generally regarded, not as an historical record at all, but rather as an historical romance in which fact and fiction are skilfully interwoven to serve the purpose the writer had in mind. It is thus quite beside the point to demonstrate that Mordecai, deported from Jerusalem in 597 B.C., would be well over 100 years of age by the time of Xerxes' reign and that his cousin Esther would be not much less! Such details, together with certain other 'discrepancies', would seem to confirm that this is an historical novel whose message matters more than its cataloguing of historical facts. S. Talmon,[1] however, argues that this description does not do justice to the composite literary nature of the book; he styles it rather as 'a historicized wisdom-tale', in which the several characters are virtually 'wisdom types' portraying the virtues of 'applied wisdom'. Such wisdom stories appear in Egyptian and Mesopotamian literature and find an echo in earlier biblical accounts, especially the Joseph story, which reveals strong wisdom elements.

But what was the purpose the author had in mind? It was to provide an historical occasion for the popular Feast of Purim, for which there was no basis in the Law, and at the same time to explain the different customs prevailing in his day with regard to the celebration of the Feast, and in parti-cular to justify its observance on 14th and 15th Adar. The section 9²⁰–10³, in which these two dates are specified, are regarded by many scholars as a slightly later addition to the book. Nothing is known for certain about the origins of this Feast of Purim, but it was probably a heathen celebration which the Jews of the eastern Dispersion took over and adapted to their own use. Attempts have been made to connect it with known Babylonian and Persian festivals and to find traces of early mythology in the several characters who appear

[1] ' "Wisdom" in the Book of Esther', *Vetus Testamentum*, vol. xiii, 1963, pp. 419–55.

in the book. Thus Esther and Mordecai are said to represent the Babylonian deities Ishtar and Marduk, whilst Vashti and Haman represent the Elamite deities Mashti and Humman. Such mythological references, however, even if they can be justified, have no meaning for the story as it is now written. The figures who appear in its pages are not gods and goddesses but men and women.

The story of the book, like the Feast itself, probably originated in the eastern Dispersion and may be based on an actual persecution of the Jews there. It may indeed have been in circulation in Babylonia as early as the fifth century B.C., and subsequently adopted, with certain modifications, by the Jews of Palestine perhaps some time during the second century B.C. Ben Sira, writing *c.* 180 B.C., makes no reference to either Mordecai or Esther in his list of heroes, nor is the Feast of Purim mentioned in 1 Macc. 7[49], where some reference might have been expected. The first significant passage is 2 Macc. 15[36], which names Nicanor's Day (cf. 1 Macc. 7[49]) as 'the day before Mordecai's day'.

The story it tells is marked by a strong nationalistic spirit that must have made inspiring reading for the Jewish people facing such odds, be it in their own land or in the far-flung Dispersion. The book makes no direct reference to God or to religion, except in its allusion to the founding of the Purim Festival. Nevertheless, its intense nationalism shows its author's concern for the preservation of his people's religion, and Mordecai and Esther are depicted as types of faith and righteous conduct. Its somewhat grim character may not be altogether attractive, but the book arises out of a situation of urgency, in which the Jews, it would seem, were being forced to give up their own identity. In the Greek version of the book there are certain 'Additions' to the Hebrew text, amounting to 107 verses, which appear under this name in the Apocrypha. For the most part these are embellishments of a specifically religious character which try to make good this apparent deficiency in the rest of the book.

For some time the claims of Esther to canonicity were not

recognized by prominent Rabbis, and even when official recognition was at last given it failed to meet with whole-hearted approval either within Judaism or in the Christian Church. In course of time, however, by reason of its witness to the origin of such an important festival, it achieved great popularity and was by some placed second only to the Torah itself.

### a. AHASUERUS THE GREAT $(1^{1-4})$

1. The book begins, as do Joshua, Judges, and Ruth, with the conventional phrase, 'And it came to pass' (cf. AV), thus giving the impression that it is a genuine historical record instead of an historical novel.

The name *Ahasuerus* represents the Hebrew *'Aḥašweroš*, which in turn represents the Persian *Kšayarša*; this takes the form *Xerxes* in Greek, i.e. Xerxes I (485–465 B.C.). The LXX mistakenly gives 'Artaxerxes' here.

*one hundred and twenty seven provinces*. These are the 'satrapies' into which the Persian empire was divided. This number is repeated in $9^{30}$ and is given as 120 in Dan. $6^2$. The historian Herodotus gives it as 20. Perhaps the larger number in our text indicates provincial sub-divisions under the control of governors (cf. $3^{12}$), or perhaps it has no reference to actual historical fact at all, its purpose being to magnify the greatness of the empire.

2. *in Susa the capital*. This phrase refers to 'the fortress' in Susa, the Persian capital, where Xerxes, like his father Darius I before him, took up his winter residence.

3–4. *the army chiefs*: lit. the army. This may refer to Xerxes' chosen bodyguard. It is generally taken to mean '(the officers of) the army', who feasted for *a hundred and eight days*.

### b. THE FEAST OF PURIM $(9^{20-32})$

In these verses the author explains how the Feast of Purim received its name and why it should be observed regularly by all Jews. It is enjoined in a letter sent by Mordecai (20–22) and confirmed in a joint letter from Mordecai and Esther (29–32); moreover, it is given a place within Jewish tradition and is accepted as obligatory by the Jewish people (23, 27). It is to be observed annually on Adar 14th and 15th (21).

26. *they called these days Purim*. The Feast is now given its name for the first time and its derivation is explained. It derives, says the writer, from the word 'pûr' (cf. $3^7$, $9^{24, 26}$). This is apparently a foreign word, for it is translated in the Hebrew text by the word *gôral*, meaning 'lot'; the Hebrew masculine plural ending 'îm' is added to give the hybrid form 'Purim'. It recalls the reversal of Haman's fortunes when he fixed by 'pur' the slaughter of the Jews (cf. $3^7$). The interpretation given by the writer may be quite fanciful or it may be true; it is quite impossible to say.

27–28. *these two days*: i.e. Adar 14th and 15th, as indicated in vv. 17–19. The Feast, though not decreed in the Torah, is nevertheless traditionally, and so legally, binding on all Jews and their descendants and also on *all who joined them*, i.e. proselytes.

31. The celebration is to commemorate the change of their lot from *fasts* and *lamenting* to feasts and rejoicing. Some commentators see here a command to observe a fast prior to the feast. In later centuries Adar 13th was in fact set aside as a day of fasting in commemoration of the fast decreed by Esther in $4^{16}$.

### 3. *The Song of Songs (Canticles)*

In the AV, RV, and RSV this book has the title 'The Song of Songs'; in Roman Catholic versions it is known as 'Canticles' after the Latin *Canticum Canticorum*. In the Hebrew text the title reads, 'The Song of Songs which is Solomon's'. This construction (like 'the Holy of Holies') expresses a superlative in Hebrew, and means here 'The best song of all'. Solomon's name appears six times in its pages ($1^5$, $3^{7, 9, 11}$, $8^{11, 12}$), and elsewhere he is said to have a reputation as a song writer (cf. 1 Kings 4³²). There is no real ground, however, for crediting him with this book. Not only is it out of character, the book itself does not make such a claim. The title, which ascribes it to him, does not necessarily imply that he was the author, and in any case its language shows that it is probably an editorial addition.

The rather peculiar language of the book, which has something in common with certain post-exilic writings, gives the clearest clue to its date; the occurrence in it of at least one Greek word (*'appiryon*, 'palanquin') in 3⁹ and a Persian word (*pardes*, 'orchard') in 4¹² suggests a date about the third century B.C. There was no small controversy about its claims to canonicity; but at the Council of Jamnia in A.D. 90 it was strongly supported by Rabbi Akiba and thereafter gained general acceptance. As part of the Hebrew Canon it was naturally in turn accepted by the Christian Church.

The book consists of a number of love lyrics of indeterminate number, often of an erotic character, expressing with perfect frankness and a complete lack of self-consciousness the courtship- and marriage-relationship. It probably contains traditional material, some of which may go back to a much earlier date; but the pattern of the book, such as it is, perhaps suggests a unity of authorship. Its descriptions of rustic scenes, its choice of language, and its topographical allusions all suggest that it originated in the north of the country rather than in the south.

The chief interest in the book centres in the method of its interpretation. Most popular has been the allegorical approach which for centuries has found vogue among both Jews and Christians. In Jewish circles the lover and his beloved were taken to represent God and his people Israel, whilst in the Christian Church they have generally symbolized Christ and his Church or else Christ and the individual soul. Such interpretation is not surprising, for in the Old and New Testaments references are to be found to the divine-human relationship in terms of a man and his bride. But helpful though this approach may be for the purpose of religious devotion, there is no hint of any such allegorizing in the Song of Songs itself. The difficulty of such an approach can be seen in the varied, and sometimes fantastic, identifications which commentators have made.

Attempts have been made in more recent times to explain the book as a collection of cultic myths in celebration of the union of the god and the goddess which for many centuries was a feature of pagan fertility religions. In Palestine such fertility rites, whose purpose was the increase of the crops or herds, were associated with Baal and his consort Anath, whilst in Babylonia the deities were Tammuz and Ishtar. The suggestion is that these myths, in the form of love lyrics, were subsequently adopted and adapted for use in the Jerusalem Temple. This, it is said, finds confirmation in the fact that the Song of Songs was for a long time read at the Feast of Passover, which has strong agricultural associations. But startling though some of the connexions may be, it is hardly credible that such pagan fertility rites, which met with such opposition in the Old Testament and which figured so prominently in the pagan environment of Greek and Roman times, should have been thus 'baptized' into Judaism and incorporated in the Canon of Scripture. Another explanation of the similarity between the two is more likely. The liturgical language of pagan fertility cults may well have become part and parcel of common speech, particularly that relating to the love-life of ordinary men and women, and so have found its way naturally into the Song. On the other hand it is quite possible that the ritual language of the pagan liturgies drew upon the language of love to be found among the common people.

Again, a number of scholars have interpreted the Song as a drama whose plot introduces either two principal characters, Solomon and a young woman called the Shulammite (cf. 6¹³) whom he tries to woo, or else three principal characters, Solomon and the Shulammite and a simple country lover whose betrothed the King tries to seduce and add to his harem. Much ingenuity has been shown in an attempt to apportion the various parts to the several characters and a 'chorus' of professional singers. This attempted solution, however, carries little conviction. There is little sense here of dramatic development, nor is 'secular' drama of this kind to be found anywhere else in Hebrew literature.

The most convincing explanation is that the book consists of a series of lyrical compositions on the theme of the love of a man for a woman. Its language is at times bold and frank, but need not shock the reader who sees the shared experience of such love as one of the highest human relationships. It takes great delight in the beauty of nature and in the nature of beauty, especially that of the human body, without descending to the vulgar or lewd or merely sensual. The suggestion has been made that these love-songs may have had their origin in eastern weddings in which the parts of Solomon and the Shulammite were played by the bridegroom and his bride. But although, as we have seen, they probably contain traditional material, there are whole sections of the Song which cannot be explained with reference to the wedding *motif*. It is safer, then, to regard them as straightforward lyrical songs, whose theme is the rapture of human love, the work perhaps of a single author. The book is a reminder, to Jews and Christians alike, that love, whether physical or spiritual, is of God.

### a. 'A LOVER AND HIS LASS' $(2^{8-15})$

This is a delightful love lyric in which a young woman speaks in rapturous tones of her beloved and recalls his words to her, in which he extols the beauties of the springtime and praises her own sweetness and comeliness.

8. Read, 'Hark! my beloved! behold here he comes'. The hyperbole of the last two lines is perfectly understandable in the language of love.

9. *a young stag*. The AV is better: 'a young hart'. The young lover looks through the window-slits in her house and peers through the lattices to catch a glimpse of her (cf. Ecclus. $14^{23}$, where the same language is used of one seeking Wisdom).

10. The young woman recalls what he had said on that occasion.

11 f. The word translated *winter* is found only here in the Hebrew Bible. The rainy season, to which reference is made, ends in April and signs of spring begin to appear.

12. *singing*. The RV translation, 'pruning', is supported by the LXX, the Vulgate, and the Targum, whilst the corresponding verb occurs with this meaning in Isa.5[6]. Reference to pruning, however, is not very appropriate, seeing that the vines, for example, are already in blossom (13). It is better, therefore, to accept the rendering 'singing', which conveys the sense found elsewhere in the Old Testament and also in cognate languages, despite the fact that it normally refers to songs of a ritual character together with their musical accompaniments.

*the turtledove* is a migratory bird whose appearance in Palestine is a harbinger of spring (cf. Jer. 8[7]).

13. *puts forth its figs*. The verb probably means 'to fill with juice', 'to mature'. The *figs* in this context are the unripe fruits which remain on the tree all winter and begin to ripen with the coming of spring. They are to be distinguished from the second crop which ripens in August.

14. *your face*: 'your appearance', 'your form'.

15. This verse does not fit easily into the context. It may well be a snippet from a rustic song sung by watchmen in the vineyards. It has been suggested, on the other hand, that the vineyard may represent the young woman and the little foxes the young men who seek to win her favour.

*b*. THE PLEDGE OF LOVE (8[6-7])

These words, spoken by the woman, declare a *love* which will never fail and which nothing can destroy (cf. 1 Cor. 13). It is as irresistible as *death*, as inexorable as *the grave*, as vehement as *fire:* nothing can extinguish it; its price is far beyond all *wealth*.

6. *a seal*. This was suspended by a cord round the neck (cf. Gen. 38[18, 25]) or worn on a finger of the right hand (cf. Gen. 41[42]; Jer. 22[24]), and was used to give the bearer's mark or signature.

The point of the simile is that the woman wishes her relationship with her beloved to be as close and as personal as it possibly can be.

*jealousy*: 'passionate love'. This line is 'parallel' in expression and meaning with the preceding line.

*the grave*: Hebrew 'Sheol' (cf. Isa. 5¹⁴ and Prov. 27²⁰ where Sheol is depicted as an insatiable monster).

*flashes*: 'thunderbolts', cf. Job 5⁷; Ps. 78⁴⁸.

*a most vehement flame*: literally 'a flame of Yah'. This is probably to be taken as an instance of the Hebrew idiom in which the divine name is used to express the superlative degree. It is not inappropriate for the writer that he should in this way associate God's name with the love of a woman for a man.

7. This verse brings the book to its climax and shows that, for all the sensuous appearance of love, for this writer it has a strong moral foundation. Much more is involved in love than the payment of a rich dowry; it is altogether priceless.

# XIII

## PROPHECY

As the post-exilic period advanced the conviction grew that 'the age of prophecy' was past and prophetic inspiration was dead. The authority of the scribes increasingly asserted itself, whilst prophecy was more and more discredited. Reason for this can be found in the circumstances of the time. The growing authority of the Law, for example, whilst in no way antagonistic to that of the Prophets, tended to detract from the authority of prophecy itself and to give it a subordinate place; again, the similarity between the prophetic oracle and the practice of divination so common in the surrounding oriental religions and a constant danger to the faith of Judaism, must have cast grave suspicion upon it; there is reason to believe, moreover, that the pronouncements of certain 'irresponsible' prophets at this time may well have been interpreted by the Jewish authorities as a menace to the safety of the state. For whatever reasons, towards the end of the Persian period the prophet no longer appeared as the charismatic figure of earlier days; for the most part he is represented as a cult official whose responsibilities were directed towards the maintenance and right ordering of the Temple worship (cf. 1 Chron. 25¹).

Despite these fears and suspicions, however, prophecy was not altogether dead. There is reason to believe that a number of oracles, now attached to the writings of the canonical prophets, are in fact the utterances of certain unnamed prophets of the Persian or Greek periods. Two such collections of oracles are contained in Zech. 9–14 and Isa. 24–27. Their inclusion in the writings of Zechariah and Isaiah respectively may be purely accidental, but it is just possible that they are the work of a 'Zechariah-school' and an 'Isaiah-school' of prophets (cf. Isa. 8¹⁶) who sought, in their oracles, to interpret and reapply their masters' prophecies to the changed circumstances of the days in which they were then living. Whether this explanation be valid or not, it would appear that genuine prophecy continued into Hellenistic times.

The name 'apocalyptic' has sometimes been given to these two passages. This is hardly justifiable, however, for apocalyptic is to be distinguished from prophecy by certain fairly well-defined characteristics[1] which are not altogether apparent in these collections of oracles. Nevertheless, such a description is understandable, for, together with other post-exilic prophecies, they show certain trends which later on become prominent features of apocalyptic thought—the idea of divine transcendence, the growth of angelology, the use of strange symbolism and ancient mythology, the re-interpretation of prophecy, the visionary form of inspiration, the message of judgement, the Day of the Lord, the destruction of the Gentiles, the coming of the Kingdom, and the resurrection of the dead. Despite this, however, it is safer to say that Zech. 9–14 and Isa. 24–27 represent a transition from the more familiar oracles of pre-exilic prophecy to the more extravagant forms of the apocalyptic writers.

### 1. *Zechariah 9–14*

At the end of 'the Book of the Twelve Prophets' there appear three collections of prophecies, each introduced by the unusual expression 'the oracle of the word of Yahweh'. Two are attached to the Book of Zechariah (9–11; 12–14), whilst the third appears as the Book of 'Malachi', the intention perhaps being to make the books of the minor prophets add up to the significant number twelve. Since Zech. 9–14 is markedly different in style from chs. 1–8 and assumes a different historical background, it is generally conceded that it is not the work of Zechariah but of some unknown prophet or prophets. It has been customary to divide these chapters into Deutero-Zechariah (9–11) and Trito-Zechariah (12–14), but their composition is probably much more fragmentary than this

[1] See pp. 219 f.

The likelihood is that they represent a variety of prophetic utterances from several writers living at different times who sought to interpret or reinterpret God's revealed word against the background of their own day. This fact helps to explain the sometimes repetitive character of the oracles and perhaps also certain inconsistencies in the ideas expressed, although such inconsistencies are a characteristic of prophecy of this kind.

Whilst these chapters are to be classed as prophecy, there are obvious indications that in form and content they already have much in common with apocalyptic. This is most clearly seen in the interest they show in the coming of God's kingdom, with its prevenient trials and tribulations. The world will be transformed and a new age will begin in which even the Gentiles will have a share; Jerusalem with its cultus will be exalted above the nations and holiness will be the mark of God's redeemed people.

There is no consensus of opinion concerning the date (or dates) of these chapters. Reference to the northern kingdom of Israel and also to Syria, Philistia, Egypt, and Assyria would seem to suggest a pre-exilic background, but these are more likely to be simply 'archaizing touches' on the part of the writer. Allusion to the Dispersion in $9^{11\ f.}$ and reference to Greece in $9^{13}$ (if this is not to be regarded as a gloss) point rather to the Hellenistic period. A number of scholars have suggested a Maccabaean date; but this is unlikely, if only because of the closure of the Prophetic Canon prior to this date, around the beginning of the second century B.C. On balance the indications suggest the period between Alexander the Great and the reign of Antiochus III, but the evidence is so scanty and the historical allusions so obscure that there can be no certainty on this point. The New Testament writers, however, were undaunted by such obscurities or by exegetical difficulties. They found in their predictions much that was in keeping with their own message and which pointed to their fulfilment in Jesus of Nazareth and the establishment of his kingdom on earth (cf. Matt. $21^5$, $26^{15,\ 31}$, $27^9$; Mark $14^{27}$; John $12^{15}$, $19^{37}$; Rev. $1^7$).

*a*. ORACLES OF JUDGEMENT AND DELIVERANCE $(9^{1-17})$

Within this chapter are three closely related oracles (1–8, 9–10, 11–17) which describe the destruction of God's enemies as a prelude to the coming of his kingdom. The events recorded in the first of these may refer to the time of the Assyrian conquest towards the end of the eighth century B.C. On the other hand, the reference may be to the conquest of Persia by Alexander the Great at the battle of Issus in 333 B.C., and his subsequent march southwards through Phoenicia in the direction of Egypt.[1] The description agrees in broad outline at least with the known events of that period.

1. *The word of the Lord* is said to be IN (not *against*) *the land of Hadrach*, which lay close to *Damascus* and bordered on *Hamath* (2). It signifies the ideal northern limit of David's kingdom (cf. 1 Kings 8⁶⁵), and the expression may imply that the prophet himself was living there.

The second part of the verse is obscure. The text reads, 'For the eye of man (*'adham*) . . . is towards the Lord', meaning perhaps that the Gentiles, like *all the tribes of Israel* in the Dispersion, look expectantly to Yahweh. The RSV follows an emendation which reads 'cities' for 'eye' and 'Aram' (i.e. Syria) for "*'adham*'.

2–4. The prosperity, *wisdom*, and coming judgement of Tyre are graphically described elsewhere, in Ezek. 27 and 28, and this is perhaps in the prophet's mind here. The historical event described in these verses may have been the conquest of Tyre by Alexander the Great.

3. The word for *rampart* is in Hebrew a pun on *Tyre:* 'Tyre has built herself a tower'.

5–6. Four of the five cities in the Philistine confederation are mentioned here, the fifth being Gath. The reference to *Gaza* may be an allusion to its five months' siege by Alexander in 332 B.C.

6. *a mongrel people.* Elsewhere this means a people half-Jewish

[1] See p. 3.

(cf. Deut. 23²), but in this context it may refer simply to foreign settlers.

7. This is a remarkable verse by reason of its universalistic outlook. The Philistines, Israel's traditional enemies, will be cleansed of impure practices; a remnant of them will survive who will be converted and incorporated with God's own people.

*the Jebusites*, i.e. the original inhabitants of Jerusalem taken over by David.

8. *my house*, i.e. 'my Temple' or perhaps better 'my people' (cf. Hosea 8¹, 9¹⁵; Jer. 12⁷ ᶠᶠ·).

9-10. This picture of the messianic Prince reflects the mysterious figure in Gen. 49¹⁰ ᶠᶠ·, and recalls the humiliation (*humble and riding on an ass*), vindication (*triumphant and victorious is he*), and world-wide rule (*his dominion shall be from sea to sea*) of the King as depicted in certain of the Psalms (cf. Ps. 2⁸, 72⁸, 89³⁸ ᶠᶠ·, 110). There, as here, he exercises a rule of *peace* (cf. Ps. 46⁹) in which the inhabitants of *Zion* rejoice (cf. Ps. 48¹¹, 97⁸). The words *humble* (or perhaps better 'afflicted'), *triumphant* (or 'acquitted'), and *victorious* (or 'saved' by God) are all reminiscent of the cult.

11-13. The promise of deliverance is repeated. The historical allusion is once more obscure, but it may refer to the Jews of the Dispersion in the years following Alexander's conquest, since the enemy named is Greece, which God will overthrow. Note that the northern kingdom of Ephraim, as well as Judah, will participate in the restoration—a hope often expressed also in the later apocalyptic literature.

13. *over your sons, O Greece.* If this is a gloss, as is generally recognized, it is of interest in showing how the passage came to be interpreted; if not, it is a clear indication of the date when this section of the book was written.

14-17 describe a theophany in which Yahweh himself comes to the aid of his people, the imagery being that of a storm with *arrows like lightning* and *whirlwinds of the south.*

15 is difficult. The words translated *slinger* (lit. 'sling-stones') may conceal the name of an enemy.

*they shall drink their blood like wine.* This is the reading of the LXX, which is preferable to the Hebrew 'they are turbulent'. The people, bespattered with the blood of their enemies, are likened to the bowls used for collecting the blood of the sacrificial animals and also to the sides of the altar where the blood was dashed.

16. The text is difficult, but the sense is fairly clear. God will deliver his people and look after them like a flock, for they are to him as precious jewels. The land to which they will be restored will be abundantly fertile.

*b.* THE LORD'S FLOCK AND THE RETURN FROM THE EXILE ($10^{3-12}$)

These verses, like $9^{11-17}$, may also relate to the period immediately following the conquests of Alexander the Great.

3. *the shepherds . . . the leaders* (lit. 'he-goats'), i.e. presumably the foreign rulers.

4. The terms *corner-stone*, *tent-peg*, and *battle-bow* provide suggestive titles for the future leaders of Israel, who will be home-born and not foreigners. It is futile to try to identify them with any known historical persons. The Targum not unfittingly finds here a reference to the Messiah.

6–7. Note that the return of *Ephraim* (called *Joseph* in verse 6) is again singled out for special mention (cf. $9^{11-17}$).

8. *I will signal for them.* Yahweh will 'whistle' for them as he once did for the Assyrians (cf. Isa $5^{26}$, $7^{18}$).

*I have redeemed them*: as in the Exodus of old.

9. Read: 'I will sow them among the nations': they will flourish and be multiplied.

10. It is just possible that *Egypt* and *Assyria* may refer here to the Ptolemaic and Seleucid kingdoms, with their large colonies of Jews, after the time of Alexander's successors. Prophecy, however, had long since associated captive Israel with both Egypt

and Assyria (cf. Hosea 9³, 11⁵, ¹¹; Isa. 7¹⁸, 52⁴), and the reference here may apply equally well to the earlier post-exilic period.

*Gilead . . . Lebanon*, i.e. the land will extend to the extreme east and north, as in the ideal days of David.

11. The language here is figurative. There will be a new Exodus with signs and wonders following.

*the sea of Egypt*. This reading is based on an emendation which is to be accepted.

12. Read with the Hebrew 'they shall walk in his name'. The RSV follows the LXX.

### c. A SHEPHERD AND HIS FLOCK—AN ALLEGORY (11⁴⁻¹⁷)

In this enigmatic passage we recognize the device known as prophetic symbolism, in which the prophet enacts his message: here, however, the symbolism is literary or visionary rather than actual. It is an allegory in which the prophet is bidden, as God's representative, to play the part of a *shepherd*, i.e. a ruler, of God's *flock*.

4 ff. The background may again be that of the Ptolemaic kingdom, but it is quite impossible to say. Foreign rulers exploit them and native rulers show them no mercy.

6. *this land*: perhaps 'the earth', emphasizing a universal judgement. But 'this land' is equally good.

7. *those who trafficked in the sheep* (lit. 'Canaanites') is suggested by the LXX. The Hebrew text is corrupt. It has been suggested that the reference may be to tax-gatherers.

The account of the *two staffs* is no doubt based on Ezek. 37¹⁶ ᶠᶠ·.

8. Many attempts have been made to identify *the three shepherds* mentioned here, but lack of historical data makes the task quite impossible. The first part of the verse is probably an interpolation, the meaning of which would be known to the writer's contemporaries.

10 *the covenant . . . with all the peoples*. God's agreement with the

Gentiles, restraining them from harming his people, is now cancelled.

12. *thirty shekels of silver*: the same sum offered in compensation for an injured Hebrew slave (cf. Exod. 21³²)!

13. *treasury* is an emendation. The text reads 'potter' or 'smelter'. The significance of this act is not altogether clear. Perhaps the meaning is that it is God and not simply the prophet himself who has been paid off in such a miserable way.

14. This may be a reference to the Samaritan schism in the fourth century B.C., or perhaps to rivalry within the Jewish nation in the Greek period.

17. Doom is pronounced on the *worthless shepherd* in poetic form, after the style of Jer. 50³⁵⁻³⁸.

*d.* GOD'S FINAL DELIVERANCE AND THE CLEANSING OF HIS PEOPLE (12¹–13⁶)

This passage (and also Ch. 14) concerns the great and terrible Day of the Lord, about which the prophets spoke and which was to find a prominent place in apocalyptic expectation. The idea of a final onslaught of the nations against Jerusalem was already familiar in the Gog prophecies of Ezek. 38–39 and in the Temple liturgy (cf. Ps. 2, 46, 48⁴ ᶠᶠ·, etc.). The interest here is eschatological, and so attempts to identify allusions with historical events are extremely precarious.

12. 1. The second collection begins here with 'the oracle of the word of the Lord'.

2. The second part of this verse is difficult. As it stands Judah apparently takes part in the siege against Jerusalem. The true sense is perhaps conveyed in the LXX reading: 'and there will also be a siege against Judah'.

3. *hurt themselves*: lacerate themselves.

5. *the clans of Judah* acknowledge that the defence of Jerusalem is of God.

6. *Judah* works havoc among the nations *round about*; *Jerusalem* remains impregnable.

7. The reference to Yahweh in the third person may suggest a different oracle at this point. A slight 'snub' is given to *Jerusalem* and *the house of David*, i.e. (descendants of the royal house), who are warned not to take to themselves *the glory* due to the inhabitants of *Judah* round about. If there is a hint here of strained relationships between Jerusalem and Judah, the historical situation is lost in obscurity. In the following verse the reprimand is forgotten.

8. They will receive supernatural help and all—even the feeblest among them—will become like David their ideal leader.

10. God grants the people *a spirit of compassion and supplication* for the great sin they have committed. But what is this sin? The Hebrew text reads, 'they shall look on ME whom they have pierced', i.e. on Yahweh who is the speaker. These words can be taken as a strong metaphor to mean that the people have hurt him grievously in profaning his name, although the expression is very strange as applied to God. Accordingly, many scholars amend, with several MSS., and read 'look upon HIM', finding here a reference to some historical figure (possibly a High Priest) in whose death the inhabitants of Jerusalem had acquiesced. Alternatively the passage may, like Isa. 53, be using metaphorical language, not unlike that of some of the Psalms, to express the eschatological meaning of suffering.

11. The reference here is to ritual mourning associated with Hadad the Canaanite storm-god (cf. 2 Sam. 8³ ff.; 1 Kings 11¹⁴, ¹⁹, ²¹) and Rimmon the chief god of Damascus (cf. 2 Kings 5¹⁸). In the fertility cults, such as that associated with the god Tammuz (known as Adonis to the Greeks), weeping or mourning for the god was a recognized part of the ritual (cf. Ezek. 8¹⁴). There was presumably a similar practice in the case of the god Hadadrimmon. The association of such lamentation with *the plain of Megiddo* is not clear. Megiddo lies to the

south-west of the plain of Esdraelon and is a strategic military strong-point. It was here that King Josiah was killed in battle (cf. 2 Kings 23²⁹ ᶠ·).

12–13. These verses are in the *ḳinah* or 'lamentation' metre and convey the sense of mourning. The royal house is represented by the families of David and Nathan (cf. 2 Sam. 5¹⁴), and the priestly house by the families of Levi and Shimei (cf. Num.3¹⁸). The divisions of the people into male and female, royal and priestly, etc., may suggest a ritual lamentation.

13. 1 f. This reference to a cleansing *fountain* recalls Ezekiel's river in 47 ¹ ᶠᶠ·; there too the waters are a purification from all *uncleanness* and in particular the worship of *idols* (Ezek. 36²⁵; cf. Num. 19⁹), which is the supreme example of uncleanness (cf. Ezek. 37²³).

2. At the time of God's deliverance both idolatry and prophecy will be rooted out.

*the names*. This means the idols themselves, not just their titles. The remarkable thing here is that prophecy as such is associated with idolatry and *the unclean spirit* which is opposed to the spirit of God (cf. Ezek. 36²⁶ ᶠ·, 37¹ ᶠᶠ·). It would appear that by this time all prophecy had fallen into disrepute and that no distinction needed to be made between the false and the true. In subsequent Jewish thought it was held that prophetic inspiration had come to an end in the time of Ezra (cf. 1 Macc. 4²⁶, 9²⁷, 14⁴¹; *Against Apion* 1. 8; *Megillah* 15a, etc.).

3. His own family will repudiate and even kill him (cf. Deut. 13⁶⁻¹⁰, 18²⁰).

4. *a hairy mantle*: the recognized garb of a prophet (cf. 2 Kings 1⁸; Matt. 3⁴).

5. Such a man will deny that he belongs to the ranks of the prophets. The emendation on which the RSV is based is probably to be accepted.

6. The ecstatic prophets sometimes lacerated themselves in a state of frenzy (cf. 1 Kings 18²⁸ ᶠᶠ·, 20³⁵· ⁴¹ ᶠᶠ·; Hos. 7¹⁴). This

prophet explains away his *wounds* by saying they were inflicted *in the house of my friends*.

*friends*: lit. lovers. This word is sometimes used metaphorically of the Baals (cf. Hos. 2⁵, ⁷, ¹⁰, ¹² f., etc.), and this may be the allusion here; more probably, however, it is to be taken literally, with reference either to his acquaintances or to his more doubtful associates (cf. Moffatt's translation: 'harlot's house').

### *e*. THE REFINED REMNANT (13⁷⁻⁹)

This poetic passage, describing the 'messianic woes' preceding the last days, has not the necessary connexion with 11⁴⁻¹⁷ that many commentators suggest. God's chosen leader will be stricken and the people *scattered*. A remnant will survive, refined like *silver* or *gold*, who will acknowledge Yahweh to be their *God*.

7. *my shepherd*. There is no need to link this with the 'foolish shepherd' of 11¹⁵⁻¹⁷.

The words *who stands next to me* suggest perhaps some kingly or High-Priestly figure. Is there any possible connexion here with the figure in 12¹⁰? Like him this shepherd is stricken, presumably killed, and the people are scattered (cf. Matt. 26³¹).

8–9. A *third* of the people will survive the trials and testings and will become God's own people (cf. Hos. 2²³). This idea of 'the righteous remnant' was put forward by Isaiah and is a fairly common notion in subsequent Old Testament prophecy.

### *f*. IN THE LAST DAYS (14¹⁻²¹)

The theme of this chapter—the siege of Jerusalem by the Gentiles and the inauguration of the kingdom of God—is the same as that of 12¹–13⁶;[1] its spirit and outlook, however, are quite different and indicate a different author. The several sections into which it is divided may have been originally separate oracles, brought together by reason of their common subject matter. Its interest in the fulfilment of earlier prophecy

[1] Cf. also Ps. 2, with its description of the onslaught of the nations.

and its stress on the supernatural intervention of God show a much closer relationship with apocalyptic than any other part of the book.

1–5 describe the siege of Jerusalem in 'the last days'.

1. *a day of the Lord*, i.e. a day of judgement. The city of Jerusalem is addressed here. Its booty will be shared out within its own gates.

2–3. *all the nations*. The onslaught of the nations on Jerusalem is a familiar eschatological idea in later prophecy and in apocalyptic. Here *half* the population goes *into exile* and half remains in *the city*. But Yahweh intervenes, as so often in the past.

4. As in Ezek. 43² God comes from the east and stands on *the Mount of Olives*, which is *split in two*, forming a *valley* running east and west. Somewhat similar descriptions of a theophany in terms of earthquake are found elsewhere in Scripture (cf. Judges 5⁵; Ps. 97⁵; Micah 1⁴, ⁸; Nah. 1⁵; Hab. 3⁶).

5 contains several ambiguities. The word *nastem*, from the root 'to flee', occurs three times in this verse and is translated so in the AV ('ye shall flee . . . yea, ye shall flee, like as ye fled'), i.e. the prophet pictures the people of Jerusalem escaping through the valley. This, however, seems to contradict verse 2, where the survivors remain in the city. The LXX and the Vulgate read *nistam*, from the root 'to stop up', and the RSV adopts this reading in the first of its three occurrences. Perhaps all three should be taken in this way: '*the valley . . . shall be stopped up* . . . and it will be stopped up as it was stopped up by the earthquake in the days of Uzziah'—presumably to carry the waters mentioned in verse 8.

*the valley of my mountains*. Perhaps 'the valley of the mountains' or, with slight emendation, 'the valley of Gehinnom', which runs south and west of Jerusalem.

*shall touch the side of it*, viz. the Mount of Olives. The Hebrew text, followed by the AV, reads 'shall reach unto Azal', which, if correct, indicates some unidentified site near Jerusalem.

*the earthquake* is that referred to in Amos 1¹.

*the holy ones*, i.e. the angels (cf. Deut. 33²,³; Ps 98⁵,⁷; Dan. 4¹³, 8¹³).

*your God will come . . . with him*. The Hebrew text reads 'my God will come . . . with thee', the latter reference being to Jerusalem.

6–11 tell of the transformation of the land when the new age begins.

6. *cold nor frost*. This is based on an emendation and is to be accepted. There will be no extremes of temperature. For the same idea see 2 Esdras 7⁴¹.

7. *it is known to the Lord*: probably a pious scribal interjection.

8. *living waters shall flow out*. The prophet no doubt has in mind Ezekiel's river in 47¹ ᶠᶠ· Here, however, it flows not only into *the eastern sea* (i.e. the Dead Sea) but also into *the western sea* (i.e. the Mediterranean).

9. The whole earth will acknowledge Yahweh as *king* and accept the Jewish creed (cf. the *Šemaʿ* in Deut. 6⁴).

10. The mountainous region of Judah will become *a plain* from *Geba* (about eight miles north-east of Jerusalem) to *Rimmon* (about ten miles north of Beersheba), representing the limits of the pre-exilic kingdom (cf. 2 Kings 23⁸). Jerusalem alone will be exalted, in fulfilment of Isa. 2¹ ᶠᶠ·. Its boundaries run from *the Gate of Benjamin* in the north-west to *the Corner Gate* (or *the former gate*, cf. Neh. 3⁶, 12³⁹) in the north-east, and from *the Tower of Hananel* in the north to *the king' swine presses* in the south.

11. *there shall be no more curse*: it will no longer fall under the 'ban' whereby all its property is devoted to destruction as a sacrifice to the god of the conqueror (cf. Joshua 6¹⁷ ᶠᶠ·).

12–15 give the fate of the nations which fight against Jerusalem, the description in verse 12 being taken up again in verse 15. The *plague* will strike men and beasts alike; in *panic* they will slay one another. Such language is fairly common stock-in-trade of later apocalyptic.

14. *Judah will fight against Jerusalem*: better, read 'in Jerusalem', i.e. Judah will join the inhabitants of Jerusalem in fighting against the nations whose spoil they will capture.

16-19 tell of the conversion of the surviving Gentiles and of their celebration annually of the Feast of Booths.

16. *the feast of booths*. At this great festival, closely associated with the New Year celebrations, Yahweh was acclaimed as *king*. Here the nations go up *year after year* to Jerusalem to acknowledge his kingship over all the earth.

17. An important feature of this feast was the libation, when water from the Pool of Siloam was poured out at the foot of the altar. By this means, it was believed, they would ensure God's gift of rain. Those nations which do not take part in the festival will have their supply of rain cut off.

18. The Egyptians, with the river Nile, are not in such great need of rain and so their punishment will be different—*upon them shall come the plague!*

20-21 indicate the holiness of Judah and Jerusalem in the new age. Even the commonest articles, such as the bells on the horses and the very cooking pots, will be considered holy.

20. *the bells of the horses*. These bells, originally used for driving away evil spirits, are to be inscribed with the same words as those on the High Priest's turban (cf. Exod. 28³⁶, 39³⁰).

*the pots . . . shall be as the bowls before the altar*. There will be so many worshippers that every pot, however common, will be used as a sacred vessel so that all may sacrifice.

21. *boil the flesh of the sacrifice*: cf. Lev. 6²⁸.

*a trader*: lit. 'Canaanite'. There is a word-play here, as in 11⁷, ¹¹, and the thought of the 'Canaanite' inhabitants of the land is perhaps not altogether absent. The immediate reference, however, is probably to those who may have sold consecrated vessels to people who came to the Temple to sacrifice. Since *every pot* is now adopted for *sacred* use, such traders will no longer be needed in *the house of the Lord*.

## 2. *Isaiah 24–27*

It is generally conceded that these chapters do not belong to
Isaiah of Jerusalem but were written at a much later date, in
the fifth, fourth, or even third century B.C. Despite the differences between them and the accepted Isaianic oracles, however, there are certain distinct similarities of thought and
language which as we have seen may well indicate a continuity
of tradition and suggest a reinterpretation of prophecy within
the setting of post-exilic times.

Alongside the writer's prediction of world catastrophe there
is a more particular reference to the overthrow of a great
city ($25^{1-5}$) which a number of scholars have identified as
Babylon. If this identification is correct—and it is little more
than a guess—it may then refer to its overthrow by Alexander
in 331 B.C. It is just possible that the account given here of the
sufferings of the Jews may reflect the treatment meted out by
Artaxerxes Ochus (359–338 B.C.) when he deported many of
them to Hyrcania and Babylonia. But this too is to surmise with
little or no factual backing. All that can be said for certain is
that these oracles are patently unlike Isaiah's genuine oracles
in their style, the circumstances assumed in the passage, and
the ideas expressed in it.

Isa. 24–27 consists of a number of eschatological prophecies
($24^{1-12}$, $24^{16b-23}$, $25^{6-8}$, $25^{9-12}$, $26^{20}-27^1$, $27^{12-13}$), broken up
by several psalms and prayers recording the hardships of
God's people and the triumphs of the Lord ($24^{13-16a}$, $25^{1-5}$,
$26^{1-6}$, $26^{7-19}$, $27^{2-6}$). The eschatological sections are of considerable significance by reason of the subsequent development
of their ideas in the apocalyptic writings. They deal in the
main with the desolation of the earth and the final judgement
of the nations resulting in the triumph of the people of God.
The whole earth, it is said, will twist and tremble at the judgement of God ($24^1$); not only men, but even the angel host ($24^{21}$)
will be punished, and the sun and moon will be darkened
($24^{23}$). In celebration of his triumph God will ordain a great
banquet to which 'all peoples' will be summoned and at which

the reproach of his people will be taken away (25⁶ ᶠᶠ·). The mythical monster 'Leviathan' will be punished and destroyed (27¹), and the righteous among his people will be raised in resurrection to share in the glories of the coming kingdom (26¹⁹).

*a.* THE TERRIBLE DAY OF THE LORD (24¹⁶⁻²³)

The theme of this eschatological prophecy is the great and terrible Day of the Lord. As in other prophetic writings the judgement of God is here depicted in terms of storm and earthquake (18–20) and the eclipse of both *sun* and *moon* (23). The judgement is to fall not only on *the kings of the earth*, but also on *the host of heaven* (21). Here ancient mythology, with its conflict between the god and other supernatural powers, is projected into the future and becomes an expression of eschatological hope. These angel hosts are astral deities which, in mythological understanding, are represented by stars, and indeed identified with them. In the end they are to be judged and confined *as prisoners in a pit* (21). The lengths to which this idea is taken in the apocalyptic writings can be seen in 1 Enoch, for example, where the story of the fallen angels is told in terms of stars which fall from heaven (86¹ ᶠᶠ·) and are finally judged and thrown into the abyss (cf. 18¹² ᶠᶠ·, 88¹ ᶠᶠ·). As in 1 Enoch so here the order of judgement is the same—first the angels and then the earthly rulers. Both accounts no doubt reflect the belief that before God judges any nation or ruler, he first judges the guardian angels whose charge they are. This idea of guardian angels is suggested, as we have seen,[1] in the LXX of Deut. 32⁸⁻⁹ and elsewhere, and finds corroboration in a Hebrew text found at Qumran. There the nations of the earth are given over into the control of angel powers. Circumstances in the Hellenistic period were conducive to the growth of such an idea; for the belief was prevalent among the Greeks that God ruled the world by the agency of intermediary beings. The notion subsequently underwent development and refinement in the Jewish apocalyptic writings, where the several

[1] Cf. p. 137, n. 1.

angels were often identified by name (cf. Dan. 10¹³ ff·, 12¹;
Jub. 15³¹ f·; 1 Enoch 89⁵⁹ ff·, 90²⁰ ff·).

### *b.* A FEAST FOR ALL NATIONS (25⁶⁻⁸)

This second eschatological passage is a sequel to the one
just considered. In the new age soon to dawn *all peoples* will
share in the triumphs of the Lord. In celebration of his victory
over his enemies God will prepare on Mount Zion a *feast* of rich
food and well-matured *wine* (6); the *veil* of mourning will be
removed (7); death will be swallowed up and the sorrow and
*reproach of his people* will be removed *from all the earth* (8).

6. The *feast* prepared by God, which finds a parallel in ancient
Canaanite mythology, is here projected into the future and
celebrates the Lord's triumph at the end of history. Fuller
reference to this 'eschatological banquet' is made in later
Jewish apocalyptic literature (cf. 2 Esdras 6⁴⁷⁻⁵²; 2 Baruch
29³⁻⁴), in the Qumran Texts (cf. *Rule of the Congregation* II. 18–
22), in the New Testament (cf. Luke 13²⁸⁻²⁹, 22³⁰ ff·; Rev. 19⁹)
and frequently in the rabbinic tradition. There it is associated
with the glories of the messianic age.

8. God, it is said, *will swallow up death for ever.* This theme is
repeated in a number of the Psalms, especially the enthrone-
ment Psalms, in which the living God, as a powerful warrior,
delivers the people from the onslaught of 'death' (Hebrew root,
*mwt*). Behind this picture there no doubt lies the Canaanite
myth of Baal's conflict with Mot (meaning 'summer heat',
and possibly also 'death') as depicted, for example, in the
Ras Shamra tablets. In this Old Testament passage, however,
there is no thought of an actual god called 'Death'; here the
word stands for all that is evil in the universe and in opposition
to God's sovereign will. In the light of a later reference to
resurrection from the dead (cf. 26¹⁹) it is possible that more is
to be read into this occurrence of the word than into that in the
Psalms, and that we are to see in it an expression of belief in
life beyond the grave. The verse finds a resounding echo in

Rev. 21⁴, which tells of the transformation wrought by the risen, exalted Christ.

### c. THE PROMISE OF RESURRECTION (26¹⁶⁻¹⁹)

In these verses the writer records both the sufferings of God's people (16) and the smallness of their numbers (17–18), for they had brought very few into the faith of Israel (18). Then, in a burst of confidence, he announces that their numbers will at last be made up, for God will restore to them the righteous members of the nation by raising them from the dead (19).

16. Read with the LXX 'WE *sought thee*, WE *poured out a prayer*'. This last phrase is obscure in the Hebrew. As it stands it may be rendered 'we poured out a whispered prayer'; a slight emendation of the text, however, would give 'we cried out because of affliction', which is perhaps to be accepted.

17–18. All their efforts to produce children of faith have proved fruitless. *The inhabitants of the world have not fallen*, i.e. (presumably) have not been overthrown. The sense of the passage, however, seems to require a different conclusion. An alternative rendering of the text is, 'the inhabitants of the world have not been born', viz. into the faith of Israel. This same picture of a woman in travail is used in the Dead Sea Scrolls (cf. *Hymns of Thanksgiving* III. 7–10) to portray the emergence, through toil and suffering, of God's people in the time of the End.[1]

19. It is better to read 'Thy dead shall live; their corpses shall rise. They that dwell in the dust shall awake and sing. For the dew of lights is thy dew, and the earth shall give birth to the shades.' Many scholars take this passage metaphorically, as in Hosea (cf. 6², 13¹, ¹⁴), and Ezekiel (cf. 37¹ ᶠᶠ·), to refer to the restoration of the NATION and not literally to the resurrection of men's bodies. It seems more likely, however, that it refers to INDIVIDUAL resurrection—not of all men, but of the pre-eminently righteous in Israel who will be raised to share in the messianic kingdom. If this is so, it is the earliest reference

[1] See p. 296.

to such a belief in the Old Testament, a belief which underwent considerable development in later apocalyptic and became a basic tenet of faith in both Judaism and Christianity.

*they that dwell in the dust.* This is the reading of the LXX and is corroborated by the Isaiah Scroll from Qumran.

*the dew of lights.* This is better than 'the dew of herbs' (AV). The reference may be to the dew of the regions of light where God is (cf. Ps. 104²), or to the dew of (morning) light which brings life to the vegetation. In either case it is a sign of the revivification of the dead to which reference is made a number of times in the apocalyptic literature (cf. 1 Enoch 22⁹; 2 Baruch 29⁷, 73²; Apoc. Abr. 19) and in the rabbinic literature.

*the land of the shades.* The typical Old Testament idea of the departed as 'shades' in Sheol is preserved here; it is a land of forgetfulness and despair where 'the dead know nothing, neither have they any more a reward' (Eccles. 9⁵). In the Isaiah passage, however, the dead will be raised from Sheol to share in the resurrection.

*thou wilt let it fall.* Take 'the earth' as the subject of the verb 'to fall', in the sense of 'to be born', as in v. 18, and translate 'the earth shall give birth to the shades'.

*d.* THE DESTRUCTION OF THE DRAGON (26²⁰–27¹)

Judgement is coming soon. Let God's people hide in safety until it is all over. When the Lord comes from heaven to punish evildoers the earth will not conceal the blood shed upon it; as in the days of Cain (cf. Gen. 4¹¹) it will make its own appeal to the bar of heaven. In 27¹ the judgement is described in terms of God's defeat of a mythical dragon. This reference recalls the ancient Babylonian (and Canaanite) account of a combat between Marduk and a great sea-monster. In the Isaiah passage, however, the myth is projected into the future and becomes part of the property of eschatology. The same idea is expressed in several other parts of the Old Testament, where the monster is variously described as the Dragon, Leviathan, Rahab, or the Serpent. Both there and in the Babylonian account it represents the mighty deep or the cosmic ocean (cf. Job 7¹², 26¹², 38⁸;

Ps. 74¹³; Isa. 51¹⁰; Hab. 3⁸; Amos 7⁴), a symbol of the powers of chaos and evil in the universe which God will one day destroy. On occasions, however, it is identified with a national world-power, as in Ps. 87⁴, where it stands for Egypt (cf. also Ps. 74¹³ ᶠᶠ·; Ezek. 29³, 32²). Some scholars would make the same identification in this passage and take *the fleeing serpent* and *the twisting serpent* to represent either Assyria and Babylonia or Babylonia and Persia. Outside the Old Testament it appears again in several apocalyptic writings, in the Dead Sea Scrolls, and in rabbinic literature. Sometimes the mythical element is uppermost (cf. 1 Enoch 60⁷⁻⁹; 2 Esdras 6⁴⁹⁻⁵²; 2 Baruch 29⁴, where two great monsters are used as food at the 'eschatological banquet'!); at other times the creatures represent men and nations (cf. Ps. Sol. 2²⁹; *Zadokite Document* VIII. 10). In the New Testament the idea is developed further; there the dragon appears as Satan, who is bound and cast into the abyss (cf. Rev. 12⁹, 20²).

# XIV

## APOCALYPTIC[1]

THE term 'apocalypse' is derived from the Greek word *apokalupsis*, meaning 'an unveiling' or 'an uncovering': in the first place it signified 'a vision', and subsequently was used to designate certain books whose contents, it was believed, were revealed by this means. Many such 'apocalypses' were issued during the period 200 B.C.–A.D. 100, most of them having been preserved within the tradition of the Christian Church. Those that have survived have been augmented in recent times by the discovery of the Dead Sea Scrolls, which have brought to light apocalyptic works hitherto unknown and also sectarian writings having much in common with the already-known apocalyptic books.[2] The actual writing of such books may have been confined to a rather narrow circle of 'wise men', but the ideas they express were certainly widespread throughout the intertestamental period.

Whilst not all of them follow the same literary pattern, they nevertheless show certain fairly well-defined characteristics which mark them out as a distinct body of literature. One such mark is their *esoteric* character, for they claim to uncover the secrets of the universe by means of dreams and visions. These disclosures are essentially *literary* in form, for tradition has it that they were preserved in sacred books wherein 'the wise' among God's people could read 'the signs of the times'. This literary device is given an air of credibility by the adoption of *pseudonymous* authorship: in most cases the author writes in the name of some worthy figure of the past, not in an attempt to deceive, but rather as spokesman of a long line of tradition

[1] For a fuller treatment of this subject see D. S. Russell, *The Method and Message of Jewish Apocalyptic*, 1964.

[2] See pp. 181 f.

which he believes he has received from ancient times. The language of apocalyptic, moreover, is often *symbolic*, making frequent use of fantastic and bizarre figures; indeed, this literature as a whole is to be understood, not in terms of sober prose at all, but as a peculiar art-form in which the language is that of highly imaginative poetry.

The description sometimes given of apocalyptic as 'the child of prophecy' is a fair one, for, despite many obvious differences, its message is essentially a re-adaptation of the old prophetic message within a new situation. It is especially interested in the predictive side of prophecy, with its message concerning the great Day of the Lord, and fills in with graphic details what the prophets had said concerning 'the latter end of the days'.[1] The apocalyptists shared with the prophets the belief that the climax of history would be revealed by the direct intervention of God, but they differed from them by working out the day and hour of its coming, announcing that the appointed time was at hand!

Throughout these writings the future hope tends to become more and more supramundane, and human destiny is viewed not only in terms of the nation but also in terms of personal survival beyond the grave.[2] The nations still come forward for judgement, as in the ancient prophecies, but now the souls of men and the very angels are also brought before the Great Assize.

Not all these developments can be traced in every apocalyptic book of this period. In particular the Book of Daniel cannot be regarded as 'typical' of this genre of literature; nevertheless it set a pattern which many other writings followed, and exercised a powerful influence both on Judaism itself and on the emerging Christian faith.

## 1. *The Book of Daniel*

The Book of Daniel is the first and greatest of the Jewish apocalyptic writings, and is the only one of its kind to find a

[1] For an examination of apocalyptic eschatology see pp. 139 ff.
[2] See pp. 148 ff.

place in the Canon of Scripture. It purports to have been written during the Babylonian Exile in the sixth century B.C., but both external and internal evidence point rather to the second century B.C. as the date of its composition.

Thus on the external side it appears in the third section of the Canon and not among the Prophets as one might have expected; the conclusion to be drawn is that the Prophetic Canon had already been closed (*c.* 200 B.C.) by the time Daniel came to be written. There is no evidence that the book was known before the second century B.C. Even Ben Sira, writing about 180 B.C., shows no knowledge of a hero named Daniel in his list of famous men (cf. Chs 44–50). The earliest reference to the book is apparently in Sibylline Oracles III. 397–400 (*c.* 140 B.C.), where allusion is made to Dan. 7, although there may be an even earlier reference in 1 Enoch (cf. 14$^{18-22}$, which may be a borrowing from Dan. 7$^{9\ f.}$). In 1 Macc. 2$^{59\ f.}$ (*c.* 100 B.C.) mention is made of Daniel and his friends by name, indicating a knowledge either of the book itself or of a source lying behind it. Reference is again made to him in a pseudo-Daniel apocalypse from Qumran where fragments of seven manuscripts, dating from about 100 B.C., have been found relating to the Book of Daniel. That is, whereas no previous mention is made of the book, there is evidence that from the second century B.C. onwards it was both known and revered.

Internally the evidence is even more varied. Linguistically the book as it stands cannot be anything like as early as the sixth century B.C. This is shown by the late style of the Hebrew, which resembles that of Chronicles, Esther, and Ecclesiastes, and also by the appearance in the text of Persian and Greek loan-words, one of which (Greek *sumphonion*) is not found in the sense used here (meaning 'bagpipes') before the second century B.C. Historically there are certain discrepancies which are to say the least surprising, if the book is a product of the exilic period. Thus, there is no confirmatory evidence in either 2 Kings or Jeremiah for the deportation mentioned in 1$^{1\ f.}$; Belshazzar was not the son of Nebuchadnezzar (cf. 5$^{11}$) but of Nabonidus, and although heir to the throne never became king (cf. 5$^{1\ ff.}$,

$8^{1}$ ff.); there is no historical evidence for 'Darius the Mede', who is said to have conquered Babylon (cf. $5^{31}$, $6^{28}$), or for the 'Median empire' which it is assumed came between those of Babylonia and Persia; the word 'Chaldean' in the sense of 'astrologer' (cf. $2^{2}$ etc.) was not so used at the time of the Exile and reflects a late Greek usage; it is most unlikely, moreover, that Daniel would have been appointed to high office in the Babylonian priesthood, as is here stated (cf. $2^{48}$), or that he, a strict Jew, would have accepted such an appointment. On the other hand there is a concentration of interest on the period from Alexander the Great to Antiochus Epiphanes (died 164 or 163 B.C.), about which the writer shows accurate knowledge. No specific reference is made to Antiochus' death (although it is anticipated in $11^{45}$), but allusion is made to his desecration of the Temple a few years earlier (cf. $7^{25}$, $8^{14}$, $9^{27}$, $12^{7}$; 1 Macc. $1^{54}$). It seems most likely, then, that the book, in its present form at any rate, is to be dated about the year 164 B.C.

The determination of the date raises the question of its literary unity, about which there is no agreement amongst scholars It is customary to divide it up, according to its literary contents, into two parts: the six stories recorded in Chs 1–6, and the four visions in Chs 7–12. The stories are told in the third person about the exploits of Daniel and his three companions under Babylonian rule; they reflect a fair measure of toleration, and present Daniel as a wise man able to interpret dreams and forecast events. The visions on the other hand are for the most part related by Daniel in the first person, reflect a Palestinian background, and indicate a more serious situation of intolerance and persecution. Despite these differences, however, there are close connexions between the two parts, as, for example, between Chs 2 and 7. Indeed in some respects ch. 7, despite its dream-form, belongs more closely to the first part of the book than to the second.

This is illustrated by the language in which it is written, for apart from $1^{1}$–$2^{4a}$, all of Chs 1–7 is in Aramaic, the rest of the book being in Hebrew. That is, whereas in content and form the break comes at the end of Ch. 6, in language it comes at the end of Ch. 7. Many suggestions have been made to explain this bilingual division. In itself such a phenomenon provides no argument for the book's composite character; nevertheless the evidence suggests that the author in the first part selected and recorded a number of earlier stories with a Babylonian background, probably in oral form and in the popular Aramaic tongue, to which he added Ch. 7 by way of interpretation; even this interpretation itself may have belonged to the same line of oral tradition. Shortly afterwards the same writer, or perhaps one of his disciples, recorded the visions in Chs 8–12, which are themselves a commentary upon, and an expansion of, the dream in Ch. 7; these visions, though literary in character, may well reflect genuine visionary experience on the part of the author. They were recorded in Hebrew, a language more expressive of the ardent nationalist outlook of the writer. The section $1^1$–$2^{4a}$, it is suggested, was then changed by the author from Aramaic into Hebrew to make his book more acceptable among those of like mind with himself, continuing aptly in Aramaic at $2^{4b}$ where the narrative records the Chaldeans' reply to the King.

Associated with the canonical Book of Daniel at an early date were three other collections of material, which appear in the Apocrypha as *The Prayer of Azariah and the Song of the Three Young Men* (inserted between $3^{23}$ and $3^{24}$ in the Greek text of Daniel), *The History of Susanna*, and *Bel and the Dragon*. These originally independent works illustrate the popular character of the Daniel cycle of stories and the reputation he possessed as a wise and godly man.

It is possible that the Daniel tradition is to be traced much farther back, however, and that the chief character of the book reflects an ancient hero of that name who is mentioned elsewhere in the Old Testament. In Ezek. $14^{14, 20}$ a certain Dan'el, in conjunction with Noah and Job, is praised for his righteousness and powers of intercession, and in $28^3$ reference is made to his wisdom and his knowledge of secret lore. The implication that he is a hero of ancient tradition has found confirmation in the occurrence of the same name in the Ras Shamra (Ugarit) tablets, dating from the fourteenth century B.C., where he appears as a righteous man who has compassion on the widows and the orphans. There can be little doubt that these two sources refer to the same character and to the prevalence over a long period of a legendary figure called Dan'el. It is perhaps less certain in what way he is connected with the Daniel of the Canonical book, but it can hardly be doubted that a relationship does in fact exist. The difference in spelling between the two forms of the name offers no real difficulty. The author of Daniel was familiar with the Book of Ezekiel and must have known its reference to this legendary hero. Both Noah (cf. 1 Enoch 6–11 etc.; Jub. 7²⁰ ᶠᶠ·, 10¹ ᶠᶠ·) and Job (cf. Ecclus. 49⁸ ᶠ·), moreover, are familiar figures in Jewish writings of the second century B.C., and it is reasonable to suppose that Daniel also, with his established reputation for wisdom and secret knowledge, should make his appearance in apocalyptic tradition. If this is so, the author may well have taken over, together with the name, material of a legendary kind associated with the ancient Dan'el.

The book reflects the religious outlook of the Hasidim, and was probably written by one of their number who regarded the opposition to Antiochus by the Maccabees as only 'a little help' (11³⁴) and looked for deliverance rather to divine intervention. Theologically its outlook and teaching fit into this background more readily than into any other—its stress, for example, on the observance of the Law in matters of food, fasting, and prayer, and its teaching concerning angels, the resurrection, and the Golden Age soon to break in. Written against a background of grievous persecution and suffering, its aim was to encourage the faithful in their time of trial and to assure them of the speedy intervention of God.

### *a.* DANIEL AND HIS FRIENDS (1¹⁻²¹)

This story of Daniel at the Babylonian court serves as an introduction to the other stories in the first half of the book. Its background portraying the Babylonian Exile was appropriate to the situation in which the Jews found themselves both in the Dispersion and in Palestine itself during the time of Antiochus Epiphanes.

1. *In the third year of the reign of Jehoiakim*, i.e. 606 B.C. According to Jer. 25¹ Nebuchadnezzar did not become King until Jehoiakim's fourth year (i.e. 605) and, on the evidence of 2 Kings 24¹⁰⁻¹⁵, did not besiege Jerusalem until a year after Jehoiakim's death (i.e. 597). There is, however, a tradition in 2 Chron. 36⁶⁻⁷ which alludes to a rebellion in the time of Jehoiakim, when Nebuchadnezzar, it is said, carried off the King and some of the Temple treasures. The author of Daniel apparently links this event with that recorded in 2 Kings 24¹, which states that Nebuchadnezzar exacted tribute from Jehoiakim for three years, reckoning these as the FIRST three years of his reign. That is, he calculates the Exile from 606 B.C. rather than from 597 B.C. In so doing it is just possible that he had in mind the fulfilment of Jeremiah's prophecy that the Exile would last for seventy years (cf. Jer. 25¹¹ ᶠ·, 29¹⁰), which, on this reckoning, would be from 606 to 537 B.C.

*Nebuchadnezzar*. The correct spelling, as the inscriptions show, is Nebuchadrezzar, with *r* for *n*. The form with 'n' would be attractive to the writer of the Book of Daniel, for he could hardly have failed to notice that the numerical value of the letters of 'Nebuchadnezzar' is equal to that of 'Antiochus Epiphanes'! This device, which is illustrated in the New Testament[1] and also in the Qumran Scrolls, would strongly appeal to an apocalyptic writer and may lie behind his choice of this particular form of the name.

2. *the land of Shinar*: an archaic name for Babylonia found elsewhere in the Old Testament (cf. Gen. 10¹⁰, 11², 14⁹; Isa. 11¹¹; Zech. 5¹¹).

*his god*, i.e. Bel, also called Marduk (cf. 4⁸; Isa. 46¹, etc.), whose Temple was in Babylon.

---

[1] Cf. Rev. 13¹⁸, where 666 ('the number of the beast') is the sum of the Hebrew letters of 'Nero Caesar'. This device, whereby hidden meanings are found in words by reference to their numerical value, is known as *gemaṭría*.

4. *the letters and language of the Chaldeans*. With the exception of 5³⁰ and 9¹ the word *Chaldean* is used in Daniel to signify a professional class of Babylonian priests described as 'wise men' or 'astrologers'. This meaning is late and reflects the usage of Graeco–Roman times. Elsewhere in the Old Testament it has an ethnic sense and refers to people of lower Babylonia who under Nebuchadnezzar's father Nabopolassar established a Chaldean dynasty which survived until Persian times. By *letters and language* is meant the mysterious Akkadian tongue with its strange cuneiform script, and the equally mysterious magical lore associated with this priestly caste of 'wise men'.

6 f. The names of Daniel and his friends, each with the ending *-el* (meaning 'God') or *-iah* (meaning 'Yahweh'), are changed into Babylonian names, some of which at least have reference to Babylonian deities. This custom of adopting a foreign name was fairly common among the Jews of Hellenistic times, especially among those with Hellenistic sympathies. No objection is offered here to a practice which in course of time became generally accepted.

8–16. This story of Daniel and his friends faring better on a plain diet than others on rich food would have a particular relevance for the Jews living in the Dispersion, who laid great store by the observance of dietary laws as a distinguishing mark between themselves and the Gentiles.

17–20. Elsewhere in the apocalyptic literature inspiration (especially that of a visionary kind) is sometimes associated with a special food or diet (cf. 'Mart. of Isa.' 2¹¹; 2 Esdras 9²³⁻²⁵). God gives these young men *wisdom* which shows itself in the ability to interpret *visions and dreams*. In this respect the influence of the Joseph stories of Genesis can be clearly seen.

*Magicians and enchanters*: names given to the Babylonian 'wise men'. Divination played an important part in Babylonian religion.

21. *the first year of King Cyrus*, i.e. 539 B.C., when he became King of Babylon and issued an edict permitting the captive Jews to return to their own land (cf. Ezra 1¹, 5¹³, 6³).

*b.* NEBUCHADNEZZAR'S DREAM $(2^{1-49})$

This chapter illustrates the claim of $1^{17}$ that God had given to Daniel 'understanding in all visions and dreams'. The similarity between this account and that of Joseph in Gen. 41 is quite striking and there can be little doubt that the writer is using this old story as his model.

Nebuchadnezzar's dream concerns four great world empires, depicted in terms of a great metal image whose destruction is near (31 ff.). There is a close connexion here with the theme of Ch. 7, which portrays the same four empires by means of animal symbolism. The most likely identification of the metals in the image is that the gold represents the Babylonian empire, the silver the 'Median', the brass the Persian, and the iron and clay together the Greek. The readers of Daniel would be aware of their own involvement in such matters, and would see in the prophecy of Nebuchadnezzar's downfall the pending destruction of the tyrant Antiochus Epiphanes. The kingdom of God, symbolized by the stone 'cut out by no human hand', would crush him as it had crushed the kingdoms that had gone before. The dream and its interpretation were sure (45).

4 ff. The language of the book changes from Hebrew to Aramaic with the quoted words of the Chaldeans in v. 4, and continues in Aramaic until $7^{28}$.

The word *interpretation* (Hebrew, *pēšer*; Aramaic, *pĕšar*), which occurs thirty times in the Aramaic section of the book, is, like the word *secret* or *mystery* (Aramaic, *raz*) which occurs nine times, one of the key words in Daniel. The latter is a Persian loan-word (translated in the Greek Versions by *mustērion*); it does not signify any ordinary secret but rather the divine purpose which lies behind the universe and all the movements of history. Both words appear frequently in the Qumran texts. The idea that these divine mysteries have been made known to a select few who are able by means of divine *wisdom* to give their interpretation, is a familiar one in the Scrolls and in the apocalyptic writings.

20–23. Daniel's response is a hymn of praise, in which he acknowledges God as the source of all *wisdom and might*.

28. *the latter days*. This phrase is found also in the Old Testament prophets, where it refers to the end of an historical era; in the apocalyptic writings it refers rather to the end of the world.

31 ff. The symbolism of metals to represent different ages or empires was traditional and fairly widespread.

Unlike the *image*, the *stone* symbolizing the kingdom of God was of divine origin, made *by no human hand*, in the end it would fill *the whole earth*.

36 ff. The metals represent successive kingdoms—Babylonian, 'Median', Persian, and Greek—down to the writer's own time. The mixture of iron with clay no doubt represents two of the rival camps into which Alexander's empire came to be divided —*iron* for the Seleucids and *clay* for the Ptolemies (cf. 11⁵ ᶠᶠ·). The kingdom of God was about to break in with destructive and recreating power.

*c.* IN THE FIERY FURNACE $(3^{1-30})$

The absence of Daniel's name from this story may suggest that it belonged to a separate tradition prior to the editing of the book. It would, however, have a dramatic relevance in the time of Antiochus Epiphanes, who also set up an image, which men were commanded to worship, having features remarkably like his own.[1] Failure to do so would be punished by death. In this connexion several forms of martyrdom are described in 1 and 2 Maccabees, among them that of burning (cf. 2 Macc. 7⁵).

*d.* NEBUCHADNEZZAR'S MADNESS $(4^{1-37})$

The king's dream of a great tree whose stump alone is allowed to remain is interpreted by Daniel with reference to Nebuchadnezzar and his kingdom, whose pride would be humbled to the dust. Nebuchadnezzar himself loses his reason

[1] See p. 41.

and for seven years is made 'to eat grass like an ox' (32). In the end he is restored and acknowledges the Most High God. This happy ending, together with the obvious piety of the King, so unlike the character of Antiochus Epiphanes, suggests that the story had its origin in pre-Maccabaean days. Its application to Antiochus, however, would be quite fitting in other respects, for the readers of Daniel would recall that Antiochus Epiphanes, meaning '(God) manifest', was popularly known as Antiochus 'Epimanes', meaning 'madman'! Like the proud Nebuchadnezzar he too would receive his deserts.

There is no independent historical allusion to Nebuchadnezzar's being stricken by madness in the way recounted here. There is, however, an Aramaic text among the fragments found at Qumran which tells how King Nabonidus was 'smitten with a malignant inflammation' for seven years, at the end of which he was cured through the intervention of a Jewish exorcist who brought him to acknowledge the name of the Most High God. In its present form this 'Prayer of Nabonidus', as it is called, may be later than the Book of Daniel, but its reference to Nabonidus and not to Nebuchadnezzar in this connexion may well represent the original tradition. Support for this conclusion is probably to be found in an even more ancient text—the so-called 'Verse Account of Nabonidus'[1]— where, in an account of his religious innovations, which included the introduction of the image of a strange god, the statement occurs: 'The king is mad'. This identification would further explain the reference in the following chapter of Daniel where Belshazzar is introduced as the son of Nebuchadnezzar, whereas in fact he was the son of Nabonidus. If such an alteration of name did take place it was probably at a stage in the story's development earlier than the editing of the Book of Daniel.

8. *Belteshazzar.* This court name, given earlier to Daniel by Nebuchadnezzar (cf. 1⁷), is said here to be derived from the name of Bel, the title of Babylon's chief god, Marduk. Such

---

[1] Cf. J. B. Pritchard, *Ancient Near Eastern Texts*, 1950, pp. 312 ff.

etymology, however, is most unlikely. The word represents the Akkadian 'Balaṭsu–uṣur' meaning 'May he protect the life of the king'.

*the spirit of the holy gods.* In the light of v. 34 we should probably read the singular 'God'. The whole phrase is reminiscent of Gen. 41³⁸, where Joseph is described as 'a man in whom the Spirit of God is'.

9. *mystery . . . . interpretation.* See 2⁴ ᶠᶠ· above.

10 ff. This picture of a great tree, hewn to the ground so that only the stump remains, probably derives from Ezek. 31, where the greatness of Egypt, represented by a mighty cedar, is humbled to the dust. Behind both biblical passages we are perhaps to find a reference to 'the garden of God' (cf. Ezek. 28²·⁹, 31¹⁰, etc.). Nebuchadnezzar, having challenged the sovereignty of the Almighty, will be brought low.

13. *a watcher, a holy one.* Both expressions are found frequently in later apocalyptic writings with reference to angels.

16. *seven times*: probably 'seven years'.

27. *by practising righteousness.* The LXX translates 'by almsgiving'. This reflects the late meaning of the word and there may be a feeling of it in this passage (cf. Tob. 12⁸ ᶠ·). Repentance and good works will do much to avert the judgement of God.

30. *I have built.* Nebuchadnezzar had a great reputation for his building schemes.

35. *the host of heaven.* These are contrasted with 'all the inhabitants of the earth' and represent the angelic heavenly powers. In the Old Testament the expression is used with reference to the stars (cf. Deut. 4¹⁹; Jer. 33²²); in later apocalyptic writings, as in 1 Enoch 18¹⁴ ᶠᶠ· and 86¹ ᶠᶠ·, the stars represent angels, and this is the likely meaning here.

*e.* BELSHAZZAR'S FEAST (5¹⁻³¹)

The purpose of this story was to encourage the faithful, and so it is to be judged not as an historical record but as a religious lesson. From the point of view of history it poses a number of difficult problems: Who was Belshazzar, and what was his relationship to Nebuchadnezzar? What historical allusions, if any, are made in the writing on the wall? Who was Darius the Mede and what was the Median empire?

1 f. *King Belshazzar . . . Nebuchadnezzar his father*. Nebuchadnezzar is represented as the father of Belshazzar, the last king of the Babylonian empire. This claim involves three discrepancies—Belshazzar was apparently never king in his own right, his father was not Nebuchadnezzar but Nabonidus, and Nabonidus, not Belshazzar, was the last Babylonian king. Nebuchadnezzar died in 562 B.C. and, after a succession of three kings, was followed by Nabonidus (555–538 B.C.), during whose reign Babylon fell (538 B.C.). The latter part of his time was spent in Tema, during which the affairs of state were left in the hands of his son Belshazzar. That he was not, however, recognized as king is indicated by the fact that the New Year Festival could not be celebrated in Babylon because of the King's absence, even although Belshazzar was himself in residence.

*the vessels of gold and of silver*. The memory of the plundering of the Temple by Heliodorus (cf. 2 Macc. 3[10 ff.]) and again by Antiochus Epiphanes (cf. 2 Macc. 5[15 f.])[1] would still be fresh in the minds of the readers.

24 ff. The word *mene*, from the root 'to count', is written once only in v. 26, and this is followed in v. 25 also by the ancient versions; the word *tekel*, from the root 'to weigh', is the equivalent of the Hebrew 'šeḳel'; and the form *parsín* is a plural or dual of the word *peres*, from the root 'to divide'. It seems likely that each represents a coin of the realm: a mina, a shekel, and a half (mina). The root meaning of each word tells its own story: the days of Belshazzar's kingdom are 'counted' or 'numbered'; it has been 'weighed' in the balance and found wanting; soon it will be 'divided' up. A double meaning is probably to be detected in this last word *peres* whose root

[1] See pp. 35, 40.

indicates not only the sense of 'division' but also the word 'Persian' (Aramaic, *pārās*)—the Babylonian empire would be divided and given over to the Persians. Another explanation is that each of the three words represents a king or a kingdom. Various identifications have been suggested. For example, the mina represents Nebuchadnezzar, the shekel Belshazzar, and the half mina the Medes and Persians; others take them to represent the three Babylonian rulers Nebuchadnezzar, Evil-Merodach (cf. 2 Kings 25²⁷ ᶠᶠ·), and Belshazzar, or perhaps even more acceptably Nebuchadnezzar, Nabonidus, and Belshazzar. The Qumran fragment entitled 'The Prayer of Nabonidus'[1] shows that some Jews at least knew this king by name; moreover, as we have seen, he and not Nebuchadnezzar may have been the original figure in Ch. 4. It is possible that when the change of name was made in Ch. 4 it was carried through also in Ch. 5. This would explain the reference to Nebuchadnezzar and not Nabonidus as Belshazzar's father.

31. *Darius the Mede*. This Darius who is described as a Mede, the son of Xerxes (cf. 9¹) and the immediate predecessor of Cyrus (cf. 6²⁸), cannot be the Persian Darius I who captured Babylon in 520 B.C. or Darius II who is mentioned in Neh. 12²². Indeed there is no historical evidence outside the Book of Daniel for any such person, nor is there any room for his supposed 'Median' empire between the defeat of Nabonidus and the rise of Cyrus. It is easy, however, to see how this conception arose. Prophecy had foretold the overthrow of Babylon by the Medes (cf. Isa. 13¹⁷, 21²; Jer. 51¹¹· ²⁸), who, before the conquest of Cyrus, had made themselves masters of a vast area. The writer may have regarded these prophecies as being in a sense fulfilled when in 538 B.C. Babylon was overthrown by Gobryas, Cyrus' general, for Cyrus' kingdom had come by that time to include that of the Medes. He takes a greater liberty, however, when he confuses the name of Cyrus (who captured Babylon in 538 B.C.) with that of Darius I (who captured the same city in 520 B.C.), and creates a fictitious

[1] See above, p. 229.

figure 'Darius the Mede', whose empire he places prior to that of Cyrus himself (cf. 6²⁸)! This agrees with his notion of four successive kingdoms—Babylonian, 'Median', Persian, and Greek—which are to be overthrown by the kingdom of God (cf. Ch. 2).

*f.* IN THE LIONS' DEN (6¹⁻²⁸)

This story of Daniel in the lions' den has much in common with that of the fiery furnace in Ch. 3, and teaches a similar lesson of forbearance and trust in God.

10. This verse no doubt indicates the practice of the Jews in the Dispersion during the Greek, and possibly also the Persian, period. Prayer was offered in a kneeling position, with the face *toward Jerusalem* (cf. 1 Kings 8³⁵, ³⁸, ⁴⁴, ⁴⁸; Ezek. 8¹⁶; Tob. 3¹¹), *three times a day* (cf. Ps. 55¹⁷), corresponding to the times of morning and afternoon ('evening') sacrifice in the Temple and the hour of sunset.

*g.* THE VISION OF THE FOUR BEASTS AND THE SON OF MAN (7¹⁻²⁸)

1–8. *The beasts.* This first vision amply illustrates the importance of symbolism and mythology in the apocalyptic writings. The four beasts are generally taken to represent the empires of Babylonia, 'Media', Persia, and Greece. Certain details, such as the fact that they emerge out of the *sea*, are not taken up in the interpretation but form part of the 'trimmings' of traditional mythology. Attention is focused on the *fourth beast*, with its *ten horns*, and on another *little horn* which *plucked up* three of the other horns *by the roots*. This beast presumably represents Alexander the Great, the ten horns ten rulers who suceeded him, and the little horn Antiochus Epiphanes, who dealt ruthlessly with three of those who stood between him and the throne.

9–12. The judgement. The picture now changes from the turbulent sea to a judgement scene in heaven. This idea of God in his heavenly Council, sitting in judgement with his angelic attendants, is a fairly common one in the Old

Testament (cf. 1 Kings 22¹⁹ ff.; Job 16 ff.; Isa. 66 ff.; Ps. 89⁷) and is found also in the apocalyptic writings. The venerable figure, called here the *Ancient of Days*, seated on his fiery throne pronounces judgement on the beasts. This reference to fire as an expression of judgement recalls its important place also in Persian eschatology. *The books* which are opened likewise recall the 'Tablets of Fate' of the Babylonian New Year Festival on which were recorded the destinies of men.

13–14. *A royal audience: one like a son of man.* In his *vision* the writer sees, coming *with the clouds of heaven, one like a son of man* who is brought before the 'Ancient of Days'. The picture is that of a royal audience and investiture in which this 'son of man', having been ushered into the divine presence, is given *dominion* over all the *nations* of the earth and *a kingdom which shall not pass away*.

Who is this 'son of man'? The Aramaic phrase *bar 'enash*, like its Hebrew equivalent *ben 'adham*, signifies a 'member of the human race'. The writer of Daniel was probably influenced by the use of the expression in the Book of Ezekiel, where it appears 87 times, and also in Ps. 8⁴ᶠ·, where man is presented both in his creaturely weakness over against God and in his divine dignity over against the Creation; for here 'one like a son of man' stands in obvious contrast to the four beasts. Over against the beastly and the bestial he represents the human and the humane to whom will be given everlasting dominion. What we have here, then, is a symbolic figure whose significance is to be interpreted later on in the chapter (see vv. 21, 22, and 28).

Another identification, however, is possible. Elsewhere in the Old Testament, as in Daniel itself and in the extra-biblical literature, it is said of the angels that they appear 'in the likeness of men', and in later apocalyptic writings the 'son of man' of Daniel appears as a supramundane creature, 'a man from heaven'. It is just possible that the same interpretation can be given here. But once again what we have is a symbolic figure and not any particular identifiable angel.

15–18. *The interpretation.* Greatly puzzled by the vision, Daniel asks an angelic attendant its meaning. Such angel interpreters are a common feature in apocalyptic tradition; living in close attendance upon God they have special knowledge of the divine secrets. The four beasts, he is told, represent four kingdoms (literally 'kings') whose authority will be taken away and given to the *saints of the Most High*. Here is the meaning of the investiture of the 'son of man' with an everlasting kingdom in v. 14. But who are these 'saints' (literally 'holy ones')? Once more, two interpretations are possible:

It is generally accepted that they represent the faithful remnant of Israel who will inherit God's kingdom (cf. 'the *people* of the saints of the Most High', v. 27). In support of this, reference can be made to such a passage as Ps. 80[17], where 'son of man' is used as a collective symbol for the people of Israel.

Another interpretation, however, is possible. It can be argued that here (as frequently elsewhere in biblical and extra-biblical sources) the expression 'the holy ones' signifies rather 'the angels' who are to be God's agents in bringing in his kingdom. The kingdoms of the world, symbolized by the beasts, are under the dominion of evil forces; in the coming kingdom the power will be given into the hands of 'the holy ones'. This idea of the defeat of evil spirits or demons by good spirits or angels in a final eschatological battle appears frequently in the apocalyptic writings and also in the Qumran Scrolls.

19–28. *Interpretation of the fourth beast.* The allusion to Antiochus Epiphanes is clear; the context lends support to the argument that by 'the saints' is meant here 'the faithful Israelites' rather than 'the holy angels', though some would argue that a redactor has changed the whole character of the passage by interpreting 'the saints' (i.e. the angels) in vv. 21 and 22 as 'the people of the saints' (i.e. the faithful Israelites) in v. 28. Antiochus will *change the times* appointed for the Jewish festivals and *the law* of Moses which was the very heart of their religion. But the period of his domination will be limited to *a time* ('a year'?), *and times and half a time*, presumably three and a half years. This number, however, is probably to be taken as a general and not a precise reference: it is simply a 'round number', being half the sacred number seven (cf. our rather loose use of 'half a dozen'). In course of time it came to be regarded as a number of ill omen. Verse 28 concludes both the vision and its interpretation and may even have marked the close of the book at an earlier stage of its development.

## h. THE RAM AND THE HE-GOAT ($8^{1-27}$)

This chapter, which is in some ways an expansion of Ch. 7, marks the beginning of the main Hebrew section of the book. From this point onwards the recorded visions reflect a situation of severe persecution, and are probably to be dated between 167 and 165 B.C., i.e. during the reign of Antiochus Epiphanes. In the end (and the end is very near) he is to be destroyed by the hand of God.

### 1–14. *The vision*

2. Daniel is transported in vision to *Susa*, the future Persian capital, which is near *the river Ulai* (i.e. Eulaeus).

3. Animal symbolism is a common characteristic of the apocalyptic literature. Here *the ram*, with its *two horns*, represents the Medo-Persian empire. The Persian *came up last*, but *was higher than the other*. The ram and the horn are symbols of power in the Old Testament. The ram was also the zodiacal sign of the Persian empire.

5. The *he-goat* represents the Greek empire. The zodiacal sign of the Seleucids in Syria was that of Capricorn (*caper* a goat, *cornu* a horn).

8. This verse records the death of Alexander and the division of his empire into the four kingdoms of Asia Minor, Egypt, Macedonia, and Mesopotamia.

9. The writer passes over the years between the battle of Ipsus in 301 B.C. and the rise of Antiochus Epiphanes in 175 B.C. Reference is made to Antiochus' campaigns against Egypt (*the south*), Parthia (*the east*), and Palestine itself (*the glorious land*).

10. Antiochus' arrogance knows no limit. He attacks even the starry *host of Heaven* and throws them *to the ground*. These words may also carry an allusion to his attack on the several religions of his realm, the stars symbolizing heathen gods (cf. Deut. 4$^{19}$; Isa. 24$^{21}$ ff.).

11. He is insolent even to *the Prince of the host*—probably a reference to God himself, although it may allude to the angelic leader of the heavenly host (cf. also v. 25). He deprives God of *the continual burnt offering* which was offered twice daily (cf. 1 Macc. 1$^{45}$) and desecrates the *sanctuary*—an allusion to the events of December 167 B.C.

12. The text is obscure. *The host* may refer to troops under Antiochus who enforced the King's command (cf. 1 Macc. 1$^{44 f.}$), or the passage may indicate that heathen sacrifices (*transgression*) were substituted for *the continual burnt offering*. *Truth* refers to the true religion.

13 f. An angel reveals the exact duration of the time of suffering. The sanctuary will be *restored* after *2,300* evening and morning offerings, i.e. 1,150 days. Such attempts to date events, and especially the time of the end, are typical of the apocalyptic writings. The significance of the number is obscure. It represents a period four months shorter than that indicated in 7$^{25}$, if the three and a half years indicated there are to be taken as an exact space of time (see loc. cit.).

*The transgression that makes desolate* is presumably the same as 'the abomination that makes desolate' in 9$^{27}$, 11$^{31}$, and 12$^{11}$. The expression *pesha' šomēm* is a play on 'Baal Shamen' (Lord of heaven), a name given to Zeus Olympius, whose altar and image were set up in the Jerusalem Temple (cf. 1 Macc. 1$^{54,\ 59}$; 2 Macc. 6$^5$).

15–27. *The interpretation*

16 f. The period from the second century B.C. onwards marks a significant development in angelology. Here, for the first time in the Old Testament, an angel is named.

23. The insolence of Antiochus is well known. He is described as

*one who understands riddles*. This may mean that he is a master of intrigue or perhaps that, like Daniel, he claims knowledge of the divine secrets.

25. *the Prince of princes*: God.

26. Apocalyptic is essentially literary in character. Daniel has to *seal up the vision* until the time of the End. The impression is thus strengthened that the apocalyptists' message was from the distant past and had been preserved through many generations. There are many references in this literature to such 'secret books' whose secrets are to be revealed in the last days.

### *i*. THE SEVENTY YEARS ($9^{1-27}$)

This passage illustrates the apocalyptists' interest in the predictive side of prophecy, and at the same time emphasizes that their message, contrary to appearance, is directed not towards the far-distant future but to the contemporary situation. Its aim is to encourage the faithful to hold their ground, for the hour of their deliverance is at hand.

### 3–19. *Daniel's prayer*

There are indications that this prayer, consisting of a confession (4–14) and a supplication (15–19), is an earlier composition which the writer of Daniel has incorporated in his book. This chapter is the only passage in Daniel where God is given the name 'Yahweh'.

### 20–27. *Gabriel's interpretation*

20–24. Gabriel interprets Jeremiah's seventy years as *seventy weeks of years*. At the close of this period, which has been determined (*decreed*) by God, the profanation wrought by Antiochus will be brought to an end, a righteous and everlasting order of society will be established, the prophets and their visions will be vindicated, and the sacred Temple will be rededicated with anointing oil. This interpretation of seventy heptads or week-years is probably given under the influence of Lev. $26^{34\ f.}$ and 2 Chron. $36^{21}$, which suggest that each year of Jeremiah's prophecy should be regarded as a sabbatical year.

25–27. The writer divides the seventy heptads into three
periods, each of which is closed by a significant historical
event. The first period is to last for seven 'weeks' (i.e. 49 years)
*from the going forth of the word to restore and build Jerusalem to the
coming of the anointed one*. This apparently refers to the period
between the fall of Jerusalem in 586 B.C. (cf. Jer. 30¹⁸, 31³⁸⁻⁴⁰)
and the return of the High Priest Joshua to Jerusalem in
538 B.C. (cf. Ezra 3²; Hag. 1¹; Zech. 3¹). The second period is to
last for sixty-two 'weeks' (i.e. 434 years), when *an anointed one
shall be cut off*. The most likely identification here is Onias III,
last High Priest of the Zadokite line, who was killed in 171 B.C.
(cf. 2 Macc. 4³³⁻³⁶). The fact that this period (538–171 B.C.)
falls short of the stated 434 years by about 67 years (434 minus
367) should not be pressed, for what we have here is a purely
schematic number; the writer's knowledge of Persian chronology was no doubt dependent on popular tradition whose
accuracy was far from trustworthy. The third period is to last
for one 'week' (i.e. 7 years), when *the prince who is to come shall
destroy the city and the sanctuary and make a strong covenant with many*.
The allusion here is no doubt to Antiochus, whose troops would
plunder Jerusalem (cf. 1 Macc. 1³¹⁻³⁸, 3⁴⁵), and who for seven
years (171–164 B.C.) would enlist the support of apostate Jews
(cf. 1 Macc. 1¹⁰⁻¹⁵). During the second half of this period (i.e.
from 167 to 164 B.C.) he would desecrate the Temple, causing
the sacrifices to cease. The exact meaning of the phrase *the
wing of abominations* is obscure, although it no doubt has
reference to the abominable Baal Shamen whose image was set
up in the Temple (cf. 9²⁷, 11³¹, 12¹¹); it may refer to the erection of the statue in a *wing* of the Temple (cf. Matt. 4⁵), or,
with a slight emendation, the text may give the sense that
'instead of' the prescribed sacrifices *abominations* would be
offered. After these things would come *the decreed end*. The
unspecified nature of this event suggests that the passage was
written some time before the rededication of the Temple in
December 164 B.C., i.e. three years after its desecration.
When, however, in due course the year 164 B.C. came and
passed by, and still the End did not appear, subsequent writers

set themselves, as Daniel had done, to reinterpret Jeremiah's prophecy in the light of the situation in their own day. Such interpretations are found in 1 Enoch, the Testaments of the XII Patriarchs, the Zadokite Document among the Dead Sea Scrolls, and the writings of Josephus.

### j. A VISION OF THE END (10¹–12¹³)

This lengthy account may be divided, for the sake of convenience, into prologue and vision (10¹–11¹), interpretation of the vision (11²–12⁴), and epilogue (12⁵⁻¹³).

#### 10¹–11¹: *Prologue and vision*

As a result of Daniel's abstemious preparation, an angel appears to him and assures him that his *words have been heard* by God.

1. *a great conflict*: either the angelic warfare alluded to in subsequent verses or the emotional strain felt by Daniel as a result of the vision.

2 f. Such practices as fasting and partaking of a special diet or drink are frequently mentioned in the apocalyptic writings as preparations for psychical experience. This allusion, together with the emotional repercussions mentioned in vv. 7 and 10 f. (trembling), 9 (a deep sleep), 15 (dumbness), and 16 (physical weakness), may well reflect the actual experience of the writer himself.

5 ff. *a man clothed in linen*: i.e. an angel, probably the same Gabriel as in 8¹⁵ ᶠ·. 'Linen garments' represent the 'spiritual bodies' of the angels. The experience of Daniel's companions recalls that of Paul in Acts 9⁷.

13 ff. The belief was widespread during this period that God had set guardian angels over the nations of the earth who formed a heavenly counterpart of the Gentile rulers into whose power he had, from time to time, delivered his people by reason of their sins. Wars on earth had likewise their counterpart in wars in heaven between the several guardian angels and their hosts.

Indeed, according to some writers, the war in heaven determined the corresponding war on earth, so that if a particular
guardian angel gained the ascendancy over his peers, the nation
over which he had been appointed gained the ascendancy over
the other nations of the earth. Thus before a nation could be
judged and punished its angel ruler must first be dealt with.
All such rulers, being subject to God's permissive will, would in
the end be judged—like the nations over which they ruled.
Reference is made in this passage to the guardian angels of
Persia and Greece (cf. v. 20), who apparently are determined
to resist the disclosure of divine secrets to Daniel and so to the
people of Israel. But the victory of Israel is assured, for Michael,
the guardian angel of God's chosen people, whose coming is a
sign that the End is at hand (cf. 12$^1$), comes to the help of the
angel Gabriel. This is the first reference to the angel Michael
in the Scriptures (cf. also 10$^{21}$, 12$^1$; Jude 9; Rev. 12$^7$).

11$^2$–12$^4$: *The interpretation of the vision*

At last the angel is in a position to reveal 'the word' referred
to in 10$^1$. This consists of a 'potted' history, as it concerns the
Jewish nation from the beginning of the Persian period to the
time of Antiochus Epiphanes. Beginning with Cyrus and his
immediate successors (2) the writer passes on to Alexander the
Great (3–4), whose kingdom is divided between Ptolemy I
(*king of the south*) and Seleucus I (*one of his princes*) (5). Allusion
is then made to the marriage of Ptolemy II's daughter Berenice
to Antiochus II, whose divorced wife, Laodice, wreaked
vengeance on her rival and her child (6). Ptolemy III,
Berenice's brother (*a branch from her roots*), takes vengeance on
the Seleucids (7–8) and then withstands his enemy's reprisals
(9). The subject of the next few verses is Antiochus III the
Great, who, after an early defeat by Ptolemy IV at Raphia (10–
12), won the support of malcontents, including certain
Jewish insurgents (*men of violence among your own people*) (14),
and finally gained control of Palestine (15–16). The marriage
of his daughter Cleopatra to the young Ptolemy V did not win
him the advantage he sought (17), and in the end he was

humiliated by the Roman *commander* Scipio at Magnesia in 190 B.C. and forced to return to *his own land* (18–19).

After brief mention of Antiochus III's son and successor Seleucus IV, and his general Heliodorus (*an exactor of tribute*) (20), the writer goes on at greater length to consider the other son Antiochus IV Epiphanes (*a contemptible person*), who obtained the throne *by flatteries* (21). Having *swept away* all opposition, including the *prince of the covenant* (no doubt the High Priest Onias III), he distributed largesse from the *plunder* he obtained (22–24). In 169 B.C. Antiochus marched against Egypt on the pretext of protecting his nephew Ptolemy Philometor, feigning friendship with him, but all *to no avail* (27). Learning of disturbances in Jerusalem *his heart* was *set against the holy covenant*, i.e. the religion of the Jews; not only did he massacre the people, he also plundered the holy Temple (28). Some months later he took part in a second campaign against Egypt only to be turned back by the Romans (*ships of Kittim*, cf. a similar use of the phrase in the Dead Sea Scrolls) (29–30). It was at this juncture that Antiochus decided to stamp out the Jewish religion, profaning *the Temple* by setting up there the image of Zeus (*the abomination that makes desolate*, see note on 9²⁷), and taking away *the continual burnt offering* (31). Some Jews succumbed, but others (described as *those among the people who are wise*) remained faithful (33). These men counted the support of Mattathias and Judas as only *a little help*, for their trust was in God (34). Through their suffering they would *refine* and *cleanse* their whole nation (35). Antiochus, the self-styled 'God manifest' (Epiphanes), disregards the *gods of his fathers* and the popular Tammuz-Adonis (*the one beloved by women*) so as to *magnify himself above all* (36–37). He honours Jupiter Capitolinus (*the god of the fortresses*), now combined with Zeus Olympius, and mans the fortresses in Jerusalem with foreign troops (38–39).

At this point in the narrative history proper ends and prediction proper begins. In an attack on Egypt Antiochus will come into Palestine and *tens of thousands shall fall* (40–41). He will thereafter plunder Egypt, but on hearing *tidings from the east and the north,* will go northwards and *pitch his tents* between the Mediterranean Sea and Mount Zion, where he will meet *his end* (42–45). These details do not accord with the known facts of Antiochus' life, and indicate the point in time at which the writer received his vision. In thus presenting past history (through vv. 1–39) in the form of future event he underlines the fact of the foreknowledge of God and so deepens faith that the immediate future as foretold in his prophecy is also in the hands of God.

The death of Antiochus is the awaited sign that the time of tribulation will soon be over. The triumph-day of God is at hand, in which *Michael*, Israel's guardian angel, has a leading part to play. But before this day dawns *there shall be a time of trouble such as never has been* (12¹)—a dramatic conflict preceding the birth of the new age which is a common feature in the apocalyptic literature. Those, however, whose names are *written in the book* of God's elect *shall be delivered*; of such are *the wise*, to whose circle our author himself belongs (2–3). These will be raised to share in the glories of the new age, whilst others will be raised *to shame and everlasting contempt* (2). The resurrection thus contemplated is not for all, but rather for *many* of those who have died. The pre-eminently good and pre-eminently wicked are raised to receive their recompense at the hands of God. For the rest of mankind, it would appear, Sheol remains the eternal resting-place.[1] In the final verse Daniel is told to *shut up the words and seal the book until the time of the end* (4). The fact that it is now being read is a sign that the End is at hand! As in the days of Amos (cf. Amos 8¹¹ f.), men will *run to and fro* seeking knowledge of God; but this book contains all the knowledge they need!

## 12.⁵⁻¹³: *The epilogue*

In these verses the writer is again concerned with the time of *the end* (6). In answer to Daniel's enquiries the angel swears an oath, in the presence of two angelic witnesses (cf. Deut. 19¹⁵),

---

[1] For a fuller treatment of life after death in the apocalyptic writings see above, pp. 148 ff.

that the present tribulations will last three and a half years (cf.
7²⁵), when the *shattering* of Israel by Antiochus will come *to an
end* (7). When Daniel confesses that he still does not *understand*,
he is told that the matter is settled and *sealed* in readiness for
*the end*, when presumably everything will be made plain
(8–9). Meanwhile the righteous and *the wicked* go their ways,
but only *those who are wise* (cf. 11³³, ³⁵, 12³) will *understand* (10).
There then follow two verses which most scholars regard as
glosses written after the expiry of the 1,150 days mentioned in
8¹⁴. According to v. 11 the day of deliverance will dawn 1,290
days (i.e. 3 years and 7 months) after the pollution of the
Temple and in v. 12 this is extended to 1,335 days (i.e. 3 years
and 8½ months). The significance of these numbers is altogether
elusive. For the seer *the end* is near, when he will take his
destined *place* in the coming kingdom (13).

## 2. *The Book of Enoch*

The idea of secret writings 'sealed up' in a book until the
time of the End was not confined to the Book of Daniel, but
was a common feature of many such books in subsequent years.
Of special significance are those writings associated with the
name of Enoch, which had a wide popularity from the second
century B.C. onwards. This Enoch tradition is represented by
a composite work known as 1 Enoch or the Ethiopic Book of
Enoch,[1] supplemented by the Book of Jubilees, and in the
early Christian centuries by the Secrets of Enoch (2 Enoch)
and the Hebrew Book of Enoch (3 Enoch). Throughout these
writings the central figure is Enoch, who records in his books
secrets he has received by divine revelation that have been
preserved for future generations

> According to that which appeared to me in the heavenly vision,
> And which I have known through the word of the holy angels,
> And have learnt from the heavenly tablets (93²).

[1] So called because it is extant only in Ethiopic. Originally written in
Aramaic (a number of fragments have been found at Qumran), it was
translated into Greek, portions of which are available, representing Chs.
1–32, 106, and 107.

These secrets concern not only crises of world history, but also the ultimate meaning of the universe, and in particular the mysteries of the sun, moon, and stars.

The Book of Enoch is an artificial composition in five parts,[1] covering a period of about one hundred years from *c.* 164 B.C. The first five chapters are probably the work of the final editor, and Chs. 105 and 108 (which do not appear in the Greek) are to be regarded as later insertions. Some scholars have found evidence for a Book of Noah within this tradition, and identify certain sections of 1 Enoch and Jubilees as belonging to it. The five parts into which the book is divided are as follows:

*a.* ANGELS AND VISIONS (Chs. 6–36). This section is probably to be dated shortly after Daniel. It tells of the fall of the angels who cohabited with the daughters of men (cf. Gen. 6[1 ff.]) and of the judgement which befalls them and their giant offspring, whose spirits, as demons, inhabit the earth. Through lust they have brought all manner of evil and have corrupted mankind. Their doom is writ! Four 'hollow places' are described in which the spirits of the departed are separated from one another in anticipation of the coming judgement: 'These places have been made to receive them till the day of their judgement and till their appointed period' (22[4]). In two visions Enoch is then conducted by angels, first to the place reserved for the punishment of the angels, and then to Sheol, to Jerusalem, and to the ends of the earth.

*b.* THE SIMILITUDES (OR PARABLES) (Chs. 37–71). These parables, or rather 'discourses', are in three parts. The first (Chs. 38–44) deals with the judgement of the wicked and the rewards of the righteous, and with the astronomical and meteorological secrets of the heavens. The second (Chs. 45–57) tells of the Son of Man,[2] or the Elect One, who sits in judgement over all the earth; in his resplendent glory he separates the wicked from

---

[1] Cf. also the Pentateuch, the Psalms, Proverbs, the Megilloth, Ben Sira, and Pirkē 'Abhoth.

[2] See p. 147.

the righteous and pronounces judgement on men and angels alike.

> This is the Son of Man who hath righteousness,
> With whom dwelleth righteousness,
> And who revealeth all the treasures of that which is hidden . . . .
> And (he) shall loosen the reins of the strong,
> And break the teeth of the sinners (46³, ⁴).

The third (Chs. 58–69) describes the rewards of the righteous, the Final Judgement, the resurrection, and the names and functions of the fallen angels; whilst the final chapters (70–71) record Enoch's translation and further visions.

This is the only portion of 1 Enoch not represented by fragments found at Qumran, and for this reason it has been conjectured that it is in fact a product of the first or second century A.D. and may even be a Jewish-Christian work. The probability is, however, that it is Jewish in origin and belongs to the second half of the first century B.C.

*c*. THE HEAVENLY LUMINARIES (Chs. 72–82). The interest of this section is in astronomical lore, with a particular concern for calendrical calculations. The writer describes the ordained movements of the heavenly bodies, whose measurement of time-divisions is of the greatest importance in fixing the calendar and so in determining the observance of religious festivals. He advocates a solar year of 364 days over against, say, the Pharisees, who adopted a lunar calendar; in so doing he agrees with the view presented in the Book of Jubilees (cf. 6²⁹⁻³⁸) and among the Qumran Covenanters. By this means it was possible to arrange for the religious festivals to fall each year on the same day.

*d*. THE DREAM VISIONS (Chs. 83–90). These consist of two visions: in the first Enoch sees the destruction of mankind in the Flood (Chs. 83–84), and in the second he traces the history of Israel, by means of animal symbolism, down to the time of the Maccabees (Chs. 85–90). When the final assault of the heathen on the Jews is repulsed, judgement follows, and the Gentiles are either destroyed or else converted to the true faith. The righteous dead are resurrected and the Messiah, symbolized by a white bull, ushers in the Golden Age: 'And I saw till all their generations were transformed, and they all became white bulls; and the first among them became a lamb, and that lamb became a great animal and had great black horns on its head' (90³⁸).

*e*. THE ADMONITIONS (Chs. 91–104). Within this section is the so-called Apocalypse of Weeks (93¹⁻¹⁰, 91¹²⁻¹⁷), to be dated in the Maccabaean period. History, from Enoch's time onwards, is divided into ten 'weeks' of unequal length. From the point of view of the writer seven of these have already passed. In the seventh week apostasy is rife; in the eighth week the righteous are victorious and the works of the wicked are brought to an end; in the ninth week the world is prepared for judgement; in the tenth week the Final Judgement is followed by an endless age of bliss:

> And the first heaven shall depart and pass away,
> And a new heaven shall appear,
> And all the powers of the heavens shall give sevenfold light . . . .
> And sin shall no more be mentioned for ever (91¹⁶, ¹⁷).

The rest of this section, which may belong to the time of Alexander Jannaeus (103–76 B.C.), consists of admonitions given by Enoch to his children, and underlines the future punishment of the wicked and the reward of the righteous.

There is an obvious 'sympathy' between this book and that of Daniel; but its complex teaching and diverse views point to a separate apocalyptic tradition as its source. This tradition, as already stated, continued into the Christian era and exercised no small influence on Christian as well as Jewish thought.

### 3. *The Book of Jubilees*

The Book of Jubilees is an elaboration of Genesis and part of Exodus, written about the middle of the second century B.C. to glorify the Law by demonstrating its strict observance by the Patriarchs. The writer's aim is to exalt the Law in his own day and so resist the encroachments of Hellenism. The book supplements the Enoch tradition by tracing back much of its secret lore (cf. 4$^{17}$) through Noah to Enoch (cf. 7$^{38 f.}$), who revealed to him and to his children after him (cf. 10$^{14}$, 21$^{10}$, 45$^{16}$) many secrets hidden from mortal men (cf. 10$^{12 f.}$): 'And he was the first among men that are born on earth who learnt writing and knowledge and wisdom and who wrote down the signs of heaven according to the number of their months in a book . . . . And what was and what will be he saw in a vision of his sleep, as it will happen to the children of men throughout their generations until the day of judgement' (4$^{17, 19}$). In form, however, it is the record of a revelation given by God's holy angel to Moses on Mount Sinai concerning the history and laws revealed in Gen. 1–Exod. 3; 'This is the history of the divisions of the days of the law and of the testimony of the events of the years, of their (year) weeks, of their Jubilees throughout all the years of the world as the Lord spoke to Moses on Mount Sinai' (Prologue).

Its name is derived from the fact that it divides history into 'jubilee' periods of forty-nine years each, which are in turn sub-divided into seven weeks of years. At the time when the book was written the belief was widespread among the Jews that world history was divided into three epochs, culminating in the Golden Age. This same idea is suggested in Jubilees. The first epoch, which lasts for forty-nine 'jubilees', closes with the flight of the Israelites from Egypt; the second (whose duration is unspecified) begins with God's revelation of the Law to Moses; the third sees the coming of the kingdom, 'when the heavens and the earth shall be renewed' (1$^{29}$). Thus the unfolding of history leads to the gradual revealing of the kingdom of God, when men will live till they are a thousand years old. The author indeed seems to believe that he is standing at the very beginning of the messianic age, when men, through their study of the Law, will return to the paths of righteousness (cf. 23$^{26}$). No mention is made of a resurrection to life in this eternal kingdom. On the contrary, concerning the righteous it is said, 'Their bones will rest in the earth and their spirits will have much joy' ($23^{31}$). In the end judgement will be meted out not only to sinful men (cf. $4^{24}$), but also to the fallen angels (cf. $5^{10}$), to Mastema (here equated with Satan), and to his evil progeny (cf. $10^8$). Angelology and demonology appear to have reached a more advanced stage here than in Enoch, and the tendency towards dualism has become more clearly defined.

# XV

# WISDOM

THE term 'wisdom literature' is usually applied to the canonical books of Job, Proverbs, and Ecclesiastes (to which may be added a number of the Psalms), and outside the Canon to Ecclesiasticus (or Ben Sira) and the Wisdom of Solomon. Since the Book of Job and at least the major part of Proverbs[1] are to be dated earlier than the Greek period they will be left out of present consideration.

Hebrew 'wisdom' has much in common with that of the neighbouring peoples of Egypt and Babylonia and can be traced back into pre-exilic times. In Jeremiah's day, for example, 'the wise' were apparently a class of teachers to be placed alongside the priests and the prophets (cf. Jer. 18[18]), and were identified with 'the scribes' whose concern was for the preservation and transmission of the Law (cf. 8[8]). It was from this class of 'wise men' or professional scribes that the so-called 'wisdom literature' arose. Thus, although it is late in its extant literary form, it represents a long line of tradition and contains much earlier material.

Basically, Hebrew 'wisdom' is not so much philosophical and speculative as it is 'existential' and practical; and, although it is often 'worldly-wise', it is nevertheless built on strong ethical and religious foundations. This is well illustrated by Ben Sira, who deals at length with questions of etiquette and conduct, and identifies 'wisdom' with the Law of God (cf. 24[23]) and 'the wise' with those who study and obey its precepts. Both here and in other wisdom books the ground of morals is to be found in the religious conviction that 'the fear of the Lord is the beginning of wisdom' (Prov. 1[7]).

---

[1] Prov. 1–9, the latest section of the book, *may* belong to the period after Alexander the Great.

The subject of 'wisdom' covers a wide range of interests, from the practical sagacity of Ben Sira to its personification or virtual hypostasization[1] in Prov. 8 and elsewhere (cf. Job 28; Ecclus. 24; Wisdom 7[22-30]). The philosophical element is now more apparent (e.g. in the Wisdom of Solomon) than in the earlier period. During this period also, following the conquests of Alexander, Chaldean 'wisdom' and Chaldean sages flooded in from the east and exercised a profound influence on Judaism, as is shown by the contents of the Jewish apocalyptic books. Thus Daniel and his companions are described as 'skilful in all wisdom and cunning in knowledge and understanding science', being instructed in 'the learning and the tongue of the Chaldeans' (Dan. 1[4]). The writer of Daniel was of a different stamp from, say, Ben Sira, but like him he was numbered among 'the wise' whose delight was in the Law of the Lord.[2]

## 1. *Ecclesiastes*

In the Hebrew Bible this book is called 'Koheleth' and in the LXX and Vulgate 'Ecclesiastes'. The form of the word (feminine singular participle of a root meaning 'to assemble') suggests that it refers to the office of assembly-president or assembly-speaker, and so to the occupant of that office. The author's function was not that of 'the preacher', as the older rendering has it, but rather of a professional teacher in the wisdom school, whose responsibility it was to teach the sons of the influential and the well-to-do of his day. He was not typical, however, of this class of wisdom teachers; he was a man of independent thought who was obviously critical of the traditional point of view.

Despite rather strong misgivings, his book in due course came to be accepted within the Canon of Scripture. One reason for this was no doubt its claim to Solomonic authorship. Another may have been the treatment it received from subsequent editors or 'glossators' who tried to make it more acceptable

[1] See p. 133, n. 1.
[2] Cf. E. W. Heaton, *The Book of Daniel*, 1956, pp. 19 ff.

to orthodox Judaism. A number of scholars find evidence for at least two such writers. The first, it is claimed, was a wisdom writer (a *ḥakham*) who added proverbial sayings in defence of the traditional presentation of wisdom; the second was a pious member of the orthodox party (a *ḥasidh*) who tried to neutralize some of the author's near-heretical statements, even though this meant the introduction of contradictory statements into the text.[1] The epilogue, $12^{9-12}$, in which Koheleth is addressed in the third person, refers to him in a complimentary manner and is probably to be credited to one of his disciples. The heterogeneous character of the work is obvious; it lacks the planning and structure of a book like Job, nor is the logic of its thought always clear. It is possible, however, that the explanation is to be found, not in the literary history of the work, with its duality of authorship, but quite simply in the inconsistency of the writer himself. On the one hand he rebels against the accepted orthodoxy of his day, on the other he refuses to renounce the faith of his fathers and continues to speak from within the Jewish tradition.

The book was apparently known to Ben Sira, writing about 180 B.C., who in one place paraphrases Koheleth's teaching; fragments of it were found at Qumran from about the middle of the same century. Its use of Aramaisms and the hint of some Grecisms, together with the general spirit of the book, suggest a date in the Greek period, perhaps somewhere between 250 and 200 B.C. Attempts have been made to find precise historical allusions in the text, but these are too obscure to form a basis for sound judgement. The place of writing may have been Egypt, but references to rain-clouds (cf. $11^4$, $12^2$) and water-cisterns (cf. $12^6$) point more surely to Palestine.

It is clear that Koheleth was deeply influenced by the spirit of the age in which he lived, but attempts to prove his direct dependence on Greek writers or specific Greek schools of thought

[1] G. A. Barton suggests as interpolations from the *ḥakham* $4^5$, $5^3$, $7^a$, $7^{1a, 3, 5,}$ $6-9, 11, 12, 19$, $8^1$, $9^{17, 18}$, $10^{1-3, 8-14a, 15, 18, 19}$, and from the *ḥasidh* $2^{26}$, $3^{17}$, $7^{18b, 26b, 29}$, $8^{2b, 3a, 5, 6a, 11-13}$, $11^{9b}$, $12^{1a, 13, 14}$. Cf. *A Critical and Exegetical Commentary on the Book of Ecclesiastes*, 1908, pp. 25 f.

are not convincing. There is perhaps clearer evidence of the influence of Egyptian wisdom-teaching, which finds some striking parallels both here and elsewhere in the Hebrew wisdom literature (cf. especially Prov. $22^{17}$–$23^{11}$). Thus the picture of old age in $12^{3-7}$, the paradoxical nature of life, as described in $9^{11}$ and $10^7$, and the injunction to enjoy life whilst there is time, as in $2^{24}$, $3^{12\ f.}$, $9^{7-9}$, can all be paralleled in much earlier Egyptian texts with whose teaching our author must have been familiar.

His aim is 'to seek and to search out by wisdom all that is done under heaven' ($1^{13}$). He does not begin with some divine disclosure which gives meaning to future events, but rather with life and experience as he knows them. In these he tries to find meaning and ultimate purpose, but the goal he seeks escapes him. The events of life—determined beforehand by God (cf. $3^{15}$) in such a way that each is followed by its opposite (cf. $3^{1-8}$)—show no agreement whatsoever between the principles of divine justice in the world and the hard facts of human experience. Koheleth is thus agnostic when confronted with the inscrutability of Providence; but he cannot be charged with atheism. His own experience may deny the commonly accepted notions of God, but for him God is still the dispenser of events and the source of all life and happiness (cf. $3^{22}$, $5^{18\ ff.}$, etc.).

Over against the transcendence of God stands the transitoriness of man. For Koheleth life is summed up in the word 'vanity'; it is empty and of no profit, with no identifiable goal. Conformity to things as they are may lead to the avoidance of trouble, but there is no meaning to existence. In particular there is no truth in the claim that length of years and increase of wealth are the measure of a man's character in the sight of God. Belief in an after-life in which the wrongs of this life are set right is pushed aside; in Sheol all are treated alike, even men and beasts (cf. $3^{19\ ff.}$, etc.). But happiness, which is God's gift (cf. $6^3$), may still be found in the pursuit of toil and in the enjoyments which life brings: 'There is nothing better for a man than that he should eat and drink, and find enjoyment in his toil' ($2^{24}$).

This, then, is a book about wisdom, human and divine, in which the writer recognizes the severe limitations of his subject. He agrees with the other wisdom-teachers of his day that wisdom has value in the practical sphere, for 'wisdom excels folly as light excels darkness' ($2^{13}$). But it is only of relative worth, for increased knowledge brings increased sorrow (cf. $1^{18}$) and such advantage as it gives is only for a brief season (cf. $9^{10}$). Life should be taken as it comes (cf. $2^{24}$, $9^{7-9}$); religious duties should be carried out (cf. $5^{1-5}$), but excesses—of good and of evil alike—should be avoided (cf. $7^{16 \text{ f.}}$). Man cannot hope to understand the mysteries of life, which are hidden from all save God, who is himself the source of all true wisdom and the spring of understanding.

### a. SUPERSCRIPTION AND PROLOGUE $\left(1^{1-11}\right)$

1. *the Preacher*: Hebrew *Ḳoheleth*, Greek *Ekklesiastes*. The Hebrew word, as already noted, is a feminine form from a root meaning 'to assemble' and expresses a title or function or office (cf. similar forms in Ezra $2^{55}$ and $^{57}$), in this case 'speaker of the assembly', the reference being to the assembly of 'the wise'. This is a more likely explanation than that the speaker represents 'Wisdom', a feminine word sometimes personified as a woman (cf. Prov. 8), for throughout the book the masculine character of Koheleth is defined either by an accompanying noun (e.g. 'son', 'king') or by a masculine form of the verb (cf. $1^{2, 12}$, $12^{8, 9, 10}$).

In this superscription, which may be from the hand of the editor, Koheleth is identified with Solomon, *the son of David* (cf. also $1^{12, 16}$, $2^{7, 9}$), a literary convention which is maintained as far as $2^{12}$. Solomon was regarded as the fountain-head of wisdom, as Moses was of law-giving and David of psalmody. The choice of this name suited the writer's purpose admirably: even wisdom like Solomon's led only to futility and disillusionment.

2–11. In this prologue to the book Koheleth presents his theme: there is no progress and so no purpose in life. In both the natural order and human experience there is a monotonous repetition, and nothing is permanent save the ever-recurring pattern of events. What appears to be new is in fact quite old: it is men's memories that play them false.

2. *Vanity of vanities*: a form expressing the superlative in Hebrew (cf. 'Song of Songs', 'holy of holies'). The word 'vanity', meaning literally 'vapour' or 'breath', occurs forty times in Koheleth and expresses the theme of the whole book—all is 'utter futility'.

3. What's the use! All men's hard toil ends in nothing: 'Double, double toil and trouble'!
    *under the sun*: cf. the expression 'under heaven' (Exod. 17¹⁴; Deut. 9¹⁴). The phrase is found in the Old Testament only in Koheleth, but appears in Phoenician inscriptions of the fifth century B.C.

5 f. Even *the sun* 'goes round in circles'! So also does the wind.
    *hastens*: lit. 'pants'. This picture of the sun running a race (cf. also Ps. 19⁵) recalls the reference in 2 Kings 23¹¹ to 'the chariots of the sun' in the Temple in Jerusalem. There may also be some connexion with the idea in Egyptian wisdom literature of the sun showing the effects of old age.

7. The *streams* keep on flowing; but *the sea* is never full. How utterly futile!

8. *The eye* sees and *the ear* hears but, like a hungry man, neither is *satisfied*.

9 f. The cyclic view of time and history, though not typical of the Old Testament writers, was nevertheless known to them (cf. 2 Sam. 11¹; 1 Kings 20²²; Isa. 29¹; Job 1⁵) and is here given at least tacit acceptance by Koheleth. It assumed different forms in the ancient world and gained prominence in the Middle East from the time of Alexander's conquests onwards.¹ What appears to be new is only a repetition of what has been.

¹ Cf. D. S. Russell, *The Method and Message of Jewish Apocalyptic*, 1964, pp. 213 ff.

11. *There is no remembrance of former things*: better, 'of former men' (RV 'of former generations'). Every generation 'starts from scratch'. It fails to benefit from the experiences of former generations and must learn life's lessons all over again. When events, similar to those in the past, do reappear, they are mistakenly thought to be new.

*b*. THE FATE OF MEN AND BEASTS $(3^{16-22})$

The theme of this passage is that man, be he good or bad, has *no advantage* over the beast. *Justice* and *righteousness* are ousted by *wickedness* (16) and give proof of this fact (18). *The fate* of both is the same (19), for both alike return to *the dust* (20–21). Let a man *enjoy his work* now, for death will bring oblivion (22).

16. *the place of justice . . . the place of righteousness*: a reference perhaps to the institutions of State and Church where *wickedness* prevails.

17. This verse, which interprets the thought of the passage, is regarded by many as an addition by the *ḥasidh* glossator, who tries to qualify Koheleth's sweeping judgement. Retribution will follow; everything is in God's hands.

18. The facts of human experience show that men *are but beasts*.

19 f. Their final destination and final destiny are the same—*the dust* and the grave. The immediate reference is to the dust from which man was made and to which he will return at death (cf. Gen. $2^{7, 19}$, $3^{19}$). Elsewhere the writer shows that he accepts the Old Testament idea of Sheol, a place of darkness and despair where 'the dead know nothing, and they have no more reward . . . there is no work or thought or knowledge or wisdom in Sheol, to which you are going' $(9^{5, 10})$.

21. The RSV is no doubt correct in reading this verse as a question (cf. LXX and other versions) rather than as a dogmatic statement (cf. AV, following Massoretic text). Concerning the fate of man and beast Koheleth is thoroughly agnostic.

*the spirit of man*: Hebrew *ruaḥ*, signifying the life-principle in both man and beast. In $12^7$ the writer says that this life-principle in the end returns to God who gave it. In neither case is there reference to the 'discarnate spirit' found in Greek thought and in later Jewish apocalyptic writings.[1] Some scholars see in this verse a rebuttal of the view expressed in Mesopotamian astral religions that man's spirit ascends to heaven at death to assume once more the nature of the stars.

22. Man cannot see beyond death. Let him at least *enjoy his work*, which is a gift from God (cf. 3¹³).

### c. NO MORAL PURPOSE IN LIFE (8¹⁰⁻¹⁷)

The theme of 3¹⁶⁻²² is continued here. The absence of an observable retributive principle in life shows that there is no moral purpose at work in the universe (10–14). All that is left to a man is that he should enjoy life while it lasts (15), for, try as he may, he will never be able to understand it (16–17).

10. The Hebrew of this verse is difficult. It is possible, however, to translate: 'Well, I have seen wicked men buried and they came (to the grave); but they that have done right (the word for 'such things' has this meaning also) have gone from (the) holy place and been forgotten in the city', i.e. wicked men have been honoured by being given decent burial (cf. Job 21³²), but righteous men who have been faithful in Temple worship have been forgotten. Most commentators, however, suggest emendations which involve only slight alteration of the text or else find support in the versions. In this way it is possible to translate: 'Well, I have seen wicked men drawing near (for 'buried') and entering the holy place; they walk around and boast (for 'were forgotten') in the city that they have done right.'

11–13. It is claimed by some that these verses are from the hand of the pious glossator, who tones down the words of Koheleth in vv. 10 and 14. Evil will not be allowed to go unpunished. The 'God-fearer' will receive his reward, but *the wicked* (like *the shadow* which ceases to be when the sun has set, cf. 6¹²; Job 8⁹) will not *prolong his days*.

14. For the thought of this verse cf. Job 9²², 21⁷; Ps. 73³; Jer. 12¹.

---

[1] See p. 152.

15. Despite the purposelessness of life men must not try to contract out of it but must *enjoy* it to the full.

16 f. Man can find no real meaning or purpose in *all the work of God*, even though in his search he gives up *sleep* and toils incessantly. *To know wisdom* is not enough; the divine purpose remains unknown.

*neither day nor night one's eyes see sleep*: lit. 'although neither by day nor night does one see sleep with one's eyes'. The meaning is clearer if, as has been suggested, the words belong to v. 17 and are to be read in parenthesis after the word 'seeking'.

### d. YOUTH AND OLD AGE ($11^9$–$12^8$)

Koheleth urges young people to enjoy the time of their youth and to reverence God before old age catches up with them ($11^9$–$12^1$). The decrepitude of old age is like the darkness of a storm (2) or like a household whose members have seen better days (3–4). With advancing years a man's powers fail and the mourners get ready for his passing (4–5). Like the snapping of a cord or the smashing of a pitcher death comes, to confirm Koheleth's judgement that life itself is utter futility (8).

9. *walk in the ways of your heart and the sight of your eyes*. This would appear to contradict the injunction in Num. $15^{39}$, and was to prove an obstacle to the book's claims to canonicity. The words which follow may represent a qualification by Koheleth not to 'overdo things', or they may be from the pen of the pious glossator.

10. 'Put aside worry from your mind and (then you will) put away calamity from your body.'

*the dawn of life*: i.e. the pride of life in the sense of 'youth'. The word may signify 'blackness of hair' and so refer to a man's younger days before his hair turns grey. Another interpretation is that it means 'gloominess' or 'melancholy'.

12.1. *your Creator*. The plural form used here is unusual but has been explained as a plural of majesty. Some commentators suggest a slight change in the text so as to read 'your   istern' or 'your well', the reference being to one's wife, as elsewhere in the wisdom literature (cf. Prov. 5¹⁵⁻¹⁸ and in Egyptian sources). Alternatively, the first part of the verse may be from the pious glossator, in which case the word 'rejoice' (11⁹) rather than the word 'remember' (1) would qualify vv. 1, 2, and 6.

2. In old age, as in a storm, warmth and light give way to cold and darkness. Cloud follows cloud in relentless repetition.

3. We are probably to find in this portrayal of old age as an impoverished household an allegory depicting an old man's failing powers. *The keepers of the house* are the arms; the '*twisted*' *strong men*, the legs; *the grinders* (lit. 'grinding women'), the teeth; and *those that look through the windows*, the eyes.

4. This verse probably refers to the onset of deafness.

*the doors* (lit. 'double doors'): probably the ears.

*the sound of the grinding*: either the noise of general conversation, or the reference may again be to the teeth.

*one rises up at the voice of a bird*: i.e. an old man's sleep is easily disturbed. A slight alteration would give 'and there shall arise for him the voice of a bird', i.e. he will acquire a high-pitched, tremulous voice.

*daughters of song*: perhaps his vocal cords, which are *brought low*, i.e. weakened.

5. Old people *are afraid* of heights and of jostling in the narrow, crowded streets.

*the almond tree blossoms*: possibly an allusion to the old man's white hair (contrast 'blackness of hair' in v. 10?). Other possibilities: 'he rejects the almond' (i.e. he has no appetite or teeth to chew it), or 'sleeplessness flourishes' (cf. Jer. 1¹¹ f., where the almond is the 'watchful' or 'wakeful' tree).

*the grasshopper drags itself along* (AV 'shall be a burden'): a picture of the old man himself, weary of limb. Other possibilities: the merest burden is too heavy for him, or the grasshopper (as an article of food) does not tempt him.

*desire fails*. The word 'desire' can be translated 'caper-berry', a fruit said to stimulate appetite. In old age its powers fail.

*his eternal home*: the grave.

*mourners go about*: professional mourners roam around looking for custom!

6. The coming of death is portrayed in two pictures. It is like a *silver cord* which snaps (cf. LXX and other versions), so that *the golden ball*, which it supports and which gives light to the house, *is broken*; or it is like a *pitcher* which is smashed when *the wheel* that lowers it into *the cistern* is *broken*. Light and water are common symbols for life (cf. Pss. 27$^{1 f.}$, 36$^9$; Isa. 35$^{6 f.}$).

7. *the dust . . . the spirit*: see note on 3$^{19 f., 21}$.

8. Once more he arrives at the same conclusion—all is utter futility!


## 2. *Ecclesiasticus* or *The Wisdom of Ben Sirach*

This book, to be found in the Apocrypha, is extant in three principal recensions—Greek, Syriac, and Hebrew. The Hebrew manuscripts cover about two-thirds of the book and have been supplemented by two fragments from Qumran covering 6$^{20-31}$. Originally written in Hebrew, it was translated into Greek for the use of the Jews in Egypt by the author's grandson, who, in a Prologue, states that he came to Egypt in 'the thirty-eighth year of the reign of Euergetes' (i.e. Euergetes II), in 132 B.C. Since his grandfather presumably wrote about fifty years earlier we can date his work about the year 180 B.C. This date is confirmed by other internal evidence, such as the eulogy in 50$^{1-24}$ of the High Priest Simon, who had apparently recently held office and who is known to have lived at the beginning of the second century B.C. Moreover, whereas the book reflects the influence of Hellenistic culture[1] on the Judaism of its day, no reference is made to the religious crisis which came to a head during the reign of Antiochus Epiphanes, although the psalm contained in Ch. 36 seems to suggest a time of great stress resulting from military oppression.

[1] See further p. 29.

The name 'Ecclesiasticus' is the title found in the Old Latin Bible. It is generally taken to signify 'the Church Book' and to derive from the fact that after the canonical Scriptures it was the most highly prized of all the *libri ecclesiastici*. In most of the Greek manuscripts the title is given as 'The Wisdom of Jesus, the son of Sirach', the author identifying himself by this name in 50[27]; its Hebrew equivalent is 'Joshua ben Sira'.

We know nothing about Ben Sira, as he is customarily called, apart from what he and his grandson tell us. It appears, however, that he was a scribe and a teacher, who devoted himself to the task of teaching 'wisdom' to all who would listen. He spent most of his life in Palestine, but was able to travel quite extensively in foreign lands (cf. 34[11 f.]), and apparently spent some time at the court of a foreign ruler (cf. 39[4]). From 51[23] we learn that he had a school or 'House of Learning', presumably in Jerusalem, where young men were given instruction how to conduct their lives aright. His grandson tells us that after a life of study Ben Sira was 'led to write something pertaining to righteousness and wisdom', so that others might benefit from his learning. This book, written in verse, is no doubt a digest of the lectures he gave to his students.

It follows no definite plan and covers a wide range of subjects —from table etiquette to the doctrine of creation, from control of one's flighty daughter to the problem of the origin of evil. The suggestion has been made that it may have been issued in two main parts (Chs. 1–23 and 24[1]–42[14]), and that three poems were subsequently added—on God in nature (42[15]–43[33]), the fathers of old (44[1]–49[16]), and the High Priest Simon (50[1-24]). In subject matter and presentation it is written somewhat after the style of Proverbs; in Ecclesiasticus, however, the old proverb in the form of a balanced couplet more readily assumes the form of a small essay. The writer makes no claim to originality, but is a keen and shrewd observer of human life as well as being a deeply religious and pious man. His observations cast much light on the life, and especially the social life, of his day.

The subject of the book is the true character of wisdom,[1] which Ben Sira accepts as a gift from God. He is thus both 'scribe' and 'wise man', who can say, in the opening words of his book, that 'all wisdom comes from God' ($1^1$). His outlook as 'scribe', however, is to be distinguished from that of the Pharisaic scribes of the Gospels: like them he was vitally interested in the Scriptures and in their legal requirements, but unlike them his interests embraced much wider concerns. In his description of the ideal scribe in $39^{1-3}$ (no doubt a self-portrait) he singles out for special mention 'the study of the law', and in the Prologue his grandson confirms that he devoted himself to reading 'the Law and the Prophets and the other books of our fathers'. Elsewhere he goes so far as to equate the Law with wisdom (cf. $24^{23}$), which in the beginning the Creator had made to dwell in Israel (cf. $24^8$). His interests, however, are much wider than the study of the Law and its legal precepts; they cover the whole of life and are concerned with all the interests of men. Nor does his teaching confine itself to purely ethical application; the wisdom he advocates is often candidly utilitarian and prudential, having worth in itself even from the purely material point of view (cf. $51^{28}$).

Ben Sira's religious outlook is for the most part that of contemporary Jewish orthodoxy which teaches, for example, that good is rewarded and evil punished this side of the grave (cf. $11^{14, \ 26-28}$). He contributes little or nothing to the solution of the problem of innocent suffering, and makes no allusion to the concerns that troubled Job and Koheleth. He makes no reference to the resurrection, or, indeed, to the hope of immortality (cf. $41^{3 \ f.}$). All that a man can hope for is that he will live on in his own good name and in his posterity (cf. $44^{8, \ 13 \ f.}$). In this he foreshadows the party of the Sadducees (cf. Matt. $22^{23}$), with whose outlook he sympathized in at least two other respects: he had a high regard for the priesthood (cf. $7^{29-31}$), whose leader Simon in particular he portrays in glowing colours (cf. $50^1 \ ^{ff.}$), and also for the Temple ritual, whose sacrifices were ordained by God and must be carefully observed

[1] See p. 133.

(cf. 33⁸, 35⁴ ᶠ·). Ritual observance by itself, however, was of little worth; not sacrifice (cf. 7⁸ ᶠ·), but only righteousness, expressing itself in filial piety and almsgiving (cf. 3³, ³⁰), could atone for sin. His sympathy with the pre-Sadducaean tradition may perhaps be suggested also in the omission from his list of famous men of the name of Ezra (cf. Chs. 44–49), who in later days was to become the prototype of the Pharisaic scribe. Ben Sira, then, is of the greatest importance, not only as an example of the traditional wisdom literature and as a record of the social life of the times, but also as a record of those tendencies in Judaism that were later to emerge under the party names of 'Pharisee' and 'Sadducee'.

## *a.* THE PROLOGUE

*through the law and the prophets and the others that followed them.* This statement, together with two others of a similar kind a little further on in the Prologue, provides a clearly defined landmark in tracing the idea of the Old Testament Canon. It indicates that the three-fold division of Scripture was recognized but that the third of these was as yet quite fluid and had not acquired a distinctive name. Such a division is implied, however, at an even earlier date in the work of Ben Sira himself, where mention is made of 'the law . . . wisdom . . . prophecies' (39¹). For a fuller treatment of the significance of this book in dating the Canon see above, pp. 177 f.

The Scriptures are here regarded as the authoritative means whereby God communicates to his people the knowledge of himself. Note the importance of Judaism as a religion of the Book during this period, particularly of the written Torah.[1]

*praise Israel for instruction and wisdom.* These words recall Deut. 4⁶, where the nations praise Israel because it has received the Law as the very ground of 'understanding' and 'wisdom'. Here too Israel is praised because it has made the Law the vehicle of wisdom and the means of instruction. 'Wisdom' is thus ethically based, and 'instruction' implies the discipline of the will, not merely the enlightenment of the mind.

[1] See further pp. 114 f.

·

*the readers . . . those who love learning*: i.e. the scribes or teachers of the Law who, like Ezra and his colleagues, 'read from the book, from the law of God, clearly' (Neh. 8⁸).

*the outsiders*: those outside the scribal profession. For other occurrences of this phrase see Mark 4¹¹ and 1 Cor. 5¹².

*by both speaking and writing.* Oral instruction was the normal mode of teaching in the scribal schools. Reference is made here also to literary activity. No doubt other extra-canonical wisdom books besides that of Ben Sira himself were produced. One example is the Book of Tobit, written probably in the third century B.C. either in Babylonia or in Egypt, which shows acquaintance with another wisdom book, 'The story of Ahikar', fragments of which were found among the papyri of the Jewish community at Elephantine in Egypt.

*in living according to the law.* The teaching of the scribes has this as its great objective, the observance of the Law. This is true wisdom.

*what was originally expressed in Hebrew*, etc. The writer is referring here to the translation of his grandfather's book ('this work') and to the Greek translation of the Scriptures, known as the Septuagint (LXX), which had not yet been completed. For an account of its suggested origin see pp. 19 f.

*the thirty-eighth year of the reign of Euergetes*: i.e. Euergetes II (169–164, 145–116 B.C.), since the first king of this name did not reign for this length of time. The writer, then, came to Egypt in 132 B.C.

*stayed for some time.* The Greek verb has the sense 'to synchronize' and suggests that the writer's stay in Egypt coincided with that part of the King's reign from 132 B.C. till his death in 116 B.C.

*I found opportunity for no little instruction.* This reading makes better sense than the received text, which may be translated 'I found a copy affording no small instruction' (RV) or 'I found no small difference of culture' (sc. between Palestinian and Egyptian Jews). The writer tells us that he found ample opportunity for instruction in wisdom in the synagogues of Egypt, which Philo, for example, describes as 'schools of prudence and courage and temperance and justice and also of piety, holiness, and every virtue by which duties to God and men are discerned and rightly performed' (*Life of Moses* II. 216).

*b*. THE PRAISE OF WISDOM (24$^{1-34}$)

In this chapter the idea of personified Wisdom closely resembles that of Prov. 8, and shows less evidence of Greek influence than does, say, the Wisdom of Solomon. Having introduced *Wisdom* as one worthy of praise in both earth and heaven (1–2), the writer allows her to speak for herself (3–22). She tells how she came forth from the presence of God and sought a home among all the peoples of the earth, but found no *resting place* until God told her to make her *dwelling in Israel* (3–8). And so Wisdom, *created* before time began (9), took her place in the city of *Jerusalem*, ministering before God in *the holy tabernacle* and in the Temple there (10–12). Having displayed her grace and beauty (13–18), she invites her listeners to come and take what she has to give and find in her satisfaction and fulfilment (19–22). The writer himself now takes up the theme, stating that Wisdom, whose *thought* is immeasurable and whose *counsel* is unfathomable, is embodied in *the Law*, by which men receive *understanding* and *instruction* (23–29). In the final section he speaks of his own share in it: he is like an irrigation *canal*, leading from Wisdom's mighty *river*, which watered his *garden* and *orchard*. At first he intended to use it for himself alone, but as the *canal* grew into *a river* and the river into *a sea*, he realized that he had to use it for the good of *all who seek instruction* (30–34).

1–2. Wisdom is here presented as a female figure (cf. Prov. 8), who is entitled to praise herself on account of her own inherent worth.

*her people . . . his host*: i.e. the people of Israel and the angelic host of heaven. She is praised in both earth and heaven.

3–22. With this whole section where Wisdom is the speaker compare Prov. 8$^{22}$–9$^{12}$, which has many points of similarity.

3. *I . . . covered the earth like a mist* (cf. Gen. 2$^6$) just as in the

beginning 'the Spirit of God was moving over the face of the waters' (Gen. $1^2$). In later Jewish writings Wisdom is more clearly identified with the holy Spirit (cf. especially Wisd. Sol. $1^{4-7}$, $11^{17}$).

4. *in high places*: i.e. in the highest heaven, of which, according to traditional Jewish belief, there were three—of meteors, of stars, and of God.

*a pillar of cloud*: the 'Šekinah' of later Jewish teaching (cf. Exod. $14^{19}$ etc.). Philo identifies this pillar with Wisdom.

7. *Among all these*. Wisdom seeks a resting-place in every people and nation but finds it only in Israel. Later rabbinic legend applies this also to the Law, which, though offered to all nations, was accepted by Israel alone.

8. According to another tradition, Wisdom, finding no resting-place, took her seat in heaven (cf. 1 Enoch $42^{1, 2}$).

10. *In the holy tabernacle I ministered*. The Law, identified here with Wisdom, finds expression in the worship of the Tabernacle. Hence personified Wisdom can be spoken of as ministering before God. Later on the Temple *in Zion* took the place of the Tabernacle.

13–17. Wisdom likens herself to several kinds of trees famed for their stateliness and beauty, and to others whose bark or sap was used for making incense or perfume.

14. *in Engedi*. This reading is preferable to 'on the sea shore' (cf. AV and RV). Engedi, on the western shore of the Dead Sea, was famed for its palm trees.

18. This verse, and also v. 24, which appear in the AV, have poor textual authority and should be omitted.

20. *sweeter than honey . . . than the honeycomb*: cf. Ps. $19^{10}$, where the reference is to the Law.

22. The practice of the Law, which is the true expression of Wisdom, will protect against *sin*. This verse concludes Wisdom's speech.

23. The writer, both here and in the verses which follow,

specifically identifies Wisdom with the Law. Everything said about the one applies equally to the other.

*the congregations of Jacob*: an echo of Deut. 33⁴, where, however, the singular 'congregation' (standing for 'the assembly of the whole people') is used. The LXX, like Ben Sira, uses the plural, having in mind no doubt the synagogues of the Dispersion.

25–27. *the Pishon . . . the Tigris . . . the Euphrates . . . the Gihon*: the four rivers mentioned in Gen. 2¹⁰ ᶠᶠ· which 'flowed out of Eden'.

27. In the first part of the verse read with the Syriac 'which makes instruction flow like the Nile'.

*at the time of vintage*: i.e. September–October, when the river is in full flood.

29. *the great abyss*: the great 'cosmic ocean', the unfathomable sea beneath the earth, cf. 24⁵; Gen. 7¹¹; Ps. 36⁶, etc.

30. The writer, continuing the thought of vv. 25–29, likens himself to a canal leading from the great river of Wisdom.

32. *I will make it shine afar*: to the Jews of the Dispersion. What he had intended using for himself alone he will use for others.

*I will again pour out teaching like prophecy*. Like the prophets he will speak as one inspired by God.

## *c*. A PORTRAIT OF THE IDEAL SCRIBE (39¹⁻¹¹)

This brief portrait is no doubt an autobiographical sketch. The ideal scribe is one learned in the Scriptures and in oral tradition (1–3; cf. 8⁸, 24³⁰⁻³², 32¹⁵, 33¹⁶⁻¹⁸, 39⁸, 44¹⁻50²⁹); he is a man of culture, with a wide experience of the world (4; cf. 29²¹⁻²⁸, 34¹¹ ᶠ·, 51¹³⁻²²); he is pious and devout, acknowledging God as the source of his wisdom (5–6; cf. 22⁷⁻23⁶, 36¹⁻¹⁷, 51¹⁻¹²); he is an apt teacher of the Law of God (7–8; cf. 51²³⁻³⁰); his name will be remembered and praised through all generations (9–11; cf. 44⁸· ¹³ ᶠᶠ·).

1. *the law . . . wisdom . . . prophecies*. The chief source of the scribe's knowledge is the Scriptures. There is at least a suggestion

here of the three-fold division of the Canon, the as-yet-undefined 'wisdom of all the ancients', representing 'the rest of the books' (cf. Prologue), coming between the Law and the Prophets instead of at the end. To the writer this was no doubt a fitting place for it because wisdom's task was to expound the Law.

2–3. The second source of the scribe's knowledge is oral tradition, particularly that dealing with subtle *parables* and mysterious *proverbs* (cf. Wisd. Sol. 8⁸). In this Ben Sira was like the writer of Daniel: E. W. Heaton calls them 'brother doctors of the same divinity'.[1]

4. The scribe is a man of culture who has travelled abroad (cf. 51¹³) and had access to foreign courts.

6. *he will pour forth words of wisdom.* Read with the Syriac 'he pours forth wise sayings in double measure', i.e. he utters not only what he has received from tradition but also what he has received by direct revelation from God. Note the scribe's independency of outlook.

7. *his secrets*: cf. 4¹⁸, 39³, also the occurrence of the word in Daniel and in the apocalyptic literature generally.

9. *his name will live.* A man lives on in his 'name', cf. 37²⁶, 44⁸, ¹⁴.

11. The Greek is difficult. The sense seems to be, 'If he survives into old age his reputation is established (for long life is the sign of divine blessing); even when he dies men's memory of him is *enough* to keep his *name* alive (for in the remembrance of the name there is life)'.

### d. PRAISE OF THE FATHERS OF OLD (44¹⁻¹⁵)

These verses form a general introduction to a noble hymn of praise in commemoration of Israel's great men of the past (44¹–49⁶).[2] In the preceding chapter the thought has been of

[1] Cf. op. cit., pp. 19–24.

[2] For the contribution of these chapters to our understanding of the idea of the Canon see p. 177.

the manifestation of God's glory in nature; now it is focused on his great works in history as exemplified in the lives of Israel's outstanding heroes. Beginning with Enoch (cf. 44$^{16}$) it praises the patriarchs (cf. 44$^{19}$–45$^5$), reaching a crescendo in its description of the High Priest Aaron and his successors (cf. 45$^{6-26}$); passing on to Joshua and the Judges (cf. 46$^{1-12}$) it extols in turn Saul, David, and Solomon (cf. 46$^{13}$–47$^{24}$), and continues Israel's history in the persons of great rulers and prophets down to the time of Nehemiah (cf. 48$^1$–49$^{13}$). Thereafter, rather strangely, it turns back to mention Enoch, Joseph, Shem, Seth, and finally Adam, perhaps suggesting the writer's acquaintance with the apocalyptic tradition, in which such names are known subsequently to have played a significant part. To this hymn he has added another in praise of the High Priest Simon, whose ministry on the Day of Atonement is described in glowing colours (cf. 50$^{1-24}$). Other historical surveys, somewhat similar to this one, are found elsewhere in Scripture (cf. Pss. 78, 105, 106, 135, 136; Ezek. 20; Wisdom 10; 1 Macc. 2$^{51-60}$; Heb. 11$^{4\,\mathrm{ff.}}$).

1. *famous men*. The Hebrew and Syriac texts read 'men of piety', signifying those who are loyal to God and his Law.

   *in their generations*: in their historical succession.

2. *great glory*. These men, like nature itself, are to manifest God's glory and majesty.

3–7. Twelve types of great men, who were *the glory of their times*, are presented in these verses—rulers, men of renown, counsellors, prophets, leaders of the people, men of learning, wise teachers, speakers of proverbs (not in the Greek text), composers of music, poets, men of ability, and men of peace. These are amply illustrated in the hymn which follows.

4. *leaders of the people*. The Hebrew text reads 'princes of (i.e. over) the Gentiles'. The writer probably has in mind a man like Joseph.

   *in understanding of learning for the people*. The Hebrew text reads 'and rulers by means of their foresight', alluding again to a man like Joseph (cf. Gen. 41 33 ff., 55 ff.) or to leaders like Zerubbabel and Nehemiah.

*wise in their words of instruction*: a reference to the work of the scribes as teachers.

At the end of this verse the Greek text has omitted a line: 'and speakers of proverbs in their keeping (of the tradition)', an allusion to the wisdom-teachers who, in their oral instruction, used the proverbial form.

5. *musical tunes*: metrical psalms accompanied by instrumental music. The writer has in mind the guilds of Temple-singers.[1]

*verses in writing*: like those in the Books of Psalms and Proverbs.

6. *rich men.* The Hebrew phrase can have this meaning, but has also, as here, a broader connotation meaning 'men of valour'.

8–9. Two interpretations are possible. Either godly men are contrasted with the ungodly (such as the evil kings of the Northern Kingdom whom Ben Sira, like the Chronicler, omits from his list), or else the reference in each verse is to godly men, some of whom have been forgotten. The contrast with 'men of mercy' in v. 10, however, seems to support the first of these.

10. *But these were men of mercy*, referring to the list which follows. The Hebrew text has 'men of piety' (cf. v. 1). The word *ḥesedh* which is used here has the same root as the word for 'Pious Ones' (*Ḥasidhim*), shortly to become a technical term signifying those defenders of the Law who took their stand against the encroachments of Hellenism.[2]

12. *the covenants*: God's gracious promises made to Abraham, Noah, Aaron, Phinehas, and David. The children *stood by* them for their fathers' sakes.

13–14. *Their posterity*, etc. The fathers live on in their children and in *their name*.

14. *Their bodies were buried in peace.* The Hebrews were very particular about their treatment of the dead and about proper

[1] See further, p. 123.          [2] See pp. 29, 45 f., 160.

burial. Behind this lay the idea that injury to the dead body involved injury to the shade whose double it was.

### 3. *The Book of Wisdom* or *The Wisdom of Solomon*

In common with the Books of Proverbs and Ecclesiastes this work is ascribed to Solomon, who was traditionally recognized as the fount of all wisdom. Apart from the title he is not referred to by name, but his authorship is assumed through Chs. 7–9 (cf. especially $7^7$ and $9^8$). In thus speaking through Solomon the author is able to rescue him, as it were, from the hands of Koheleth, whose outlook and beliefs he severely criticizes (cf. $1^{10}$–$2^{20}$). In literary form the book goes a stage farther than Koheleth in departing from the simple proverb, and assumes the character of a theological treatise with a philosophical bent and a technical vocabulary.

The writer was a Jew of the Dispersion, probably of Alexandria, who lived in the later part of the second or the earlier part of the first century B.C. This is indicated not only by the general contents and teaching of the book (see below), but also by its use of Hellenistic thought-forms and by its style and vocabulary. Hebrew religion and Greek philosophy flow into one, producing a form of Jewish apologetic of considerable significance for our understanding of the intertestamental period. It is addressed in the first instance to Greek-speaking Jews to convince the pious among them that the Greek philosophical spirit of the age, which had tended to weaken the faith of some, could in fact be interwoven with the conventional piety of Judaism to form an even stronger faith, and at the same time to admonish backsliders by demonstrating Israel's religion as the true religion, and so the true wisdom, over against both Jewish apostasy and Gentile idolatry. By so doing the writer may have hoped to convince even some Gentiles of the veracity of Judaism and the folly of idolatry.

The book's nineteen chapters fall into three parts, the first two of which are mostly in poetry and the last mostly in prose. Part I (Chs. 1–5) draws a contrast between the righteous and the ungodly and their respective destinies, demonstrating the advantages of wisdom over wickedness. The writer denounces the ungodly who deny immortality and judgement, or who indulge in riotous living and persecute the righteous (cf. $1^{16}$–$2^{24}$). The righteous will inherit immortality and be vindicated on the judgement day. The wicked, even in this life, are miserable and their end is death; for them old age and many children will be no compensation; in the end they will see the folly of their ways (cf. $3^1$–$5^{23}$).

Part II (Chs. 6–9) consists of a hymn in praise of wisdom, introduced by an admonition to seek it and followed by a prayer to receive it. The admonition is addressed to the leaders of the earth, who are reminded that by love of wisdom kingdoms are established and immortality assured (cf. $6^{1-25}$). Speaking in the name of Solomon the author tells how he had himself received wisdom, whose many characteristics he now describes (cf. $7^1$–$8^1$), and had sought her like a bride (cf. $8^{2-20}$). The prayer for wisdom which ends this section is a confession of human weakness and an acknowledgement of divine mercy (cf. $8^{21}$–$9^{18}$).

Part III (Chs. 10–19) demonstrates the part played by wisdom in the history of Israel from the Creation up to the time of Moses (cf. $10^1$–$11^1$), and praises God's mercy in his punishment of the Egyptians and his deliverance of his own people (cf. $11^2$–$19^{22}$). This latter section contains a powerful denunciation of idolatry (cf. $13^1$–$15^{17}$). In $11^{15}$–$12^{22}$ the principle is worked out that in God's dealings with men the punishment is made to fit the crime, for 'one is punished by the very things by which one sins' ($11^{16}$). The story of the Exodus and the punishment of the Egyptians further illustrate that 'through the very things by which their enemies were punished, they themselves received benefit in their need' ($11^5$). Thus, the very water which was a plague to the Egyptians became for the Israelites a source of blessing (cf. $11^{4-7}$).

There is no complete agreement about the unity of the book or about the language in which it was originally written.

The philosophic and poetic style of Chs. 1–9 is quite different from the rather bombastic rhetorical style of Chs. 10–19, and this may suggest a double authorship. The claim, however, that Chs. 1–9 were originally written in Hebrew is not convincing. In its present form at any rate the book is almost certainly the work of a single author who wrote in Greek, and this was probably the original language of the whole work.

The religious teaching of the book shows clearly the influence of Greek thought. This is seen in the writer's treatment of the idea of wisdom, which he personifies under the influence of the Stoic conception of the universal *Logos*. Indeed the process of personification is taken a stage further than in Ben Sira, so that wisdom is now presented as a substantial reality alongside God himself, sharing his properties and characteristics.[1] Stoic influence is to be seen again in the enumeration of the four cardinal virtues of 'self-control and prudence, justice, and courage' in 8⁷, and in the doctrine of the all-pervasive wisdom (cf. 7²²ᶠᶠ·) which is identified with the spirit of God (cf. 1⁴⁻⁷, 9¹⁷). Platonic influence is also evident. Thus, the world is said to have been created 'out of formless matter' (11¹⁷), and the perishable body (cf. 9¹⁵, 15⁸) is distinguished from the pre-existent (cf. 8²⁰) and immortal (cf. 3¹⁻⁵) soul. The doctrine of immortality, as distinct from the Hebrew notion of resurrection, is found elsewhere in some Jewish writings of this period,[2] but is developed much more fully in the Book of Wisdom (cf. 2²³, 3⁴, 5¹⁵, 6¹⁸, 8¹⁷, 15³). Echoes of this book can be heard in Paul's letters (cf. Rom. 9¹⁹⁻²³ with Wisd. 11²², 12¹²⁻¹⁸ and 1 Cor. 6² with Wisd. 3⁸), but it cannot be certain that he made direct use of it. More important than isolated texts is its general teaching concerning wisdom, which prepared the way for the Christian understanding of revelation and in particular for the Christian doctrine of the Incarnation.

---

[1] See p. 133.

[2] E.g. Jub. 23³¹; 1 Enoch 103⁴; Ass. Mos. 10⁹ ᶠ·; Apoc. Abr. 12, 14, 21. Josephus ascribes this belief to the Essenes (cf. *War* II. viii. 11 (155)). The evidence of the Dead Sea Scrolls in this connexion is not too clear, but seems to indicate belief in resurrection rather than immortality; cf. p. 173, above.

*a*. SEEK THE LORD AND LIVE ($1^{1-15}$)

1. *rulers of the earth*. The writer has in mind not so much Gentile rulers as those apostate Jews in Alexandria and elsewhere who by accepting Greek ways had won for themselves positions of authority in the State. One such in later years was Tiberius Alexander, nephew of Philo, who held high office under the Emperor Nero. This is no humble address to his 'betters'; on the contrary, in a series of strong imperatives he 'cracks the whip' at their heels with bold disdain (cf. also $6^{1-3}$).

4. *a deceitful soul . . . a body enslaved to sin*. Divine wisdom cannot make its abode in a man who is given over to sin. According to Hebrew 'psychology' man is not a dichotomy of body and soul (or spirit), but a unity of personality. In this verse the distinction between these two terms is not to be pressed; nevertheless the tendency throughout the book is away from the typically Hebrew conception in the direction of the Greek, which distinguished between body and soul as separate and distinct parts of man's being (cf. also $8^{20}$, $9^{15}$).

5. *disciplined spirit*. The idea of discipline is closely associated with that of instruction.

6. *wisdom is a kindly spirit*, etc. She is mild and humane but will not leave wickedness unpunished.

7. *holds all things together*. This idea of a world-soul or world-principle holding all things together is a Stoic belief. It was taken over by the Alexandrian Jews and appears frequently in Philo. In this verse it is used with reference to the spirit of the Lord. Elsewhere in the wisdom literature it is associated with wisdom (cf. $7^{24}$, $8^1$) or with the word of God (cf. Ecclus. $43^{26}$), and in the New Testament it is related to the cosmic work of Christ (cf. Col. $1^{17}$; Heb. $1^3$).

10. *a jealous ear*. In the Old Testament God is said to be 'jealous' for his honour and for the welfare of his people. Here, for the same reason, he keeps careful watch over men's words and thoughts.

11. *a lying mouth destroys the soul*: i.e. leads to spiritual death. There is no suggestion here of physical death being the result of sin.

13. *he does not delight*, etc.: cf. Ezek. 33¹¹. He is still thinking of spiritual death, but the thought of physical death is not far from the mind.

14. *the generative forces*, etc. The text refers rather to the natural processes of the world which, contrary to popular opinion, are not inherently evil.

*the dominion of Hades is not on earth.* Hades, or the underworld, is here personified. Its powers are limited to the nether regions and are not operative on earth.

15. *For righteousness is immortal.* So *ipso facto* are righteous men. Here is the writer's solution to the problem of innocent suffering—the promise of immortality—for, as he says later, 'God created man for incorruption, and made him in the image of his own eternity' (3²³).

*b.* THE HOPE OF IMMORTALITY (3¹⁻⁹)

In this passage of great beauty the writer expresses his faith in the life beyond, not in terms of the Hebrew doctrine of bodily resurrection (cf. Isa. 26¹⁹; Dan. 12²), but rather in terms of the Greek doctrine of the immortality of the soul. No mention is made either of 'shades' or of Sheol. *The souls of the righteous*, having left their bodies behind, are at once in the presence of *God*, where they await the judgement (cf. 4²⁰ ᶠᶠ·). It is now clear that their death was not a punishment. Nor indeed was their suffering in this life; it was a disciplining, a testing, a refining, an *offering* accepted by God. In the after-life, by the *grace and mercy* of God, they will share in the messianic kingdom, abiding in his *love* and under his watchful care.

1. *the souls of the righteous*, etc. For this belief in the immortality of the soul (or spirit) as opposed to resurrection see also Jub. 23³¹; 1 Enoch 103⁴, 104² ᶠᶠ·; Ass. Mos. 10⁹; Apoc. Abr. 21.

*no torment.* The contrast is probably between their bliss in heaven and their anguish on earth. But since in other writings of the period reference is made to the torments of the wicked in the after-life, this may also be the allusion here (cf. 1 Enoch 99¹¹, 103⁷ ᶠ·; Ass. Mos. 10¹⁰).

2. *In the eyes of the foolish.* Those who are morally foolish have no true spiritual discernment.

4–6 The writer sweeps away the age-old notion that suffering presupposes sin and is a punishment from God. On the contrary it is God's way of disciplining his own people.

6. *like gold in the furnace*: cf. Mal. 3³; 2 Cor. 13⁵; James 1¹².

*like a sacrificial burnt offering.* Their suffering is a sacrifice offered to God and accepted by him; cf. 2 Tim. 4⁶.

7. *their visitation*: used here in a good sense to indicate the time of their deliverance, cf. Ps. 106⁴, etc.

*shine forth.* Frequently in the literature of this period the righteous dead are said to be 'resplendent' or to dwell in 'shining light' (cf. Dan. 12³; 1 Enoch 104², 108¹¹ ᶠᶠ·, etc.).

*sparks . . . stubble.* The simile should not be pressed to signify that the righteous take vengeance on the wicked. The picture given here is a fairly common one in the Old Testament, cf. Isa. 1³¹ (LXX); Jer. 5¹⁴; Obad. 18; Zech. 12⁶; Mal. 4¹.

8. *They will govern . . . and rule*: in the messianic kingdom (cf. Dan. 7¹⁴, ²⁷). There is no need to find here reference to an earthly kingdom; indeed the context precludes such an interpretation.

9. The hope of immortality is based on the *grace and mercy* of God.

*his elect*: the heavenly company of the righteous, God's chosen ones, who will inherit the kingdom, cf. 1 Enoch 62⁸·¹⁴, etc.

*c.* THE NATURE OF WISDOM (7²²ᵇ–8¹)

In describing the nature and functions of wisdom the writer adopts the language of the Stoic philosophers, who spoke in terms of a divine power immanent in the world and operative behind the many and diverse activities of Creation (cf. also note on 1⁷). In so doing he comes very close to presenting wisdom as a hypostasis;[1] nevertheless she remains *an emanation, a reflection, an image* of God, rather than a divine being standing alongside God. Though possessing many personal attributes (22–23), she is not a person as God himself is. She is rather a divine principle or presence through which God is seen and known by men, which *pervades and penetrates all things* and is a perfect revelation of God (24–26). Though able to *renew all things*, she herself does not require to be renewed and makes men *friends of God* (27). Her beauty none can excel (28–30), whilst in her ordering of the universe she does *all things well* (8[1]).

22*b*–23. The writer ascribes to wisdom 21 attributes ($3 \times 7$, both sacred numbers), some of which the Stoics associate with the 'Logos of the many names'. It is unlikely, however, that he consciously identifies these two concepts.

22. *in her there is a spirit*, etc.: signifying the life-principle which is in her. In 9[17] she is identified with the holy Spirit.

*unique . . . manifold.* These two terms reflect the Stoic idea of the one world-soul with its many manifestations.

*subtle*: in the sense of 'spiritual' as opposed to 'material'.

23 f. *penetrating through all spirits*, etc. Wisdom enters those who have a spiritual affinity with her. Like the world-soul she *penetrates all things* by reason of her *pureness*, i.e. her 'spiritual' or 'immaterial' essence.

25 f. Wisdom shares in the very nature of God and possesses his divine attributes. As the breath is to the body, the river to its source, the reflection to the light (cf. Heb. 1[3]), the image to the object (cf. Col 1[15]), so is she to God.

27. *Though she is but one . . . she renews all things.* Like God himself (cf. Ps. 102[26 f.]), omnipotent wisdom, though the source of all change, remains unchanging and unchangeable, the one enduring power by which all things live.

*friends of God and prophets.* According to the Stoics the wise were called 'friends of God'. Philo likewise uses the phrase and points to the 'prophet' Moses as the supreme example.

[1] See p. 133.

Wisdom brings *holy souls* into the same intimate fellowship with God.

28. *lives with wisdom*: as in marriage.

30. *against wisdom evil does not prevail*: cf. John 1⁵, 'The light shines in the darkness, and the darkness has not overcome it'.

8. 1. This verse again suggests the notion of the world-soul which extends through all Creation. The word translated 'orders' is a favourite one with the Stoics. The world is both sustained and governed by wisdom.

*d.* A PRAYER FOR WISDOM (9¹⁻¹⁸)

In this beautifully written chapter the author, in the name of Solomon (8, 12), prays for the gift of wisdom. In face of the majesty and power of God (1–3) he acknowledges his own weakness and lack of understanding of the universe which God has made (5–6, 13–16). Only by wisdom—which he identifies with the spirit of God (17)—can men learn his ways (6, 11, 17 f.), for from the creation of the world she was with God (9) and knows and understands all things (11).

1 f. *by thy word, and by thy wisdom.* Although the expressions 'word' and 'wisdom' are used here in close conjunction, we are not to read into this passage the Logos (=Word) doctrine of the Greeks or of Philo.¹ The writer's reference to the 'word' is thoroughly Hebraic, and is probably an echo of Ps. 33⁶. To him 'wisdom' is God's agent in Creation.

4. *wisdom that sits by thy throne.* In 18¹⁵ it is said of the 'all-powerful word' that it 'leaped from heaven, from the royal throne'. In this verse it is personified wisdom, which shares the creative power and rule of God; cf. also vv. 9 f. and Prov. 8³⁰.

8. *a copy of the holy tent . . . from the beginning.* According to biblical tradition David received from God a plan of the Temple which he passed on to Solomon (cf. 1 Chron. 28¹¹⁻¹⁹), just as Moses had received a plan of the Tabernacle (cf. Ex. 25⁹, ⁴⁰). The writer, however, may have been influenced here

¹ See pp. 134 f.

by the Greek idea of heavenly archetypes associated with the name of Plato (cf. also Heb. 8⁵). In later Jewish theology the heavenly Jerusalem, for example, is viewed as a counterpart of the earthly (cf. 2 Bar. 32²ᶠᶠ·; 2 Esd. 10⁴⁴ᶠᶠ·, and also Gal. 4²⁶; Heb. 12²²; Rev. 3¹², 21², ¹⁰). According to rabbinic tradition the Temple was one of seven things which existed before Creation.

11. *she knows and understands all things.* Wisdom like God himself is omniscient.

*guard me with her glory.* As an 'emanation of the glory' of God (cf. 7²⁵) she illuminates his path.

15. In this verse as elsewhere in the book (cf. 8²⁰, 9¹⁵), the author tends to think in Greek rather than in Hebrew terms. But the distinction should not be pressed. To him the body is a hindrance to the soul; but it is not inherently evil and the source of sin. For the use of somewhat similar language cf. I Cor. 15⁵³; 2 Cor. 5¹⁻¹⁰.

17. *sent thy holy Spirit*: see note on 1⁷.

*e.* THE PUNISHMENT OF THE EGYPTIANS (18⁵⁻¹⁹)

The Egyptians *resolved to kill* the children of the Israelites, but instead they saw their own firstborn slain and were themselves destroyed *by a mighty flood* (5). Warning dreams were sent to prepare the Israelites for what would befall them (6), and to acquaint the Egyptians with the reason for their impending destruction (17–19). God's judgement is carried out upon the *doomed land* of Egypt by his *all-powerful word, a stern warrior* from the heights of *heaven* who *filled all things with death* (15).

5. This verse further illustrates the principle enunciated in 11¹⁵–12²². Those who *resolved to kill* the Israelite *babes* (cf. Exod. 1¹⁶) or throw them into the Nile (cf. Exod. 1²²) would themselves be punished in like manner.

*one child*: Moses (cf. Exod. 2³). The rescue of this one child would lead to the death of many. R. H. Charles, on the basis of a similar tradition in Jub. 48⁴, omits the words 'and rescued', and reads 'In retribution for even a single child that was exposed, thou didst take away ten thousand Egyptians'.

6. *known beforehand to our fathers*. The patriarchs are probably meant (cf. 9¹, 12²¹, 18⁹, ²²). According to the literature of the intertestamental period, dreams or visions giving antecedent knowledge were vouchsafed to ancients such as Eve (Apoc. Mos. 2²), Enoch (1 Enoch 1²; Jub. 4⁹), Abraham (2 Baruch 4⁴), Isaac (Test. Abr. 5), Rebecca (Jub. 35⁶), and Jacob (Jub. 32¹⁶⁻²⁶).

*the oaths*: i.e. God's promises.

9. *in secret . . . offered sacrifices*: a reference to the Passover. There is no biblical record concerning the secret character of this festival, which was observed in the homes of the people.

*singing the praises of the fathers*. The author reads back into the age of the Exodus the custom prevailing in his own time of singing Psalms at the Passover.

13. *their magic arts*: cf. Exod. 7¹¹, 8⁷, 9¹¹. The names 'Jannes' and 'Jambres' (or 'Mambres') are given in Jewish legend and also in 2 Tim. 3⁸ to the Egyptian magicians who tried to match the miracles performed by Moses.

*God's son*: cf. Exod. 4²² ᶠ·

15 f. *thy all-powerful word*, etc. This daring presentation of God's word as *a stern warrior* is a poetical personification and not a hypostasis in any true sense of that word. This idea of God's destructive word is found several times in the Old Testament (cf. Ps. 147²⁹; Jer. 23²⁹; Hos. 6⁵), but here the personification is much more strongly marked.

*carrying the sharp sword*, etc. These words recall the description of the destroying angel in 1 Chron. 21¹⁶.

*touched heaven while standing on the earth*: possibly an exaggeration of the phrase 'between the earth and the heaven' in 1 Chron. 21¹⁶. The gigantic stature of the angels is a characteristic of later Jewish and Christian angelology, cf. Test. Reub. 5⁷; 2 Enoch 1⁴, 18¹; Gospel of Peter 41; Acts of John 90.

19. Those destined to die would be made fully aware beforehand of the reason for their impending doom. This was part of the divine judgement. Cf. Nebuchadnezzar's dream in Dan. 2.

# XVI

## PSALMS

THE early origin of psalmody is attested by many sacred poems scattered throughout the Old Testament, from the Song of Deborah in Judges 5 through the historical books and prophetic writings, and also by the presence of similar poems in Babylonian and Canaanite sources. That they continued to be written in the intertestamental period is attested by the so-called Psalms of Solomon (*c.* 50 B.C.) and the Hymns from Qumran, and indeed by their presence in almost every book in the Apocrypha. But whereas the biblical psalms for the most part had their setting in the Temple and its cultus,[1] a number of them had a closer affinity with the Wisdom Schools, whose influence is particularly evident in the composition of 'post-Psalter' psalms such as those in Ben Sira (cf. $39^{12\,ff\cdot}$, $42^{15\,ff\cdot}$, $51^{1\,ff\cdot}$, etc.).

### 1. *The Book of Psalms*

The Psalter, which stands first among 'the Writings' in the Hebrew Bible, is made up of 150 psalms, not all of which, however, originally stood as independent units. As the LXX shows, 9 and 10, for example, were at one time a single work, whilst the refrain in $42^{6,\,11}$ and $43^{5}$ indicates that 42 and 43 really belong together. It is not so much a collection of psalms, however, as it is a collection of collections, a 'hymn book' composed of smaller 'hymn books', with the addition of a number of separate psalms. As it stands, it is divided into five books (1–41, 42–72, 73–89, 90–106, 107–50), probably in imitation of the five-fold Pentateuch, the first four being concluded by a doxology.

At an earlier stage, however, it may have been divided into

---

[1] See below, and also pp. 121 f.

three books (1–41, 42–89, 90–150), whose development it is very difficult to trace, if only because in each case there has been much revision and adaptation of earlier material. The first of these (1–41), which normally uses the name 'Yahweh' with reference to God (hence the name 'Yahwistic Psalter'), probably belongs to the post-exilic period and is the earliest of the three. With the exception of numbers 1, 2, and 33 these psalms are ascribed 'to David', signifying that they belonged to a Davidic collection rather than that they were actually written by him (1 is an introduction to the completed Psalter; 2 serves as an introduction to the 'Davidic collection' and may have had the title originally; 33 seems to be a later addition). The second stage of development was the addition of 42–83 which largely avoid the use of the sacred name and substitute the word ' 'Elohim', meaning simply 'God' (hence the name 'Elohistic Psalter'); this substitution is quite clear in 53, which repeats 14, and in 70 which repeats $40^{13-17}$. This collection itself contains three earlier psalters—one ascribed to David (51–72), one to Korah (42–49), and one to Asaph (50, 73–83), the names once more indicating collections called after 'patrons' rather than designating actual authors. If, as seems likely, this Davidic collection (51–72) originally followed on the earlier Davidic collection (1–41), this would give added point to the words of $72^{20}$ ('the prayers of David the son of Jesse are ended') as a conclusion to this joint collection, and bring together the divided Psalter of Asaph (by linking 50 with 73–83). A varied appendix of six psalms (84–89), in which the name 'Yahweh' is retained, has been added to this collection, four being ascribed to Korah (84, 85, 87, 88) and one each to David (86) and Ethan the Ezrahite (89). The third stage of development (probably in the Hellenistic period) was the addition of 90–150, a miscellaneous collection, of which seventeen are ascribed to David and one each to Moses (90) and Solomon (127); among the rest some minor collections of a liturgical character can be detected, particularly the 'Pilgrim Psalms' or 'Songs of Ascents' (120–34) and the 'Hallelujah Psalms' (104–6, 111–13, 115–17, 135, 146–50).

These several stages of development are difficult to date, but several factors indicate that the Psalter attained its present form somewhere around 200 B.C. or at the latest 100 B.C. For example, the Greek text of the Psalms, dating from about this period, substantially agrees with the Hebrew text; 1 Macc. 7[17] (c. 100 B.C.) quotes 79[2 f.], apparently as authoritative Scripture; the allusions to the Psalms in the Hymns from Qumran strongly suggest that they were well established; and the fact that the Psalms of Solomon (c. 50 B.C.) were not included confirms that by that time the collection had been closed. The dating of individual psalms is even more difficult, widely diverse answers having been given by scholars. In recent years, however, the tendency has been to trace back a considerable number into pre-exilic times and to limit severely or even exclude altogether the possibility of psalms from the Maccabaean period.

The earlier use of the psalms does not concern us in this volume, except to repeat that from the beginning many were closely associated with the cult as vocal accompaniments to specific cultic acts. It is within this same context that they are to be understood also in post-exilic times, and it was primarily for this purpose that these several collections were made. There is evidence that in the fourth century B.C., for example, at least some psalms were being used in this way by special 'guilds' of singers and musicians (cf. 1 Chron. 16[8 ff.]), who in due course lost their identity and were fused together, their separate 'hymn books' being incorporated into larger collections. In the Hellenistic period the psalms continued to play an important part in the Temple ritual, a tradition which was in years to come followed by both the Jewish synagogue and the Christian Church.

Reference has been made above [1] to the place of choral singing and orchestral music in the Temple services, and to the part played in them by Levitical choirs such as those of Asaph and Korah, each with its own choirmaster and 'hymn book'. Fifty-five psalms, moreover, are ascribed 'to the chief musician';

[1] See pp. 118 ff.; 123.

since some of these are among the seventy-three ascribed to David, presumably such psalms were to be found in both collections. This translation, however, is not altogether certain; it may signify rather a musical direction and be translated 'regarding the musical rendering', or it may have some other unknown cultic reference. Some of the headings to the psalms are clear enough, but others remain quite obscure. The words *maskil, mikhtam, mizmor, shiggaion, tehillah,* and *tephillah,* for example, refer to various types of hymn or psalm; other expressions indicate the musical instruments used, of which there were three groups, percussion, wind, and string; others again may suggest the tunes to which the psalms should be sung, some of them perhaps popular melodies, such as 'The Hind of the Morning' (22), 'Lilies' (45, 69), 'The Dove of the Far-off Terebinths' (56), and a vintage song 'Destroy not' (57, 58, 59; cf. Isa. 65$^8$). Thirty-four psalms have no heading of any kind and are generally known as 'orphans'. It seems likely that in the Hellenistic period most of the singing was done by trained choirs, with interjected shouts or 'Hallelujahs' from the worshipping congregation. Some psalms were presumably devised for antiphonal singing (e.g. 120–34), whilst in others the worshippers responded with a repeated refrain (e.g. 118$^{1-14}$, 136).

The services accompanying the offering of the twice-daily sacrifices were carefully ordered, not only as regards the ritual, but also as regards the offering of praise. Thus, according to early Jewish tradition, each day of the week had its specially prescribed psalm—24 on Sunday, 48 on Monday, 82 on Tuesday, 94 on Wednesday, 81 on Thursday, 93 on Friday, and 92 on Saturday—each one chosen by reason of its particular appropriateness to the day. So also on the occasion of the great Feasts. According to later rabbinic sources the Levites sang 7 on Lots, 135 on Passover, 29 on Weeks, 47 on New Year, 12 on Tabernacles, 30 on Dedication, and 81 on New Moons. In addition, the so-called Songs of Ascents (120–34) were used at the three great Pilgrim Feasts of Passover, Weeks, and Tabernacles; the *Hallel* (or Praise) Psalms (113–18), as they are called in the synagogue liturgy, were sung then also, and on Dedication and the New Moon Festivals.

The liturgical use of the Psalms is thus well attested. But they are much more than mere 'accompaniments of ritual': in their expression of piety and in their teaching concerning the nature of God they are an unconscious epitome of the Jewish faith. In a number of them this piety expresses itself (cf. 19[7-14], 25, 51, 106) in a love for the Law of God whose observance is perfect wisdom (cf. 1, 49, 112, 119, etc.). This relationship between Law and wisdom has a long history, and the indications are that such psalms had their setting in the Wisdom School rather than in the Temple. Throughout the post-exilic period, and possibly even as early as pre-exilic times, the 'wise men' set themselves up as apologists of the Law.[1] Formerly they had applied themselves to the task of giving *torah* in the sense of 'instruction', but now they applied themselves to the task of interpreting in terms of wisdom the revealed Torah of God in the form of sacred Scripture. This process can be traced from Jeremiah (cf. 8[8]) and Deuteronomy (cf. 4[5-6]) through the Psalms (cf. especially 1, 19[7-14], 119), Proverbs (*passim*), and Daniel (cf. 1[8], etc.) to Ben Sira (cf. 19[20], 24[23], etc.), where wisdom is virtually identified with the Law of God. 'Here', writes S. Mowinckel, 'we are face to face with a learned psalmography which is not derived from the Temple singers but is of a truly private nature and has no longer any direct relation to the cult.'[2] The resultant religion, which we find set forth in these psalms, is that of a genuine legal piety, characterized by a devotion to the revealed will of God and a thirst after righteousness.

The psalms listed below have been chosen for comment because of the peculiar insight they give into the religious beliefs and practices of the Jewish people who used them, in public worship and in private devotion, during the inter-testamental period.

[1] See p. 114.
[2] *The Psalms in Israel's Worship*, vol. ii (English translation by D. R. Ap-Thomas, 1962), p. 110.

*a*. THE LAW OF THE LORD (PSALM 19⁷⁻¹⁴)

Ps. 19 consists of two separate hymns brought together, quite fittingly, for use in public worship. The first deals with the glory of God in Creation (1–6) and the second with his glory in the Law (7–14).[1] This second section continues the thought of Ps. 1 and finds fuller expression in Ps. 119. Vv. 7–10 are a hymn in praise of the Law, which brings manifold blessings and in which the psalmist finds his greatest joy; in vv. 11–14 he prays that he may be kept blameless and offers his worship as a sacrifice of praise.

7–10. These verses provide an excellent example of genuine piety based on the Law, whose observance is no mere formal acceptance of rules and regulations but rather a joyful response to the revelation of God's holy will. Six times over the covenant name 'Yahweh' (Lord) is repeated, emphasizing that the Law is the gift of God's grace (cf. also v. 14).

This divine gift is described under six names which, in this context, are to be taken as practically synonymous—*law*, *testimony*, *precepts*, *commandment*, *fear*, and *ordinances*. Each of these is further defined and its true character revealed—it is *perfect* (complete, without blemish), *sure* (dependable, trustworthy), *right* (straight, undeviating), *pure* (clear, shining bright), *clean* (pure, free from the contamination of idolatry), and *true* (reliable, stable). In a series of participial clauses the psalmist then describes the effect of each on the worshipper— it gives new vitality and makes wise those who are gauche and inexperienced (7); it delights the heart and gives light to the eyes (8); it gives unfailing guidance and leads to the goal of righteousness (9). Such a gift is more precious than *gold* and more desirable than the choicest *drippings of the honeycomb*.

9. *the fear of the Lord*: indicating man's response to the revelation of God. It is the Hebrew equivalent of our word 'religion'.

11–14. The psalmist's contemplation of the Law, which warns him against evil and brings its own *reward*, leads him to

[1] For the meaning of 'law' see p. 112.

acknowledge his sinfulness and to pray for deliverance. Expressing his confidence in the forgiveness of God he offers his prayer
and his *meditation* as an *acceptable* sacrifice to Yahweh his *rock*
and his *redeemer*. The piety thus disclosed is no perfunctory
performance of religious duties, but a ready response to the
grace in and goodness of God.

11. *in keeping them there is great reward*: the reward, as the following verses show, is to be found in the forgiveness of his sins
and his protection from evil.

12. *errors . . . hidden faults*: sins inadvertently committed (cf.
Lev. 4¹ ff·, 5² ff·; Num. 15²² ff·), for which provisions are made in
the Law.

13. *presumptuous sins*: for which the Law provides no remedy (cf.
Num. 15³⁰ f·). The reference, however, is probably to 'presumptuous men' from whose *dominion* he prays to be delivered lest,
by giving way, he falls into *great transgression*.

14. *acceptable*: an expression commonly used with reference to
animal sacrifice (cf. Exod. 28³⁸; Lev. 1³ f·). He offers *the meditation of* his *heart* as a spiritual sacrifice to God (cf. Rom. 12¹).

*b.* 'LORD, I BELIEVE' (PSALM 73)

This psalm, with profound spiritual insight, describes the
writer's pilgrimage from the depths of doubt and despair to
confident faith in God and an unutterable joy in his presence.
Reference in v. 17 to *the sanctuary* indicates its use in public
worship; but it is didactic rather than cultic in character and
has affinity with the Wisdom Schools.

The faith the psalmist now professes (1) had been seriously
challenged (2), he tells us, by the bewildering mystery of the
prosperity of the wicked (3), whose lot he describes at some
length (4–12). He himself had suffered grievously, so that only
the thought of his godly associates kept him from utter despair
(13–16). Then, entering the Temple, his doubts were miracu-
lously dispelled, for there he saw as never before how precarious
and unstable was the lot of the wicked and how stupid he

himself had been (17–22). None of the pleasures enjoyed by the wicked could compare with the communion he enjoys with God and which nothing can destroy (23–26). The wicked will perish, but he will recount the saving mercies of the Lord (27–28).

1. Read with the RSV margin, 'God is good to Israel', the word 'Israel' being further defined by the words that follow.

4–12. This problem of the prosperity of the wicked is, of course, to be found elsewhere in the wisdom literature, especially in Job and Proverbs, and finds an echo in later writers still. Its presence here gives no indication as to the date of the psalm, but its message was no doubt seen to have a particular relevance at the time when Hellenism was challenging the old-established Jewish faith, for 'it was above all the wealthy and educated classes who allowed the spirit of an alien culture and of "enlightenment" to pervade their own lives and so gave offence to the devout poet'.[1]

10. This difficult verse may be translated, 'Therefore people turn to them and abundant water is drained by them', i.e. the crowds drink in their words as a thirsty man drinks water.

13–16. His faith in God almost reached breaking-point, for he was *stricken* and *chastened* continually. But he was kept from betrayal by the thought that it might undermine the faith of others.

17–22. *the sanctuary of God.* His entry into the Temple, possibly on some festival occasion, brought 'the moment of truth'. Standing in the presence of God he saw everything in a new light. The wicked and their ways were but a fleeting *dream*, insubstantial phantoms.

24. *afterward thou wilt receive me to glory.* The English word *glory* has 'heavenly overtones' not found in the Hebrew, and later Christian interpretation should not be read into it. The verse is difficult to translate, but it may be rendered 'afterward

[1] A. Weiser, *The Psalms*, Eng. trans. 1962, p. 509.

thou wilt receive me with honour'. Many find here a reference to life after death (cf. also Ps. 16[10] and 49[14 f.]), observing that the word translated *receive* is that used to describe Enoch's and Elijah's translations into heaven. But it is doubtful whether the text as it stands can convey this meaning. If reference to a life beyond is conceded, what we have here is the glimmering of hope rather than the shining of certain faith. It is safer, however, to take it to mean that God will in this life honour and vindicate his servant. This sense is brought out in an attractive emendation suggested by D. W. Thomas, who, with the interchange of only two letters in the text, reads 'thou wilt receive me along the path of honour'.[1]

28. *that I may tell of all thy works*: probably a reference to the recitation of this psalm in the public worship of the Temple.

### c. A TIME OF TROUBLE (PSALM 79)

This psalm, which has much in common with 44 and 74, is a national lament occasioned by an assault of Israel's enemies on Jerusalem and its Temple. Such psalms, of which there are several in the Psalter (cf. 12, 14, 44, 58, 74, 79, 80, 83, 89, 144; also Lam. 5), make use of the word 'we' and follow a fairly well-defined pattern. Thus in Ps. 79 the invocation of Yahweh's name (1) is followed by a lamentation giving a graphic description of the people's distress, brought about by some national disaster in which 'the heathen' plunder and kill, and then mock those who remain (1–4); next comes a supplication for deliverance (5, 9, 11), accompanied by a plea for the destruction of the enemy (6f., 10, 12) and a prayer for forgiveness (8, 9), for it is the 'honour' or 'glory' of God's name that is at stake (9); the psalm concludes with an expression of thanks and praise to God (13).

Psalms of this kind, which follow a set literary pattern, may have originated in the cult (cf. the reference in v. 1 to the defilement of the shrine) and subsequently been applied in turn to certain crises in history. On the other hand they may

[1] *The Text of the Revised Psalter*, 1963.

have arisen out of some actual historical situations. In this latter case three possible dates have been suggested for the devastation described in 1–4, when the *Temple* was *defiled* and the city laid *in ruins*—the capture of Jerusalem by the Babylonians in 586 B.C., some unknown or little-known catastrophe in the Persian or early Greek period, or the profanation of the Temple by Antiochus Epiphanes in 167 B.C. The havoc wrought by Antiochus, however, was less severe than that described in this psalm (cf. 1 Macc. 1²⁹⁻⁴⁴, 4³⁶⁻⁶¹), whilst the information available for the period from Ezra onwards is too vague to serve as trustworthy evidence. The most likely date is 586 B.C. which finds support in the reminiscences within the psalm of such passages as Lam. 5 and Jer. 10²⁵ (cf. vv. 6 f.). Its significance for the intertestamental period lies not in the date of its composition but rather in the use to which it was put in later years, v. 3 being quoted in 1 Macc. 7¹⁷ with reference to the treacherous slaughter by Alcimus in 161 B.C. of sixty members of the Hasidim.[1]

2. *thy saints.* The word used here is *ḥasidhim*, meaning 'the pious ones' or, more accurately, 'the loyal ones'. Both here and in several other psalms it describes those who were loyal to Yahweh within the Covenant he had made with his people. Later on, in Maccabaean times, it designated a particular party within the State.

3. Quoted in 1 Macc. 7¹⁷. Proper burial of the dead was a matter of the greatest moment. To leave a body unburied (cf. 1 Sam. 31¹⁰ ff.; Jer. 22¹⁹) or to mutilate or destroy it (cf. Lev. 20¹⁴, 21⁹; Josh. 7²⁵; Amos 2¹) was the severest of punishments. Behind this notion of respectful treatment of the corpse there probably lay the idea that such disrespect involved injury to the shade whose double it was.

4. *a taunt . . . mocked and derided.* The oriental is particularly susceptible to mockery (cf. also v. 10). The gibe, like the curse, undermines one's strength.

[1] See p. 51.

5 f. The psalmist blames the enemy for this terrible devastation; later on (9) he puts it down to the people's sin. But there is no contradiction here. Either way, it is for them a judgement of God.

8 f. *the iniquities of our forefathers*: probably in the sense of 'our former iniquities'. There is a deep consciousness here of penitence and the need for forgiveness.

10. *avenging*. This sentiment of divine vengeance, which appears frequently in the Old Testament, is to be judged against the background of a society in which retaliation and blood revenge were an acknowledged part of the system of justice; cf. also vv. 6 and 12.

## 2. *The Psalms of Solomon*

This collection of eighteen psalms, originally written in Hebrew, is extant in a Greek translation and in a Syriac version derived from the Greek. They were probably the work of more than one author, but their uniformity of religious outlook and aspiration indicates that they are the product of a closely knit group of deeply religious and pious men. In form and sentiment they can be compared with the canonical Psalms, 'the wicked' or 'the sinners' being set over against 'the pious' or 'the poor', to whose number the authors themselves belong. The presence of technical musical directions form another link and suggest that they may have been sung as part of the synagogue liturgy (cf. $8^1$, $17^{31}$, $18^{10}$). They stand in the Hasidic tradition and are generally believed to belong to the party of the Pharisees, whose teaching concerning man's freedom of choice (cf. $9^4$), the resurrection of the dead (cf. $3^{16}$, $13^9$, $14^6$), and the messianic hope (cf. 17, 18) they amply illustrate.

'The wicked', about whom the writers have much to say, included not only the Gentiles but also, and more particularly, those Jews who outdid the Gentiles in wickedness. They were apparently members of the wealthy (cf. $12^4$, $15^7$) priestly class, who appropriated Temple offerings (cf. $1^8$, $2^3$, $8^{12\,f.,\,26}$) and supported the claims of a non-Davidic line of kings (cf. $17^{7\,f.}$). They are charged with hypocrisy (cf. $4^{17,\,22}$) and gross sensuality (cf. $2^{13\,ff.}$, $4^{4\,ff.}$, $8^{9\,f.,\,24}$) and are judged to have no part in the life to come (cf. $14^{4\,ff.}$, $15^{11\,ff.}$). It is not difficult to recognize in this description, and especially in the telling portrait in Ps. Sol. 4, the Pharisees' traditional enemies, the Sadducees.

Reference is made in several of these psalms not only to rival factions within the State, but also to a foreign invader who captures Jerusalem (cf. $2^{1\,f.}$, $8^{18\,f.}$) and later dies an ignoble death (cf. $2^{30\,f.}$). It is generally agreed that this alludes to Pompey's capture of the city and profanation of the Temple in 63 B.C.[1] and to his death in Egypt in 48 B.C. The events leading up to the plunder of Jerusalem and the destruction of the Temple are graphically portrayed:

> When the sinner waxed proud, with a battering-ram he cast down fortified walls . . . .
> Alien nations ascended Thine altar,
> They trampled it proudly with their sandals ($2^{1\,f.}$).
> Distress and the sound of war hath my ear heard,
> The sound of a trumpet announcing slaughter and calamity ($8^1$).

The 'traitors within the gate' are roundly condemned, because at the approach of the invader

> They opened the gates to Jerusalem, they crowned its walls . . . .
> He captured her fortresses and the wall of Jerusalem ($8^{19,\,21}$).

No wonder the psalmist mourns, for

> The Lawless One laid waste our land so that none inhabited it,
> They destroyed young and old and their children together.
> In the heat of his anger he sent them away even unto the west,
> And (he exposed) the rulers of the land unsparingly to derision ($17^{13\,f.}$).

The devout psalmists deplore the entanglement of their nation in the web of international politics, resulting in bloodshed

[1] See p. 85.

and war. They condemn the profligate priesthood and the presumptuous Hasmonaean House, which had usurped the throne of David, and look forward to the appearing of the Messiah of David's line, who will destroy evil rulers, purge Jerusalem from its enemies, gather together all the tribes of Israel, and rule over them for ever in righteousness and wisdom. These messianic expectations are set forth in Ps. Sol. 17 and 18, where the word 'Messiah' (cf. 17$^{36}$), for the first time in Jewish literature, is used to describe the ideal ruler of the coming kingdom.[1] Here is how the psalmist describes him:

> A righteous King and taught of God is he that reigneth over them;
> And there shall be no iniquity in his days in their midst,
> For all shall be holy and their King is the Lord's Messiah.
> For he shall not put his trust in horse and rider and bow,
> Nor shall he multiply unto himself gold and silver for war,
> Nor by ships shall he gather confidence for the day of battle.
> The Lord himself is his king, and the hope of him that is strong in the hope of God.
> And he shall have mercy upon all the nations that come before him in fear,
> For he shall strike the earth with the word of his mouth even for evermore, he shall bless the people of the Lord with wisdom and gladness.
> He himself also is pure from sin, so that he may rule a mighty people, and rebuke princes and overthrow sinners by the might of his word.
> And he shall not faint all his days, because he leaneth upon his God; for God shall cause him to be mighty through the spirit of holiness and wise through the counsel of understanding with might and righteousness.
> And the blessing of the Lord is with him in might, and his hope in the Lord shall not faint.
> And who can stand up against him? He is mighty in his works and strong in the fear of God.
> Tending the flock of the Lord with faith and righteousness; and he shall suffer none among them to faint in their pasture (17$^{35-45}$).

It is a thoroughly human figure that is here portrayed, ruling over an earthly kingdom, with Jerusalem as its centre.

[1] See p. 146.

But stress is laid not so much on the political and military as on the moral and spiritual side of his character: he is righteous and pure from sin and his hope is in the Lord. So also in Ps. Sol. 18, where, in the heading, he is once more given the name 'Messiah'—blessedness will mark the coming of his reign (cf. 18⁷). In this coming kingdom sinners will have no part (cf. 15¹⁵); the humble poor alone will share in it and will be raised in resurrection to the joys of eternal life (cf. 3¹⁶).

## 3. *The Hymns from Qumran*

These hymns or psalms of thanksgiving consist of eighteen columns, supplemented by many fragments, some of them very minute. They have no divisions between them, and so it is difficult to say where one hymn begins and another ends. It seems likely, however, that they represent some twenty-five or thirty compositions, although the original number must have been considerably larger. As to their use, there is ample evidence that the Qumran community sang God's praises at their festivals and other observances of worship; there can be little doubt that these hymns were used in this way.

It has been conjectured that they were written by the Teacher of Righteousness, the founder and leader of the Qumran community, or by one or more of his disciples. Some of them tell of persecution and betrayal, after the style of Jeremiah's 'confessions'. This fact, together with the frequent use of the personal pronoun 'I', may reflect the experience of such a man as the Teacher of Righteousness, but in some cases the reference may well be to the community as a whole. The problem of authorship is thus an open question; but it can be safely asserted that, even if they do not owe their origin to the Teacher, they bear the stamp of his teaching and the mark of his personality.

Most of them begin with the words 'I thank Thee, O Lord', and correspond in form to the 'hymns of individual thanksgiving' in the biblical Psalter. Indeed, in their expression of piety and their religious ideas generally they have much in common with the Book of Psalms from which they make frequent quotations. Despite their similarity in form, however, they show a considerable variety of theme. Thus, the writer bows in adoration before God, whose greatness in Creation accentuates the weakness and sinfulness of man. He gives thanks for the gift of the holy Spirit, which enables him to be a father to the community whose members have suffered as he himself has done, and also for the special knowledge of the divine will granted to him, whereby he is made 'a discerning interpreter of wonderful mysteries'. In particular he rejoices that God has seen fit to deliver him out of the power of 'the wicked' who have afflicted and persecuted him. Such men are in league with Belial the prince of demons, and will be overthrown in 'the time of judgement', when God will appear to do battle with the ungodly. The eschatological teaching of these hymns will be seen to have much in common with that of the apocalyptic literature. In column III, for example, a graphic picture of the birth of the messianic kingdom, under the figure of a woman in travail, is followed by an equally graphic description, in typically apocalyptic language, of the divine judgement which in the end will come upon the earth. Another link with the apocalyptic literature is to be found in their teaching concerning 'the two spirits' in man—the spirit of truth and the spirit of wickedness—which war against each other within the human heart. So also is their interest in angels, whom God has appointed to rule over the elements and in whose company the faithful will one day stand. The following hymns[1] have been chosen to illustrate a few of these themes.

## a. 'PERSECUTED, BUT NOT FORSAKEN' (COL. II$^{20-25}$)

I thank Thee, O Lord, for Thou hast placed my soul in the bundle of the living,
And hast hedged me about against all the snares of the Pit.
Violent men have sought after my life because I have clung to Thy Covenant.
For they, an assembly of deceit, and a horde of Satan,

[1] The translations are from G. Vermes, *The Dead Sea Scrolls in English* (Pelican Books, 1962).

Know not that my stand is maintained by Thee,
And that in Thy mercy Thou wilt save my soul since my steps pro-
ceed from Thee.
From Thee it is that they assail my life,
That Thou mayest be glorified by the judgement of the wicked,
And manifest Thy might through me in the presence of the sons of
men;
For it is by Thy mercy that I stand.

*b*. THE BIRTH OF THE KINGDOM (COL. III$^{7-10}$)

(And I was) like a woman in travail with her first-born child,
Upon whose belly pangs have come and grievous pains,
Filling with anguish her child-bearing crucible.
For the children have come to the throes of Death, and she labours
in her pains who bears the Man.
For amid the throes of Death she shall bring forth a man-child,
and amid the pains of Hell
There shall spring from her child-bearing crucible a Marvellous
Mighty Counsellor;
And the Man shall be delivered from out of the throes.

*c*. THE TERRORS OF THE END (COL. III$^{19-20, 29-32a, 36}$)

I thank thee, O Lord, for Thou hast redeemed my soul from the
Pit,
And from the Hell of Abaddon Thou hast raised me up to ever-
lasting height . . .
The torrents of Satan shall reach to all sides of the world.
In all their channels a consuming fire shall destroy every tree, green
and barren, on their banks;
Unto the end of their courses it shall scourge with flames of fire,
And shall consume the foundations of the earth and the expanse
of dry land.
The bases of the mountains shall blaze and the roots of the rocks
shall turn to torrents of pitch;
It shall devour as far as the great Abyss . . . .
The war of the heavenly warriors shall scourge the earth;
And it shall not end before the appointed destruction which shall
be for ever and without compare.

# CHRONOLOGICAL TABLES

*By* R. J. COGGINS

In the tables which follow, these points should be noted:

1. Precise dating in the history of Israel is impossible before the ninth century. In particular the biblical dates of the kings of Israel and Judah, given in 1 and 2 Kings, contain inconsistencies which have been resolved in various ways. The dates given here are therefore bound to be approximations. For discussion of the main problems reference must be made to the appropriate sections of each volume.

2. Where names of prophets are given, e.g. Amos, Hosea, this should be understood as referring to the lifetime of the prophet and *not* to the composition of the book which bears his name. This can very rarely be dated with any certainty.

3. The column headed 'Archaeological Evidence' simply lists the main points at which archaeological discovery has thrown light upon the history of Israel. For fuller information, with translations where appropriate, reference should be made to such works as D. W. Thomas (ed.), *Documents from Old Testament Times* (Nelson, 1958), and J. B. Pritchard (ed.), *The Ancient Near East* (O.U.P., 1959).

| DATE | ISRAEL | NEIGHBOURING POWERS | | ARCHAEOLOGICAL EVIDENCE |
| --- | --- | --- | --- | --- |
| | | | *Egypt* | |
| 1800 | | | | |
| 1700 | Abraham | Babylonian Power c. 1700 | Hyksos Period c. 1720–1550 | Mari Documents 1750–1700<br>Law Code of Hammurabi c. 1700 |
| 1600 | | | | |
| 1500 | | Hurrian (Horite) Power | XVIIIth Dynasty 1570–1310 | |
| 1400 | Jacob<br>Descent into Egypt c. 1370 | Hittite Empire | | Nuzu Documents<br>Tablets from Ras Shamra (Ugarit)<br>Tell-el-Amarna Letters |
| 1300 | | ✗ Qadesh-Orontes c. 286 | XIXth dynasty 1310–1200<br>Rameses II 1290–1224<br>Merneptah 1224–1216 | Merneptah Stele |
| 1200 | Exodus c. 1250. Moses<br>Entry into Canaan c. 1200<br>Joshua | | XXth Dynasty 1180–1065<br>Rameses III 1175–1144<br>Defeat of the Sea Peoples | |
| 1100 | Judges Period | Rise of Philistine Power | XXIst Dynasty 1065–935 | Wen-Amon c. 1100 |
| 1000 | Saul c. 1020–1000. Samuel<br>David c. 1000–961<br>Solomon c. 961–922 | | XXIInd Dynasty 935–725<br>Shishak 935–914 | Gezer Calendar |

PATRIARCHAL PERIOD

| DATE | JUDAH | Prophets | ISRAEL | NEIGHBOURING POWERS | | | ARCHAEOLOGICAL EVIDENCE |
|---|---|---|---|---|---|---|---|
| | | | | *Egypt* | *Assyria* | *Damascus* | |
| | Rehoboam 922–915 | | Jeroboam I 922–901 | | Revival of Assyrian Power | | |
| | Abijam 915–913 | | | | | | |
| | Asa 913–873 | | | | | | |
| 900 | | | Nadab 901–900 | | | Ben-hadad I ?900–860 | Melqart Stele |
| | | | Baasha 900–877 | | | | |
| | | | Elah 877–876 | | | | |
| | | | Zimri 876 | | | | |
| | ehoshaphat 873–849 | Elijah | Omri 876–869 | | Shalmaneser III 859–824 | Ben-hadad II ?860–843 | Black Obelisk of Shalmaneser |
| | | | Ahab 869–850 | | ✗ Qarqar 853 | | |
| | Jehoram 849–842 | Elisha | Ahaziah 850–849 | | | Hazael 843–796 | Moabite Stone |
| | Ahaziah 842 | | Joram 849–842 | | | | |
| | Athaliah 842–837 | | Jehu 842–815 | | | | |
| | Joash 837–800 | | Jehoahaz 815–801 | | Adad-Nirari III 811–783 | | |
| 800 | Amaziah 800–783 | | Jehoash 801–786 | | | Ben-hadad III ?796–770 | |
| | Azariah (Uzziah) 783–742 | | Jeroboam II 786–746 | | | | Samaria Ivories and Ostraca |
| | | Amos | | | | | |
| | | Hosea | | | | | |
| | | | Zechariah 746–745 | | | | |
| | Jotham 742–735 | Isaiah (active c. 742–700) | Shallum 745 | | Tiglath-Pileser III 745–727 | Rezin c. 740–732 | |
| | | Micah | Menahem 745–738 | | | Fall of Damascus 732 | |
| | Ahaz 735–715 | | Pekahiah 738–737 | | | | |
| | | | Pekah 737–732 | | | | |
| | | | Hoshea 732–724 | | Shalmaneser V 727–722 | | |
| | | | Fall of Samaria 721 | XXVth Dynasty 716–663 | Sargon II 722–705 | | Siloam Inscription |
| 700 | Hezekiah 715–687 | | | | Sennacherib 705–681 | | Taylor Prism of Sennacherib |
| | Invasion of Judah 701 | | | | | | |
| | Manasseh 687–642 | | | | Esar-haddon 681–669 | | |
| | | | | | Ashur-bani-pal 669–633? | | |
| | | | | Sack of Thebes 663 | | | |
| | | | | XXVIth Dynasty 663–525 | | | |
| | | | | Psammetichus I 663–609 | | *Babylon* | |
| | Amon 642–640 | Zephaniah | | | | Nabopolassar 626–605 | |
| | Josiah 640–609 | Jeremiah (active 626–c. 580) | | | | | |
| | | Nahum | | | | | |
| | | Habakkuk | | | | | |
| | Jehoahaz 609 | | | Necho II 609–593 | Fall of Nineveh 612 | ✗ Carchemish 605 | Babylonian Chronicle |
| | ✗ Megiddo 609 | | | | | Nebuchadrezzar II 605–562 | |
| | Jehoiakim 609–598 | | | | | | |

| DATE | JUDAH | Egypt | Babylon | Persia | ARCHAEOLOGICAL EVIDENCE |
| --- | --- | --- | --- | --- | --- |
| 600 | Jehoiachin 598–597 (deported) Jerusalem captured 597. First Deportation Zedekiah 597–587[1] Fall of Jerusalem 587[1]; Temple Destroyed; Second Deportation | Psammetichus II 593–58 Apries (Hophra) 588–569 | | | Lachish Letters |
| | Ezekiel | | | | 'Jehoiachin' Tablets from Babylon |
| | Third Deportation 581 The Exile | | | | |
| | 'Deutero-Isaiah' | Amasis 569–525 | Amel-Marduk 562–560 Nabonidus 556–539 Fall of Babylon 539 | Cyrus 550–530 | Cyrus Cylinder |
| 500 | Return of some Jews? 537 | Egypt conquered by Persia 525 | | Cambyses 530–522 Darius I 522–486 | |
| | Temple rebuilt 520–515 Haggai Zechariah 'Trito-Isaiah' | | | | |
| | | | | Xerxes 486–465 Artaxerxes I 465–424 | |
| | 'Malachi' | | | | |
| | Governorship of Nehemiah 445–433 432–? Sanballat I, Governor Samaria Ezra's Mission 398[2] | | | | |
| 400 | | Egypt independent 401 | | Artaxerxes II 404–358 Darius III 336–331 | Elephantine Papyri   Samaria Papyri |
| | Alexander the Great conquers Palestine 333–2 | Conquests of Alexander: ✗ Granicus 334; ✗ Issus 333; ✗ Gaugamela 331 | | | |

1 or 586.

2 This may also be dated at either 458 or 428.

# HELLENISTIC PERIOD

| DATE | JUDAH | NEIGHBOURING POWERS | | | ARCHAEOLOGICAL EVIDENCE |
|---|---|---|---|---|---|
| | | *Ptolemies* | *Seleucids* | | |
| 300 | Ptolemies rule Palestine | Ptolemy I Soter 323–285 | Seleucus I 312–281 | | Zeno Papyri |
| | | Ptolemy II Philadelphus 285–246 | Antiochus I 281–261 | | |
| | | | Antiochus II 261–247 | | |
| | | Ptolemy III Euergetes 246–221 | Seleucus II 247–226 | | |
| | | | Seleucus III 226–223 | | |
| | | Ptolemy IV Philopator 221–203 | Antiochus III 223–187 | | |
| | | | ⚔ Raphia 217 | | |
| 200 | Seleucids rule Palestine | Ptolemy V Epiphanes 203–181 | ⚔ Panium 198 | | |
| | | | Seleucus IV 187–175 | | |
| | Profanation of the Temple 167 (?168) | | Antiochus IV Epiphanes 175–163 | | |
| | Maccabaean Revolt | | | | |
| | Book of Daniel 167/4 | | | | |
| | Rededication of the Temple 164 (?165) | | | | |
| | | | *Seleucids* | | |
| | *Hasmonaean Rulers* | | Antiochus V Eupator 163–162 | *Rom* | |
| | Judas Maccabaeus 166–160 | ?Qumran Sect established | Demetrius I Soter 162–150 | | |
| | Jonathan 160–143 | | Alexander Balas 150–145 | | |
| | | | Demetrius II Nicator 145–139, | | |
| | Simon 142–134 | Jewish Independence granted 142 | 129–125 | | |
| | | | Antiochus VI Epiphanes 145–142 | | |
| | | | (Tryphon 142–139) | | |
| | | | Antiochus VII Sidetes 139–128 | | Qumran Scrolls (?) |
| 100 | John Hyrcanus I 134–104 | | | | |
| | Aristobulus I 104–103 | | | | |
| | Alexander Jannaeus 103–76 | | | | |
| | Alexandra Salome 76–67 | | | | |
| | Aristobulus II 67–63 | | | | |
| | Pompey captures Jerusalem 63 | | | | |
| | Judah added to the Roman Province of Syria | | | Overthrow of Pompey 48 | |
| | Hyrcanus II 63–40 | | | ⚔ Philippi 42 | |
| | | | | ⚔ Actium 31 | |
| | Antigonus 40–37 | | | | |
| | Herod the Great 37–4 B.C. | | | | |

# THE HOUSE OF THE MACCABEES (HASMONAEANS)

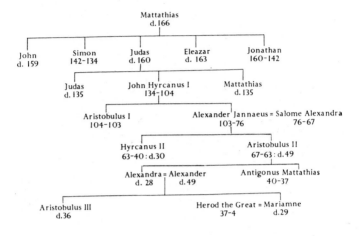

## HEROD'S FAMILY

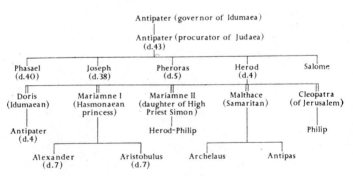

(The above table is incomplete. Herod in fact married ten wives.)

# A SELECTED BIBLIOGRAPHY

## HISTORY AND RELIGION

W. F. ALBRIGHT, *From the Stone Age to Christianity* (2nd ed., Baltimore, 1957).

—— *The Archaeology of Palestine* (Pelican Books, revised ed., 1960).

E. R. BEVAN, *The House of Seleucus* (2 vols., London, 1902).

—— *Jerusalem under the High Priests* (London, 1904).

—— 'Syria and the Jews', in *Cambridge Ancient History*, vol. viii, ch. 16 (Cambridge, 1930).

J. BRIGHT, *A History of Israel* (London, 1960).

F. F. BRUCE, *Israel and the Nations* (Exeter, 1963).

R. H. CHARLES, *Religious Development between the Old and the New Testaments* (London, 1914).

F. V. FILSON, *A New Testament History* (London, 1965).

W. FÖRSTER, *Palestinian Judaism in New Testament Times* (Edinburgh, 1964).

F. C. GRANT, *Ancient Judaism and the New Testament* (Edinburgh and London, 1960).

J. GRAY, *Archaeology and the Old Testament World* (London, 1962).

C. GUIGNEBERT, *The Jewish World in the Time of Jesus* (London, 1939).

R. T. HERFORD, *Talmud and Apocrypha* (London, 1933).

A. H. M. JONES, *The Herods of Judaea* (Cambridge, 1938).

M. NOTH, *The History of Israel* (2nd ed., London, 1960).

G. F. MOORE, *Judaism in the First Centuries of the Christian Era* (3 vols., Cambridge, Mass., 1927–30).

S. MOWINCKEL, *He that cometh* (Oxford, 1959).

W. O. E. OESTERLEY, *The Jews and Judaism during the Greek Period* (London, 1941).

S. Perowne, *The Life and Times of Herod the Great* (London, 1956).

C. F. PFEIFFER, *Between the Testaments* (Grand Rapids, 1959).

R. H. PFEIFFER, *History of New Testament Times, with an Introduction to the Apocrypha* (New York, 1949).

H. H. ROWLEY, *The Relevance of Apocalyptic* (3rd ed., London, 1963).

D. S. RUSSELL, *Between the Testaments* (London, 1960).

—— *The Method and Message of Jewish Apocalyptic* (London, 1964).

E. SCHÜRER, *History of the Jewish People in the Time of Jesus Christ* (5 vols., Edinburgh, 1892–1901; abridged paperback ed. in one vol., ed. by N. N. Glatzer, New York, 1961).

N. H. SNAITH, *The Jews from Cyrus to Herod* (Wallington, 1949).

V. TCHERIKOVER, *Hellenistic Civilization and the Jews* (Philadelphia, 1959).

S. ZEITLIN, *The Rise and Fall of the Judaean State* (Philadelphia, 1962).

## THE LITERATURE

### TRANSLATIONS

Revised Standard Version of the Old Testament (Nelson, 1952) and the Apocrypha (Nelson, 1957).

R. H. CHARLES (ed. by), *The Apocrypha and Pseudepigrapha of the Old Testament* (2 vols., Oxford, 1913; reissued 1963).

H. DANBY, *The Mishnah* (Oxford, 1933).

W. O. E. OESTERLEY and G. H. BOX, *Translations of Early Documents* (London, from 1916).

H. ST. J. THACKERAY and R. MARCUS (ed. by) *Works* of Josephus (Loeb Library, London, 1961).

G. VERMES, *The Dead Sea Scrolls in English* (Pelican Books, 1962).

### INTRODUCTIONS

#### A. THE OLD TESTAMENT

G. W. ANDERSON, *A Critical Introduction to the Old Testament* (London, 1959).

A. BENTZEN, *Introduction to the Old Testament* (2 vols., Copenhagen, 1948).

O. EISSFELDT, *Introduction to the Old Testament* (3rd ed., London, 1965).

A. WEISER, *Introduction to the Old Testament* (London, 1961).

(The last three of these include an introduction to the Apocrypha and Pseudepigrapha.)

B. THE APOCRYPHAL LITERATURE

L. H. BROCKINGTON, *A Critical Introduction to the Apocrypha* (London, 1961).

B. M. METZGER, *An Introduction to the Apocrypha* (New York, 1957).

W. O. E. OESTERLEY, *Introduction to the Books of the Apocrypha* (London, 1935).

C. C. TORREY, *The Apocryphal Literature* (New Haven, 1945).


C. THE DEAD SEA SCROLLS

F. F. BRUCE, *Second Thoughts on the Dead Sea Scrolls* (London, 1956).

M. BURROWS, *The Dead Sea Scrolls* (London, 1956).

—— *More Light on the Dead Sea Scrolls* (London, 1958).

F. C. CROSS, *The Ancient Library of Qumran* (London, 1958).

A. DUPONT-SOMMER, *The Essene Writings from Qumran* (Oxford, 1961).

J. T. MILIK, *Ten Years of Discovery in the Wilderness of Judaea* (London, 1959).

E. F. SUTCLIFFE, *The Monks of Qumran* (London, 1960).

The articles contained in *The Interpreter's Dictionary of the Bible* (New York, 1962) and in *Peake's Commentary on the Bible* (London, 1962) are most valuable.

# TEXT INDEX

## I. OLD TESTAMENT

## II. APOCRYPHA AND PSEUDEPIGRAPHA OF THE OLD TESTAMENT

## III. NEW TESTAMENT

# SUBJECT INDEX

PRINTED IN GREAT BRITAIN
AT THE UNIVERSITY PRESS, OXFORD
BY VIVIAN RIDLER
PRINTER TO THE UNIVERSITY